Population on the Loose

POPULATION ON THE LOOSE

By Elmer Pendell, Ph.D.

Co-author of *Society Under Analysis*
and of *Population Roads to Peace or War*
The latter, in a later edition, is called
Human Breeding and Survival

A FOREWORD

By Walter B. Pitkin, Ph.D.

Author of the Best Seller, *Life Begins at Forty*
and of *Must We Fight Japan?*
Author also of about 30 other books and of
hundreds of magazine articles

THREE CARTOONS

By Jay N. (Ding) Darling, Litt.D.

Syndicated Cartoonist
Formerly Chief, Biological Survey, U. S. Department of Agriculture
(Cartoons used by co-operation of Dr. Darling and courtesy of *Des Moines Register*)

Wilfred Funk, Inc.
New York
1951

Contents

FOREWORD: The Bear Trap—Walter B. Pitkin

INTRODUCTION: The Setting

PART I: OUR PROBLEM IS REPRODUCTION

Chapter
1. Too Much of a Good Thing 1
2. It's a Small World 31
3. Expansion Fever 73
4. Nightmare in the Isle of Dreams 90
5. Crowding? Who? — Me? 111
6. Joe Martin Is a Bachelor 144
7. Too Many Fathers 175
8. Prospects for Posterity 190

PART II: NOT MUCH HAS BEEN DONE ABOUT
              REPRODUCTION

Chapter
9. Joe College Has Learned About the Bees and
        Flowers 227
10. Joe's Dad Has Joined the Do-Better Club 256

PART III: CIVILIZATION REQUIRES REPRODUCTION
              CONTROLS

Chapter
11. Parenthood Should Be Planned 288
12. Priestly Rationalization 292
13. There Can Be Acres for All 313
14. Aw! Gordon! Let 'Em Get Married! 327
15. World Aid to End the Need for Aid 357

The hell they brew by two and two is hell for me and hell for you!

POPULATION ON THE LOOSE means REPRODUCTION UNRESTRAINED

Earth's area is finite; man's reproduction power is infinite

If 1% more people would add less than 1% more product, overpopulation exists

To exploit all our resources now is to eat a week's rations in one day—and then go hungry!

As a rule, the fewer qualifications people have for parenthood the more children they have

Civilizations collapse because problem makers multiply faster than problem solvers

Our own civilization must end if average heredity continues to weaken

Reproduction is something that can easily be overdone

Quality of men; quality of earth; harmony between men's numbers and earth's abundance—
for these we strive

The misguidance of COUPLES has resulted in the calamities of NATIONS

One characteristic of Catholic countries is gnawing hunger

Population conditions, worldwide in their problem aspects, have their cause in the behavior of pairs

Only population control can keep any country's numbers right, or the quality of its citizens high

The Bear Trap

In June 1950, we stepped into a bear trap. We yelled for help. Friends helped us pry the jaws apart. In six months of the struggle we lost six billion dollars and spent six billion more on struggles to come.

It was an unusual bear trap. Not the kind men set to catch bears. No. This trap was set by a bear to catch men. Kipling sized up this bear long ago as "the bear that walks like a man."

When a bear traps a man, that's news. Even more startling is the news behind the news; especially the news about the teeth of the trap and the bait the Bear puts into it. The bait is a live man in agony crying for help. The teeth are cheap men ready to spring on the unwary creature that rushes in to help the bait.

Our veterans of the southwestern Pacific recognize the trap. A G.I. in our front line would hear a buddy moaning for help somewhere out in front. He, our kindhearted G.I., would rush out to help the sufferer; and then the Jap snipers would kill him. The low moans had come from a clever mimic, or even from a phonograph record made in advance. Today the Kremlin is pulling this trick on us, using whole nations instead of supposedly wounded soldiers. And we are falling for the trick on a continental scale.

Behind the trick is a grand strategy. The Russians are using men by the tens of millions to destroy us. They are, in short, using population as a weapon. Moscow is cashing in on population on the loose. To see just how the trick may work out, we must go back to elementals. First we must observe how men grow cheap.

Men grow cheap by overbreeding. As Malthus pointed out long ago, the supply of people easily outruns the supply of food. If a couple brings into the world four children who grow up, mate and, in their turn, bring into the world four more children for each couple, generation by generation this breeding stock increases at the rate of 2, 4, 8, 16, 32, 64 . . . n.

The 10th generation thus is made up of 1,024 people, and the 20th numbers 1,048,576. All these, mind you, from one original pair of breeders. Yet this is a trifle when contrasted to the rate of population growth resulting from a pair that breeds six children who grow up to breeding age and then breed, for each couple, six more children. At this rate, in terms of couples, we should have this progression: 3, 9, 27, 81, 243 . . . n. The 10th generation would comprise 39,366 people instead of the paltry 1,024 descendants of the first-named breeding pair; and the 20th generation would have 2,326,952,934 members, all sprung from the original pair. This is just about the present population of our whole world.

Like the house fly, man could bury the earth 100 feet deep with his offspring within a few generations, if only he could make full use of his sexual equipment. Luckily for all creatures, however, including man, neither fly nor man gets a chance to breed hundreds of billions. So we shall content ourselves in the following remarks with the first and lowest genetic progression of 2, 4, 8, 16, 32, 64 . . . n, which has been realized here and there for a few short years under extraordinary circumstances, but never for long. It is easy to show how space and work and food combine to limit the spawning horde.

Imagine a large, fertile valley with excellent climate. Into it come twenty couples, all young and fecund. The valley is lost to the world. Immense mountains hem it in. Unscalable cliffs bar all who would leave or enter. Never mind how the original pioneers got in. That's one of Nature's mysteries.

Each couple lives at some distance from the others; so each has within easy range abundant food for work and play—*Lebensraum,* as one later group called it. I assume that each pair has the same luck with offspring; each of the original pairs has four babes tough enough to survive and breed. By the 20th generation, then, the valley contains 20,971,520 people, over and above parents and grandparents still living.

A brilliant Englishman, Sir Arthur Keith, some years ago studied the area a man needed for food before we had hit on the trick of plowing soil and planting crops. He found something which I could not believe until I had repeated, in full outline, Keith's calculations. He showed that, before the rise of agriculture, the whole earth could not have supported more than 20 million people.

Not until some 25,000 years ago did anybody plow and till. So, during 975,000 years out of the past million, there could not have been more men on the whole earth than half the inhabitants of our imaginary valley, bred within 400 years.

Think that over. Among other results, there will be deep respect for Benjamin Franklin's familiar observation that every species contains within its sex equipment the power to engulf the whole world within a few generations, if the species only gets a chance.

This does not quite complete our survey of what is

behind the news. In some parts of the world the actual increase of men has crowded the valleys much more than in other parts. Where men have become most numerous in relation to food, the men are cheap; where food is still plentiful in relation to men, men are dear. That is the main reason for the contrast between cheap men and dear men, but we must see not only the *fact* of cheapness and dearness of men, and the *reason* for the fact, but also the consequences.

What is a dear man? One who has cost much to bring up; one who has acquired many expensive habits, among which are skills other people are willing to buy at high rates. As a result, the dear man holds himself dear. Life means much to him. He has many things to do. He enjoys doing them. His is life more abundant—because his parents rear him so that he is exposed to many things, has many experiences, and gains insights into many matters. Yes; he has the full life.

At least 75 million Americans have been, with some ups and downs, living this life. Ours is the highest living level on earth; but we need not go into that, for it is an old story.

Dear men are few in the world as a whole, probably about 150 million as a total. For every dear man we find about 14 cheap men. Where cheap men greatly outnumber dear, the people are weak, ignorant, superstitious, and fearful. So, strong men arise to rule them in their weakness. Most of these rulers rule absolutely by default. No cheap men can stand up against them.

A large proportion of the 150 million dear men live in the United States, Canada, Australia, and New Zealand. Not long ago there were millions of dear men in Britain and in Germany, but two world wars have changed that. Britain and Germany today are about as cheap as Japan. Cheap men, herded for war by Mussolini and Hitler, forced the dear Britons to use up their old wealth in self-defense. Now, being cheap, they have no defenses left. They live on the bounty of the dear Americans. It irks them, but they will grow used to it.

The Eurasian land mass contains at least 1.8 billion cheap men. Africa has 150 million, at least. Latin America has close to 130 million.

Of course the world does not divide neatly between dear men and cheap men; there are some between—in the lands already named, which predominate in one or the other of the two extreme categories, and in Switzerland, Holland, Denmark, Sweden, France, and Eire; in Belgium, Austria, Norway, and Argentina. Men grow cheaper as we move eastward from the Rhine. Russia is the Great Slave State, and beyond Russia lie the slums, where humanity cheapens to zero, and perhaps below.

We Americans have on hand 22,796 tons of coal for each and every person. The Italians have only 6 tons for each of them.

We Americans have on hand 87 tons of iron for each of us. The Italians have only $\frac{1}{8}$ ton each.

Why wonder that the Italians are cheap and we are dear? Or that Italians all try to move in on us?

We have about 60 times as much iron and 200 times as much coal as the Japanese. Of course the Japs are cheap.

We have, alas, a rising birth rate; but we still lag far behind the Russians, who, for many years, have had one of the highest in the world. No wonder we are dear and the Russians cheap. No wonder Stalin can raise giant armies and pack prison camps with slaves.

Most Americans are rich enough to move around often and far. They travel more widely than do any of the cheap men. Farther, indeed, than most other dear men. They have more miles of automobile highways than all other people on earth combined, and more cars to drive over them and more gasoline to burn.

Americans have bigger and better schools than all

cheap people and than most other dear men. We eat more and better food than all other people. We enjoy more pleasures in the midst of softer comforts, too.

I am not arguing now that all these pleasures and comforts are good for us in the long pull; or that we are intelligent in our pursuing them. But we are still in possession of good things which intelligent people use to wide advantage.

Make all allowances for recent rise in values and for inflation up to the end of 1950. You find that each American, from babe to centenarian, has an average capital investment in the United States of just under $8,000. But each Chinese has an average investment in China of only a little more than $5.

Cheap men want the things that dear men have, so, when cheap men have a chance they risk a struggle, in order to get the good things. Cheap men now think they have a leader in the Kremlin who can help them get the good things.

The long struggle ahead has a surface pattern and a depth pattern. On its surface it is a war between democracy and totalitarian tyrants. Some innocents say it is a war between Democracy and Communism. But Communism is only one of many Old World totalitarianisms. It happens to be the newest, the biggest, and the strongest. But all over Eurasia, Africa, and Latin America thousands of lesser but zealous despots rule cheap subjects, often with much skill and scant public discontent. Most African chiefs buy slaves and sell their own tribesmen into slavery at a pinch. Arab sheiks have all the powers Hitler strove for. And don't belittle Trujillo and the many wee dictators south of the Rio Grande.

In its depth pattern the struggle is an effort of cheap men to overcome dear men. The most powerful organization among the cheap men is the Slave State, ruled by the Kremlin. That organization has made Murder, Inc., seem like a retirement plan for Unitarian clergymen.

The Great Bear of Moscow deals death to all he touches, either his own kind or outsiders. But he sets his traps most carefully for the dear men, and especially the block of dear men of the United States. The rim of Asia is the trap-line; thence to the south of Europe and north again to East Germany. And the cheap men of Eurasia are the bait.

What matters it to Stalin if a hundred million cheap men of China die? And, in fact, what does it matter to Mao Tse-tung? There will be fewer, then, to eat the scarce food, and Chinamen may grow dearer as their dying countrymen cheapen the men of the West.

And that is Stalin's game, to bleed the dear men of those things that make them dear—and thus to reduce them to common clay on which the Great Bear may more comfortably walk. And so begins the long war of attrition.

Korea was a bear trap. Tibet was another. So is Indo-China. And so is China. Soon the Kremlin will set still another and another; all baited with cheap men. There are open trap jaws in Iran, in Yugoslavia, in Italy, in East Germany. They are only slightly camouflaged, for the victim walks with proud head high, and pays little attention to the footing.

Analyzing our predicament, we find difficulties like the following.

The cheap men can earn little else but their own food, so they go without most good things, including self-respect. The common Korean lives on about $40 a year. Some 30 million of his breed are packed into a peninsula about once and a half as big as Florida, and since it is mountainous they have to grow their food on a fraction of that area. So it is that the Koreans are cheap. They spend nothing on bringing up their babies, nothing on schools, nothing on doctors and nurses, nothing on public health, nothing on preventive medicine. They work all day to get food for the next day, so that they can work all day to get food for the next day. . . .

The Kremlin planners gave these cheap men rifles and ammunition. They ordered them to live off the country, as all Koreans learn to do as children. Moscow gave them no airplanes, but did send in tanks and many excellent cannon. It was soon plain that the Kremlin, using the cheap men as tools, counted on sheer numbers of cheap men to overwhelm the dear men we sent to fight them. It is unlikely that each cheap man cost, all in all, more than one-tenth as much as one American soldier cost us.

At 1950 prices we had to spend upward of $3,000 a year just to maintain one soldier in Korea. Food and clothing alone costs ten times as much as the food and clothing of a Korean Red. Yet even these items were as nothing beside the clutter of goods and services we furnished to our soldiers in the Far East, in order to keep up the same high level of living in war as in peace, in Seoul as in St. Louis. We had to send the American level of living along with the guns. An American army lugs into the battlefield many of the comforts of home. It has thus put itself at a grave disadvantage.

A G.I. has his cold beer, his pop, his raincoat, his change of clothes and suits, his cigarettes, chewing gum, mouth wash, pin-up girls, phonograph, company mascot (dog or goat), comics, pictorials, pocket camera, fountain pen, and a hundred other items of the dear life.

But he cannot lug all these dear things, good and bad, around on his person. He wouldn't have time to pack them up, and he isn't strong enough to carry them. So somebody else has to lug them around for him. This is why, in Korea, we have had to keep behind the lines 42,000 men to supply 16,000 men up in the firing lines. In percentages, this means that only 27 soldiers, out of every 100 we send to Korea, do the shooting.

Now look at the Red armies. There, 6,400 cheap men stay behind the firing lines to support and supply 10,800 men up in front who do the shooting. That is, out of every 100 soldiers, 62 are up in front.

By tricking us into wars against cheap men, be they from satellite lands or from Russia, the Kremlin hopes to bankrupt us. It knows that, in a garrison State, nobody has the time, money, or energy for creating the new wealth that makes for better living. To finance many dear men in a war against cheap men, our workers at home must give up many comforts and luxuries. So they tend to grow poorer and poorer. If the Kremlin can keep us embattled for a decade we may grow cheap enough to give up in disgust.

The great Bear Trap is population on the loose. It is a world of cheap men, too poor and so too weak to fight off tyrants.

So much for what is behind the news. Now back to recent events in Asia.

The Korean War has become a war with China. Uncle Sam has taken the bait in the second trap in the trap line, and now hears the hunter safe and chuckling behind the border bushes. News came on November 5, 1950, that the Chinese Communists declare they are going to fight us to the last ditch in Korea. It may be bluff, and it may be fact. In any case it cuts into our surpluses.

There are various ways in which the dear men of America may be weakened and perhaps defeated. One is to reduce their wealth—reduce it so that American morale can be broken; reduce it so that we cannot produce the vast amount of equipment that is required to blow up armies and cities. Recent wars have been won by fighting forces that had a superiority of equipment. Equipment is most easily available to people who have

surpluses of goods. Our equipment can be less effective
if our wealth is dissipated.

Our policies relating to the occupation of Japan
showed Russia the way. We spend half a billion dollars a
year in Japan, and as the Japanese population increases
from 75,000,000 to 80,000,000, now to 84,000,000, and
soon to 90,000,000, the cost to America mounts higher
and higher.

We shall probably follow the same pattern in Korea.
The Korean minister recently went to Truman and asked
for relief for some ten million of his countrymen whose
properties had been bombed out by United Nations gun-
fire! We are asked to support people we come to defend!
We pay damages for freeing them. If we perform according to precedent we shall soon be supplementing the
incomes of both South and North Koreans, both allies
and previous foes—the whole 30,000,000 of them; then
35,000,000, and soon 40,000,000.

And after that comes China!

According to the precedents which we have established, all that is necessary for Stalin to win the big war
is that America win enough victories over the cheap men
of the satellite countries. The more people we free, the
more we become slaves.

Our downfall will be hastened if we capture enough
prisoners. We captured 70,000 North Koreans. How
many million Chinese will we capture?

Meanwhile the hunter baits another trap or two. We
poured $125,000,000 into Indonesia in 1950—a bribe to
keep down the rising Russian influence. And we are com-
mitted to send two billion dollars' worth of equipment
into Indo-China.

How bad do the flies have to get before one quits using
fly swatters and grabs a shovel to bury the garbage heap?

In keeping with the expanse of territory we undertake
to cover, our armies must increase. The Director of Se-

lective Service has a goal of 3,000,000 men under arms by June, 1951. He has urged that service be lengthened from 21 to 30 months. Our program, he said, is for an "indefinite" period, perhaps for "a generation." We shall need 750,000 additions a year to keep the army at 3,000,000 strength; and with 34 per cent of draftees unfit, only 800,000 able-bodied men per year reach the draft age. Yet the talk in Washington, even before China was definitely in the war, pointed to a still higher total: armies of 4,000,000 to 6,000,000. Men used to migrate to America to avoid Europe's universal military service. To what universe can they migrate now?

Armies are expensive. The bigger they are, the more they reduce our wealth. Already, in November 1950, Administration planners were talking of a 1951 military budget of 60 to 75 billion dollars, and of total Federal expenditures amounting to about a third of the total income of all our citizens.

As we squander our wealth vainly trying to help the helpless, what are we doing to end the causes of helplessness? Nothing. Even less than nothing. Men who call themselves statesmen utter noises that are full of sound and fury, signifying nothing. Stassen wants to talk things over with Stalin. Scores urge Truman to have a chummy peace chat with Joe. Willkie wanted us to exchange orchestras with Moscow, so that, through lovely music, Russians and Americans might come to understand each other and so live in peace forever and ever. Senator Flanders and twenty-seven other alleged statesmen urge us to try God; but they do not suggest just what God will try. As long as people fail to face facts and interpret them intelligently, just so long will we muddle along from crisis to crisis and from chaos to chaos. After we have swapped our business suits for loincloths and have bartered away our prefabricated dwellings for prefabricated fox holes, some of our brighter citizens may conclude that we made a mistake somewhere along the line. Yes, we did just that. We neglected to observe all facts, to read their implications, and then to act on the basis of this new insight. Thus downward the course of empire.

POPULATION ON THE LOOSE is not a war book. Nor does it offer a pat solution to all the problems of world population. But it begins what we should long ago have finished; it faces the facts; it reads aright their implications; and it shows a way toward at least some decisive lines of action. No book could do more.

WALTER B. PITKIN

ACKNOWLEDGMENTS

A man cannot build a book alone; I am indebted to many.

There are 337 names in the index at the end of this volume. Probably half of them are names of men on whose work I have drawn. I am appreciative to these friends.

I extend thanks to publishers who have graciously permitted quotations.

To Walter B. Pitkin for the foreword, "The Bear Trap," in which he has shown the immediate application of population forces in shaping the present war and world tension.

To Walter B. Pitkin and Mrs. Pitkin, to S. S. Fisher, E. A. Hooton, Margaret Sanger, and A. B. Wolfe for suggestions concerning subject matter.

To Jay N. Darling for his generosity in permitting the use of his cartoons.

To Jacob O. Kamm, head of the School of Commerce at Baldwin-Wallace College, who arranged my teaching load to give me time for work on this book.

To Mrs. Mary Snodgrass Wood and to Mrs. Eugene Weaver for efficient secretarial aid.

To Ken Penner for the title, *Population on the Loose*.

To Dan Mihuta for the graph on page 221.

To Orie V. Vande Visse, Jess Petty, Bobby Engel, Lois Cross, Irwin Cochran, and Bob Mihuta for assistance in proofreading.

To John Ferguson for alert co-operation in type selection and arrangement.

To Melvin Arnold for his considerate handling of various editorial problems.

ELMER PENDELL

Department of Economics
Baldwin-Wallace College
Berea, Ohio

The Setting

Hunger is pinching the faces of hundreds of millions of human beings because of the fact, widely recognized now, that the world has too many people; but the main trouble is that the distress is not static; it intensifies. Even since 1940, while the plight of the world has been bad and getting worse, its people have increased by more than 200,000,000. The increase alone is more than the total population of all North America.

To Americans such matters are more important than ever before, because America has undertaken what many interpret to be a sort of stewardship of the world. Our government is sure to make a reproachful failure of the job—just as it has made a shameful fiasco of our Puerto Rican stewardship — until Americans see population forces in the role of cause.

Population causes frequently lead to political consequences. Sometimes people have bartered their freedom for the promise of food. Sometimes people have rebelled against government because their poverty was too bitter. But neither the promise of food nor the struggle for freedom has often given any sound basis for hope—because both food and freedom depend largely on conditions of reproduction. Yet governments, including the American state and national governments, have rarely done anything to correct reproduction conditions; in fact, governments have more often gone against the real interest of their people in these fundamentals.

We have been reluctant to frame our thinking in terms of the relationship of men to the earth; we have clung nostalgically to the habit of personalizing human beings, because that's the way we love them. In America, time was when humankind of almost any level of intellect or education or wealth or health was welcome. Men were scarce, and therefore desired. That era is gone!

In these times of too great abundance of men, when men, from the mere fact of their existence, stand in the way of the happiness of other men, the burden of proof has shifted. Among men who were shown in the 1950 census as having five or ten children, there were many who should have had no children at all, and more who should have fathered fewer than they did.

And in many foreign lands, where men have become lemmings rushing into the sea, the burden of proof is still more clearly on the man who would increase his country's population. He should be required to prove by his own achievements that any children he may have will probably be assets to the world.

Those are matters to be shown. The facts presented in the pages ahead seem to me to show them.

We are the key men of the world's development; you and I. We live at a critical time. The thousands of years of civilizations have been necessary to our present accumulation of knowledge — knowledge of population forces. Without this much experience, men could not see what we can see. Probably more capable men have gone before us, but their inherent capacity, without the knowledge, was not enough. Probably there will be more knowledge available in the future, but it will come too late, because, unless we set the course now, the inherent capacity for guiding human destiny will be in too few heads. The combination of knowledge and inherent capacity to use the knowledge is here in the world of our time.

In the pages that follow I cite and quote information from everywhere. In many instances I use newspaper items and magazine articles where I might have used more scholarly sources or none at all. My hope is to make the reader aware that population facts are all around us. I think that after you read this book you will recognize everyday happenings, which for most people remain isolated and meaningless, as parts of a pattern which reports the prospects and points the requirements for policy. And after these pages become a part of your mental equipment I think that never so much as a week will go by in which you will not be reminded by newspaper or magazine or radio that population is ON THE LOOSE!

Chapter 1

Too Much of a Good Thing

Dr. S. Chandrasekhar wrote to me thus:

"I have recently completed an extended survey of India and Pakistan, travelling from Karachi to Calcutta, and from Lahore to Trivandrum. The appalling population conditions are hard for even myself, an Indian, to understand, especially after a seven year sojourn in the U. S."

Dr. Chandrasekhar is an American-educated Indian economist who is Chairman of the Department of Economics in Annamalai University in South India. His letter continues as follows:

"... Our food scarcity bordering on famine conditions is too well known to need repetition here. The tremendous lack of clothing, housing, and ordinary sanitary facilities to meet the needs of a growing population are too tragic to dilate upon. . . . Were I to describe the conditions under which large segments of our people live . . . this letter would become a lament. I don't know whether an American can imagine, but picture to yourself a tiny hut, fifteen feet by twelve feet, inhabited by six to eight people, without the most elementary sanitary facilities. They cook, eat, live and sleep in this one room. The whole set-up is a constant invitation to disease and death. . . . Especially when you multiply this picture fifty million times you roughly get the grim tragedy that life in India is. I am all for birth control, but in a country where religious obscurantism and fanaticism hold sway, there is no intelligent way out. Americans will make an inexcusable blunder if with India before them as a horrible example they allow similar population conditions to develop in their own uniquely prosperous land, which for us Indians and for most of the world seems like, and is, an Utopia. Of course, I am being pessimistic, for I know that Americans are too intelligent and rational to allow any such quantitative population problem to develop."

Dr. Chandrasekhar may have too high an opinion of the intelligence and rationality of Americans in thinking they will not allow a similar quantitative population problem to develop here. There are large segments of Americans who reproduce without use of intelligence or reason. And this is a point to remember: Thoughtless or misguided reproduction by a large minority can overpopulate America in a very short time. We must have a further discussion of America's prospects, but to keep the thought processes orderly, let us for the moment keep the focus on the Orient.

Fairfield Osborn, on page 98 of *Our Plundered Planet,* an important book published by Little Brown and Company in 1948, remarked that

"In China live a people many of whom are gifted in agriculture and skillful in maintaining terraces and other good land practices, yet they have come up against an enemy within their own gates—that of overpopulation."

That applies in India too, and in fact, in most of Asia, but I think it is important to get the implications of that fact. *Overpopulation* is an *enemy,* says Osborn. Yes, but overpopulation is made up of people, and the plain truth is that when men are in such numbers as to make it impossible to get enough food for self and family then those men are enemies, each of the others. An enemy is anyone whose actions are likely to injure one, and when the neighbors are in such numbers that their mutual helpfulness is more than offset by their claims on the mutual product, then those neighbors are enemies.

The situation in India is one of those I had in mind in saying, in the Introduction, that "in these times of too great abundance of men, when men, from the mere fact of their existence, stand in the way of the happiness of other men, the burden of proof has shifted." In India, by one's reproduction one subtracts not alone from the happiness of his fellowmen, but from their very life. They die at an average age of 27—compared with 64 for Americans.

India had a total population of 389,000,000 in 1941, probably 416,000,000 by 1950. That is a density of about 260 per square mile, to compare with about 48 per square mile for the United States. India's birth rate was 32 per year per 1000 inhabitants in 1940, and, though declining, is nevertheless about 28 or 29 now. Ominously high!

The housing conditions are almost beyond imagination. Dr. Chandrasekhar tells us in his book *India's Population* (The John Day Company, N. Y.) that of the 66.4 million occupied houses, not more than 2% are brick; not more than an additional 7% have substantial walls, roofs, doors and windows. Over 90% have walls of mud, reeds, or matting, with thatched roofs and no floors except the ground itself; most of them with a doorway but no door, and with no window openings at all. The average villager takes his baths in any nearby pond, spring, ditch or river, and since outdoor privies are rare, the calls of nature are attended to by the vast majority in the open fields.

As to the extreme cases one cannot think of even any animal conditions that are comparable. In Bombay a woman doctor investigating for the city government found six families living in one room 15 by 12 feet. Children and adults totaled 30 persons; and three of the six women were expecting additions to the families.

As to education, in 1941, only 12% of the population were literate enough to read and write a postcard.

Disease rates are high, death rates are high; the infant mortality rate is 160 per thousand—more than four times that in the U. S.

The vast majority of people never get enough to eat, and there are no surpluses to protect them against the years of special shortages when millions starve to death. In producing such food as they do get they push the land too hard; give too little attention to soil conservation; and as their numbers grow, the earth source of their living becomes poorer.

India's hell on earth has been supported by the socio-religious mores. The Code of Manu, probably written between 242 B. C. and 500 A. D., is in point. J. O. Hertzler reports it in *The Social Thought of the Ancient Civilizations*. Women were to be subservient to the will of men; they must do nothing independently. A female must be subject to her father in childhood; then to her husband; and if her husband is dead, to her sons. And a woman must do nothing to prevent the rapid appearance of offspring.

That ancient code still has an influence, ill-fitting as it is.

There are too many people in India, sharing the earth; and each hundred million of them makes the conditions harsher for the other hundreds of millions of them.

A curious malapropism—a distortion of language—is seen occasionally in recent years in the term "human resources." The expression probably originated because of its emotional tone: a seemingly complimentary connotation in classifying human beings as resources, because resources are helpful. But most human beings are, in net effect, the opposite of helpful. A resource is a *basis of benefits*. When people are in excess numbers, any random portion of them is, for the rest of them, exactly the opposite of a *basis of benefits*. They constitute not a resource but a liability.

When Wilbert E. Moore, apparently by assignment, used the term "human resources" in an article in the Milbank Memorial Fund *Quarterly* for January 1950, he had to adopt an industrialist employer viewpoint in order to give the word any sense at all. And even at that he had to recognize that human beings are resources only if they have the right training and are in the right places—and that in the early days of transition they have to be forced to the activities in which they may thereafter be resources even to the employer.

In a companion article Conrad Taeuber used the term "human resources" in the title, and once in the body of the article—without any analysis of the phrase, and apparently with tongue in cheek, for his material very definitely shows that an obstacle to the efficient use of agricultural resources is the pressure of population on those resources.

A user of the term "human resources" might say in a sweeping generalization that a man would be in a bad way with *no* other people in his country; that *a* man is better off with *all* the people now in the world than he would be with *none;* that therefore the other people as a whole are resources.

But actual problems do not arise in such terms. When the alleged scholars talk about "humanity's obligation to make the best use of human resources" they are usually talking about the people who are starving in China's current famine; or the great numbers of undernourished Italians for whom Marshall Plan money was intended to be a pacifier; or those emaciated inhabitants of India who produce too little food ever to get enough to eat.

It is dangerous to permit our sympathy for the personal suffering of these people to lead to the pretense that is carried in the term "human resources" that they are, *or ever can be,* of any net benefit to the rest of humanity.

Many people have recognized the liability aspect of people when they are too many.

Some writers, clear in that, are nevertheless muddy-minded in habitually advocating migration.

Oddly, there have been instances of inconsistent writers who have referred to people as "human resources" and who, in spite of that, have espoused emigration. If those segments of the population that might migrate were really a *basis of benefits,* then in a land where benefits are scanty there would be little sense in suggesting their migration. To recognize that their going would be good riddance is, if one is consistent, an admission that they are not resources.

But though any random hundred million of the people of India are a source of suffering for the rest, there isn't any place for them to go! And even if they were to go somewhere the benefits from their departure would be very temporary because of the birthrates of those who would remain.

Sidman P. Poole of the University of Virginia, in the *Journal of Geography* for February 1949, shows that if twenty million people were to migrate out of India, the relief from population pressure would last no more than five years! And he points out that installation of sanitary facilities, new hospitals—in fact, humanitarian advances in general—by the very process of saving lives, make worse the overall tragedy of population increase which invites disaster.

Should we try to educate? Should we send in engineers and some agricultural analysts? Arrange for a redivision of the land? Divide up the purchasing power of the princes? How far would these palliatives get? From the productivity of the New Delhi golf course which Governor General Rajagopalachari recently ordered plowed up, how long can any benefits be felt? The basic trouble is excessive parenthood.

Should we, perhaps via the United Nations, attempt to spread the practice of birth control? The Government of India as such seems not likely to interfere with such a campaign. If in some sort of international negotiations, trade benefits or other benefits to India were conditioned on curtailment of population—so that the country's national legislators would have those benefits to point to as offset for religious opposition, the Government of India itself might initiate a birth control or other population control program. The new Government of India did appoint a "Health Survey and Development Committee." The Committee recently reported. It recommended that the government provide instruction regarding contraception for reasons of health. But as to providing such instruction on *economic* grounds, the committee said:

"Some of us are of the opinion that, on economic grounds also, contraception is justified in the interests of the individual and of the community and that the State should provide facilities for imparting knowledge regarding birth control when desired for such reasons. The others, while they fully appreciate the importance of relating population to the economic resources of the country, feel that the active promotion by the State of contraceptive practices for economic reasons will be justified, in view of objections to it on religious grounds in certain quarters, only if there is substantial support from public opinion."

Many of the highly educated people of India think the situation calls for birth control. One of them is Dr. Hriabai Joshi, wife of India's executive director on the International Monetary Fund.

"India, its villages and cities," she says, "must be taught birth control to keep in check a population which has grown so rapidly that its size is now the basis of most of India's problems. I want to spread education in family planning to every corner."

Let us narrow the spotlight down to one division of India, namely Bengal. It is in the narrowest part of the eastern panhandle reaching toward Burma, and now belongs partly to Pakistan, partly to India. Its 70,000 square miles makes it almost precisely the size of North Dakota, though North Dakota has 650,000 residents and Bengal has nearly a hundred times that many. Bengal's 61,000,-000 inhabitants get their living on its 25 million acres of cropland. Eighty-nine percent of that cropland is used in growing rice, the yield being about 820 pounds per acre. There are 1.8 acres of rice land per family. Rice consumption averages 344 pounds of rice per year; undernourishment is general.

A study by Professor P. C. Mahalanobis, published in the *Asiatic Review,* showed that in the famine of 1943 the landless laborers and fishermen suffered most, and landlords were least affected. Professor Mahalanobis emphasized that the famine only accentuated a condition of deterioration already prevailing.

•

India's population predicament is typical of the Orient. It is paralleled in China. And in China, as in India, for those who trust their reason there is some disfavor and suspicion, growing out of the traditions. Confucius did not solve anything when he commented: "To die without offspring is one of the three gravest unfilial acts." That served as an accelerator to a machine that had no brakes. For many centuries the Chinese death rate balanced the birth rate, maintaining a population of about 60,000,000. Then, after 1600 A.D., the deaths were reduced and population increased in three centuries to 400,000,000. Now it is probably 450,000,000. Birth rate is at an unethically high 40 per 1000 per year, and death rate almost as high.

We are told by A. J. Jaffe, of the U. S. Bureau of the Census, that China has an average of 49 droughts, 48 floods, and 20 epidemics per century. In the summer of 1949 the dikes of the rivers weakened, and rampant waters billowed over vast Chinese valleys, drowning thousands, destroying the huts and crops of millions. The crops were part of the food reliance of hundreds of millions.

In the vicious pressure of people on resources individuals cease to have value. A dying man is left to die. If a person from the Western Hemisphere rescues him, the Chinese expect the Westerner to take care of the person he has saved. During December 1948, according to *News Exchange* of the Planned Parenthood Federation of America, 3879 children were found dead from cold and hunger on the streets of Shanghai.

Claude B. Hutchison, Vice-President of the University of California and Dean of its College of Agriculture, in 1946 headed a 5-months investigation of Chinese conditions by an American-Chinese agricultural mission. There was only about half an acre of tillable land per inhabitant in China, and only four-fifths of an acre for each farm inhabitant. In its report, the mission recommended, among other things, serious consideration by the Chinese government of measures to deal with the population pressure. And it declared that unless the overpopulation can be eased none of its other recommendations can improve the deplorable living conditions. Said investigation leader Hutchison in a 1947 letter to me: "There can be little doubt that most, if not all, of China's basic difficulties stem from the fact that there are too many people in China in relation to her natural resources—especially her land."

•

One of the most densely populated large areas in the world is Java, in the East Indies, which now, with Sumatra, forms the Republic of Indonesia. Java contains 51,032 square miles—about the same as Alabama—but it has 46,000,000 inhabitants, which is 16 times the population of Alabama.

Java is one of the areas that gave rise to the phrase, "the wealth of the Indies," the wealth that induced Bartolomeu Diaz to poke a ship's nose around Africa, and later lured Columbus to the Americas. The wealth is still produced there, now in the form of cinchona bark, cocoanut, kapok, palm oil, pepper, rubber, tea, and tin. But to what benefit? Because of uncontrolled reproduction the people have the miseries of deepest poverty; they are hungry, they are diseased, they are ignorant.

In the *New York Times Magazine* for March 2, 1947, Foster Hailey had an article which was entitled "Too Many People on Too Little Land." Though he was writing about the world, significantly he was writing in Batavia, Java.

He had gone there after an extended tour of Asia, where on one-tenth of the earth's surface one-half of the earth's people live, with so little food and so little shelter from the weather that misery is everywhere.

Perhaps the most significant part of Hailey's report is the observation that efforts to teach improved techniques of food production have fallen far short of the increasing need as population has expanded.

There are many who believe that the way to reduce the birth rates of the overcrowded countries is to improve the levels of living of their masses. Hailey's observation shows that improvement of levels of living is not being accomplished.

And there is a phase of the problem that is not often grasped. A point that must be repeatedly stressed is that any little improvement that is achieved must be temporary, because *its primary effect is in a higher survival rate.*

In *Hygeia* for February 1948 Halbert L. Dunn explains why that which cannot happen in Asia did happen in some western countries. In his article, "Are There Too Many People in the World?" he shows that in those western countries the *death* rates declined, but for year after year, decade after decade, generation after generation, in spite of a high survival rate and a rapid multiplication of the population, the resources of the lands were sufficient to *keep* the productivity high and the level of living high. Finally the birth rates began to fall. Says Dunn:

"It was almost three-quarters of a century after death rates began to decline before birth rates, also, commenced to fall."

Dunn finds many indications that "forebode disaster to the human race unless the present trends in population change," and he emphasizes that "humanity must face squarely the dilemma of increasing worldwide population pressures and establish control policies. Otherwise, a host of human locusts will destroy the resources of the earth which support it."

The Pollyanna plan to reduce birth rates indirectly, via (1) increase of production, and (2) improved level of living, is shown to have greater obstacles to practicability than a Rube Goldberg invention. Dunn points out that if good health and sufficient food are introduced into areas now writhing with people, the birth rate cannot be expected to drop nearly as fast as the death rate, so the populations, already vast, will double, treble, and quadruple within a few decades.

What Foster Hailey was saying is that to the extent that there has been an actual increase in productivity, there has also been an actual increase in population that has sopped up all the increase in goods and has left the people of Asia with practically no margin of income above subsistence. Millions of them don't even get a subsistence; they die.

Hailey tells of the little four-year old Java girl with a gaping raw hole in her cheek that exposed all her teeth and gums on one side. The Dutch nurses had had her almost well two months before, and sent her home; but there wasn't enough food and again she had become a victim of noma, a tissue disease brought on by starvation. When and if they got her well again, they would have to send her home again. What else could they do, since the sick were too many for their facilities?

Hailey thought that scientific birth control would help, but, he commented, religious objections would probably prevent the widespread practice of scientific birth control that would be necessary.

Remarkable, isn't it, that people build up such religious patterns and dogmas, and such fantastic interpretations about them, that they cannot face a problem in an objective, straightforward way, but must advocate a way of life that is laden with anguish!

•

Korea is another fertile spot that could be a haven of contentment except for its overpopulation. Instead, it is just another microcosm of Asia. With the size of Minnesota, it contained about 15,000,000 inhabitants when the Japanese took over in 1910, and 24,300,000 in 1940. The overall population density is about that of India.

Of the total population in Korea, 70% are in agriculture and forestry, 8% in commerce, 5% in industry and mining. The Japanese Government, by loans and subsidies, attempted to get their own farmers to migrate to Korea, says Andrew J. Grajdanzev in *Modern Korea,* but with very little success. Seventy-one percent of the Japs who went to Korea concentrated in 50 cities. Their chief occupation in Korea in 1939 was government service. Sixteen percent of them were in industry, and only 5.3% in agriculture.

The poverty of Korean farmers is shown in a comparison of gross value in dollars of production per farm per year: for Korea, $153; for Japan, $248; for the U. S. in 1940, $1,828.

The comparative levels of living of Korea, Japan, and the U.S. are also reflected in the value of livestock production: 6% of all agricultural production in Korea; 8.2% in Japan; 47.8% in the U.S.

In Korea, as in various other areas where poverty prevents a longtime view, there are destructive land practices. Thirty-two and two-tenths percent of the land area of Korea is under regularized cultivation, 18.6% is in permanent meadows and pastures. The rest can be used in permanent ways only with much less production per unit of labor. But in the forested areas there is a vicious practice of burning off the grass and bushes, and planting potatoes or grain. The denuded land, often having a considerable slope, soon loses the best of its soil through erosion, and is abandoned. Progressively the basis for production in Korea becomes less.

•

Japan, in its population policy, has been openly our enemy for a generation. Walter B. Pitkin's population analysis, entitled *Must We Fight Japan?*, was published in 1921. Japan, the size of California, would have been overpopulated, with its 56,000,000 inhabitants—350 persons per square mile—even if it had all been tillable. But actually only one-sixth of the land was tillable. Even as long ago as 1921, one acre had to feed nearly 4 persons. Pitkin estimated that with its population growth at that time of 700,000 per year, and an increasing base, by 1940 the Japanese would have at least 17,000,000 more mouths to feed—a total population of 73,000,000. History since 1921 has verified that calculation. And, said Pitkin, "There is little doubt that with the Japanese the encouragement of a high birth-rate is a national policy." Were we warned of the approaching aggression, or weren't we?

The attack on Pearl Harbor took place December 7, 1941. On January 6th of that year the Associated Press had reported from Tokyo:

"One hundred young Japanese couples were being selected today for a subsidized marriage experiment in encouraging earlier marriages and larger families. The welfare ministry will advance each of the couples a loan of $70 to $100. If the wife becomes pregnant within six months, no interest will be charged. The principal, which otherwise would have to be repaid, is to be reduced 20 percent with each child born."

The Japanese government apparently expected an increase in population to result from that baby bonus experiment. Yet they could not have expected to use that increase in population to help fight the war which was so soon to torture the world. The Japanese were already in an undeclared war with China, but that war, too, would be over before the prospective baby crop could grow up. That baby bonus project of the Welfare Ministry seems to have been a part of a plan for aggression, either by battles or by migrations, of the 1960's, or battles of the 1970's, or both.

It seems to me that questions raised by Richard U. Light may have special significance in our relations with Japan. Light is President of the Council of the American Geographical Society. In the January 1949 issue of the *Geographical Review* he asked (and I quote by permission of the *Geographical Review*) : "Will nations deliberately overpopulate, to justify their 'right' to a larger share of the earth's area?" "Will the crowded nations, unable longer to maintain or re-settle their excess humanity, persuade their more moderate neighbors to break into their agricultural savings and distribute largess out of blind pity?"

Many people are impressed by labels. Some of my students were puzzled that the Japanese government's aggression planners were called a "Welfare" ministry.

On August 14, 1945, the Japs accepted the surrender terms of the Allies. But when, on December 15th of 1945, the subject of birth control came before the parliament, "Welfare Minister" Hotoshi Ashida opposed it.

The census of October 1, 1948, showed a total of 78,-000,000 Japanese. In 1947, the births outnumbered deaths by 1,500,000. A United Press dispatch from Tokyo dated February 12, 1948, conveyed a sinister and none too subtle defiance:

"Overcrowded Japan, which went to war to seize greater living space and resources in Asia, will have a population of 95,000,000 in 1960 if last year's population increase is maintained, the government said today. The Welfare Ministry said there was every reason to believe that the population increase of 1,500,000 in 1947 will continue as the country is rehabilitated."

Nine days after that "Welfare Ministry" announcement, Hotoshi Ashida, who as Welfare Minister had set the postwar reproduction policy for the country, was elected Premier of Japan! Are we warned of the prevailing Japanese ideal — aggression in the 1960's and 1970's — or aren't we?

The *News Exchange* of the Planned Parenthood Federation, in its issue of April 1948, stated that some birth control consultation offices had been set up in Japan. At the same time, said *News Exchange,* "the little good that can be done with limited supplies and medical help is being undone by the paternity bonus." The bonus system had been expanded under the occupation authorities, the report continued, and the labor unions had included among their demands larger subsidies for children. The American *Stars and Stripes* has reported, without noting the implication, that a newly formed "democratic" union in Osaka had demanded and received from the Japanese Government a marriage bonus of Yen 20,000 for its members. *News Exchange* for February 1949 told of 2,500 unwanted children in Japan who had been sold into slavery by their parents through a single broker.

Who is financing Japan's eventual aggression? You are! The United States is spending more than $1,500,000 a day to keep the Japanese barely at subsistence level.

•

Where were the American occupation forces, while
Japanese parasitism expanded and the next Japanese aggression was getting under way? MacArthur's advisers
were split wide apart. Those within the Supreme Com-
mand for the Allied Powers who opposed birth control
and sterilization, according to a friend who wrote to me
about it from Tokyo, claimed that industrialization puts
an "automatic" brake upon the growth of population.
Although the Japanese population is still increasing rapidly, the birth *rates* in Japan have lately been declining.
Those opponents of birth control said the decline in
the Jap birth rates was the effect of neurosis, which
tends to develop in highly industrialized societies. Consequently, they said, there is no need to do anything to
control the population; let worry do the controlling.

That line of thought has the musty smell of the grave
of William Godwin, a century and a half old. Said Godwin: "There is a principle in human society, by which
population is perpetually kept down. . . ."

Malthus responded, "This principle, which Mr. Godwin thus mentions as some mysterious and occult source
. . . will be found to be the grinding law of necessity;
misery, and the fear of misery."

He detailed the misery as cold, hunger, disease, war,
and vice. He did not mention neurosis specifically, but
it fits under disease, which he did name as one of the
kinds of misery which hold population within the bounds
of the food supply.

This should be said: unlike the 1949 proponents of
planned neurosis for Japanese women, Malthus did not
advocate disease; rather, as a population check he thought
of it only as a melancholy reality.

Notice that the influence for sterilization by worry does not operate alone. In fact that influence must always be a relatively small part of the impact of a nerve-jangling environment. When the strains and tensions become so severe as to affect reproduction in any substantial proportion of women, those same strains and tensions will be in the chain of cause to a whole gamut of other population checks: if contraception is tabooed there will nevertheless be crude and dangerous experiments to prevent pregnancy; there will be a high rate of abortions, too; and there will be widespread starvation. Anyone who offers neurosis as a means of holding population down is also prescribing abortion, starvation, and all sorts of desperate attempts to prevent pregnancy. That is true because of the inevitable correlation among those misery-induced checks to population. A society cannot have one of them without having the others; an "expert" cannot prescribe one of them without implying the others.

Besides those results of overpopulation, if the distressed people have any chance of success in war, they will have war; and if they have any place to go, many of them will try to migrate.

But of course, as long as Americans supplement Japanese food production, increasingly and sufficiently, many of the strains of overpopulation and the prescribed neurosis will not apply, and the Japanese numbers will increase.

Finally, in the forces of the Supreme Commander for the Allied Powers, the antihuman aspects of the program of planned neurosis are becoming clearer. *News Exchange* quotes Bill Costello, who spoke on CBS from Tokyo: "After more than three years the vocabulary of the occupation has suddenly been enlarged by the term 'population problem.' . . . Now that the occupation is settling down for a long pull, there is a growing conviction that something has to be done about regulating Ja-

pan's population growth. After all, the U. S. is paying
the grocery bill. . . ."

According to the *U. S. News and World Report* for
September 9, 1949, the Occupation authorities had by
that time become uncomfortable. American goods and
American troops were helping to prevent hunger, unemployment and political unrest. "But U. S. officials are
beginning to worry. . . ." ("Beginning" is what the writer
said! ". . . beginning to worry about what will happen
once that assistance is stopped." They were worried that
"Japan will turn out once more to be a major trouble
spot in Asia unless the population problem can be
solved."

In the United Nations *World Magazine* for June 1949
Dennis Warner remarked that in three postwar years the
Japanese produced 7,500,000 children, a number "almost
exactly equal to the total population of Australia. . . ."
By 1970 a Japanese population of 100,000,000 is expect-
ed; perhaps 110,000,000. "That this problem overshad-
ows all the reforms of the Occupation, most of General
MacArthur's senior advisors freely admit."

Writer Warner stated that Japan would find the added
millions "catastrophic." "And so would other countries
of the Pacific . . . ," but the paradox is that this alone, "of
the multitudinous problems that confront General Mac-
Arthur, has remained untouched."

And why?

Fewer than one-fifth of Americans are Catholic, and
many of the 26,000,000 have evidenced a disapproval of
the Pope's position in population matters, yet as a political pressure group the Catholic Church is formidable.
According to writer Dennis Warner, MacArthur's advisers think the papal power takes the case out of the General's hands.

"Birth control is almost a forbidden subject in the influential Catholic world," said Warner. And he quoted

one of the senior officers in Occupation Headquarters as follows: "For General MacArthur to give even the slightest comfort or assistance to advocates of birth control would result in his immediate recall and discharge."

However, a CDN dispatch from Tokyo, dated November 4, 1949, said that MacArthur had side-stepped the birth control issue by insisting that birth control is strictly a matter for the Japanese to decide; and "when a Catholic women's organization protested pro-birth control statements by two of his advisers, General MacArthur ... quickly disavowed his advisers."

The Hotoshi Ashidas are not unopposed among the Japanese. There are many of them who favor population control. The campaign for it has been led notably by two women: Dr. Fumiko Amano, and, in the parliament, a Mrs. Kato. Hotashi Ashida is out of the government now. Under accusation of taking ten million dollars in bribes he resigned as Prime Minister. The Japanese Government on March 24, 1949, openly espoused birth control, and birth control became legal on April 1st, 1949. *News Exchange* of the Planned Parenthood Federation for April 1949 reported that the Japanese Welfare Ministry is showing a short movie on the necessity for and methods of birth control and claims to be in the process of setting up about 800 birth control clinics. There seems to be a possibility, then, that the Welfare Ministry, a sham up to now in its welfare aspect, will, at long last, become genuine.

The birth control movement seems to be progressing rapidly, yet, so far, it falls far short of the need. Insight clearer than that of most Americans as well as of most Japanese is evidenced by *Yomiuri,* one of Tokyo's largest newspapers, which on April 9, 1949, advocated compulsory limitation of families, and called on the Japanese Government to outlaw births above a designated limit for each family.

•

What sort of an Orient—and a world—can we expect if the Orient, and the world, continue without programs to reduce the numbers of births? *Life* made the answer clear in an editorial of April 26, 1948, entitled: "Coming: A Hungry 25 Years." This quotation from that editorial is made by permission of Time, Inc., the publishers of *Life*:

". . . Europe is only part of the world food problem. In Asia, whatever we do, and we must do our utmost, there simply will not be enough to go around.

"To make matters worse, the outlook for the intermediate period of four to six years is almost equally bleak. So, in fact, are the prospects for the next 25 years. This world food situation is not just a question of war-ravaged fields, floods here and droughts there. The Malthusian circumstance is that the population of the world has increased by 200 million people just since Hitler charged into Poland. India's population alone has grown by 35 million, partition riots notwithstanding. Everywhere, population is on the increase. The world's population is now about 2¼ billion. Twenty-five years from now, in 1973, it is almost sure to be nearly 3 billion. Our food problem is not merely one of recovering a lost position. It is the much greater problem of increasing our supply vastly beyond all previous records."

And so, without population control, we face increasing cause for worry for twenty-five years—and then, apparently, complete hopelessness of meeting the problems that will have developed.

Suppose we fall in line 100% with *Life's* only expressed prescription—attempting to increase our supply of food vastly beyond all previous records. If, 25 years from now, we have 3 billion people on earth, and have used every resource to the fullest, the world will nevertheless be worse off than it is now. There will be no reserves; nothing to turn to—and the reproduction tendencies will still be with us. So, after that, the dark! What an outlook!

•

It is not my purpose to make this volume an encyclopedia, but to give reports of typical conditions and to show how the facts have come to be what they are. It is unnecessary, then, to report all the Asiatic countries, and equally unnecessary to specify all the countries in Europe. The southern countries in Europe are in a condition which, though not as bad as conditions in Asia, is nevertheless loaded with suffering. Let us take a look at Italy, the land of Leonardo.

There are those who attribute the present low level of living in Italy to the Fascist regime. It is doubtful if under any form of economic organization the Italian level of living could have been very much better in the face of the large increase in population that had to be supported somehow from the inadequate Italian soil. However, there is some appropriateness in fastening the guilt on the Fascists, since they undertook to encourage an ever-increasing population. Laws were passed against the spread of information on birth control and the sale of contraceptives. There were tax exemptions for families with large numbers of children. There were special taxes on bachelors as well as high rates for their income taxes. Married men were given job preference. Newly married couples could get government loans which were scaled down as their families increased, and written off at the birth of a fourth child. Local governments, under central government stimulation, held baby races, and gave the winners prizes of medals, diplomas, and cheap housing. In Rome, honeymooners were presented with five-day free tickets on all the city's streetcars and buses, and the national government railways granted an 80% reduction to honeymooning couples.

Mussolini himself encouraged reproduction by giving special honors to mothers of a large number of children. Illustrative is a celebration of December, 1933, in honor of 92 champion mothers who had averaged 14 living children apiece. Each was given a large money prize in addition to the regular bonus of 500 lira for every child born after the 7th.

Mussolini sowed the wind; now his survivors reap the whirlwind. Ralph H. Blodgett in his *Comparative Economic Systems* text, pages 451 to 456, informs us that from 1926 to 1935 there was in Italy a decrease in per capita consumption of 10% of wheat, 14% of meat, 15% of olive oil, 6% of butter and lard, 21% of sugar, and 11% of fruit and vegetables. Clothing and furniture sales were off 33%. "The poorest Italian people had very little to eat and some of them got along on one miserable meal per day of bread and greens." The dwellings of the rural people were hovels or caves, which they shared with their domestic animals. The accommodations of the urban dwellers were almost as bad, and overcrowding was the rule. The estimated shortage of housing was nine million rooms. The number of calories in the Italian diet was lower than anywhere else in Europe except Poland. That much reduction in level of living took place before the ravages of World War II.

Conditions have become increasingly Orientalized. The *Wall Street Journal* for June 11, 1947, said:

"The citizen of Turin, for example, in March paid over 600 lira for a pound of cheese. ... That 600 lira is only a little less than what he earns for a day's work of eight hours even if he is a skilled worker. He may have the benefit of family allowances and a canteen at his place of work, but a worker can barely make ends meet unless members of his family also bring in wages."

Italy was one of the countries favored by the half billion dollars appropriated in the emergency legislation passed by the U. S. Congress in December 1947 and in the Marshall Plan program. After the Marshall plan— what?

Says *Life,* November 24, 1947 (and all my quotations from *Life* are made by permission of Time, Inc., the publishers of *Life*) :

"The general diagnosis of Italy's primary illness—'Too many people on too little land'—becomes distressingly specific in the case of the Italian peasant."

And illustrating with the tiny village of Alberobello, *Life* says,
"the peasants there are too many and the land is too poor."
Again:

". . . in the economically grim south, the pastoral loveliness of the rolling Apennine foothills gives scarcely a clue to the peasant's fierce and constant struggle with the resistant land. . . . the 5,000 residents of Tolve get only a bare subsistence from the sparse vineyards around it."

But it isn't the rural areas alone that are in poverty, says *Life*:

"The worst city slums of the Western world are in Italy, and the worst slums of Italy are in Naples. In 'beautiful Napoli' there are literally miles of tenement streets, festooned with laundry, stinking with filth which runs in open gutters, and inhabited by families who sometimes live a dozen or more to a room."

John P. Leacacos, European correspondent for the Cleveland *Plain Dealer,* told us in the Sunday edition November 23, 1947:

"There's something a little phony mixed in the current presentation of the Italian emergency. Not that anyone can deny the crisis in Italy. It's here on every side. But in the near-hysterics of some State Department arguments, one basic fact is sloughed over:

"Namely, that Italy has been more or less in a virtual emergency for 30 years and in a desperate one for the last four.

"In other words, you can't escape the past. No number of Marshall plans, as far as they apply to Italy, are ever going to succeed if the United States does not first realistically realize, before committing itself in effect to underwriting Italian recovery, that it will have to pick up all the bad checks of Italian history."

Leacacos summarizes these historical bad checks in part by calling attention to Italy's population. He says the country now has 47,000,000 people and has the largest birth rate in Europe outside of Russia. "As Italian politicians like to say, the main trouble with Italy is 15,000,-000 more mouths to feed than the country can support."

The *U. S. News and World Report for* December 10, 1948, makes the comment, "What to do with too many people is the big problem in Italy. Homes and jobs abroad for 1,200,000 must be found soon." But as the productive areas of the world have filled up, the welcome for migrants has grown thin. And that 1,200,000 figure was just an entering wedge. Further along in that article we find this: "The plan to export 1,200,000 people by

1952, even if it works, will leave in Italy an additional 1,800,000 workers needing jobs."

An Associated Press item of April 16, 1949, reported a gloomy interview with an ERP official. Italy's population is expanding at a rate of 400,000 to 500,000 a year, the official said; her postwar emigration has averaged less than 150,000.

There are too many people reproducing too fast, as Scripps-Howard writer Ludwell Denny wrote from Rome. Evidence of the deep poverty is in the crowded hovels in southern Italy, and in the desperately low average annual income. The possible new jobs, he said, would not take care of much more than half the population increase, and the outlet for continuous Italian emigration is limited.

Elizabeth Wiskemann also, in *Foreign Affairs* for October, 1949, stressed the high birth rate at the foot of the Italian boot.

Time, dated December 19, 1949, told of the land hunger of the Italian peasants, impelling thousands of them to violent seizure of estates all over Italy. Provincial committees had been re-allocating lands under a three-year-old law—but the process had been slow. Yielding to the popular pressure, Italy's legislative body, in December of 1949, passed a new land law which provided for the expropriation of poorly used land. Also, the Italian Government, with ECA help, is spending in one project $1200 per family to re-equip and re-educate the farmers. About a quarter of a billion of U. S. dollars are now being channeled into similar projects.

In the face of Italy's continuing population increase, however, there can be no reasonable hope that the benefits will for very long outlast the spending.

•

The *German* struggle for living room must be an old story to every reader. It was primarily an effort to get outlets for manufactured products, and sources of raw materials. England resisted, because the same markets and raw materials were part of the support of Englishmen.

Both Germany and England had increasing populations. Consequently, neither could maintain the level of living that had developed before 1914 without encroaching on the spheres of influence of the other. The nominal victory of the Allies in World War I was accompanied by upsets in the delicate economic balance with the rest of the world. Because of those upsets there was never a full restoration of the English level of living. Germany never recovered either. The Second World War, in its inception, was a resumption of the German struggle for resources and markets.

The density of population is suggestive of the difficulties. The United Kingdom has 520 persons per square mile, and Germany 465. Both, then, are much more heavily populated than Italy with its 380 people per square mile. However, both Germany and England have more mineral resources than Italy, and a larger proportion of their surface is cultivable. But none of the three can support itself. Each must depend on food and raw materials for manufacturing, from elsewhere. And there must be markets abroad.

The markets and the food supplies become increasingly difficult to hold, as population increases in the areas on which the manufacturing countries depend. That is further explained in the next chapter, "It's a Small World." But in part the anemia of both the English and the Germans results from the increasing foreign sales of United States manufacturers, who have used the opportunities created by both wars to cut in on markets erstwhile supplied by England and Germany.

The German population has been increasing rapidly

in spite of war deaths. The four zones of occupation, which in 1939 had a population of 56,615,000, had increased 16% by 1947, to 65,911,000.

Clearly the Germans face a starvation problem.

What is the way out? On November 5, 1947, Dr. Otto F. K. Dibelius, of the German Evangelical Church, Bishop of Berlin and Brandenburg, spoke in Cleveland before more than a hundred clergymen. He thought of three possibilities:

"If 20 or 30 million Germans were allowed to emigrate —and I don't think any country in the world would allow such an immigration—the people remaining in Germany would have a chance to live off the production of German land."

"Or if German industry were allowed to develop to a higher degree than ever before, then, like the British, it could pay in exports for the imported necessities of living."

"The only other possibility is to let about 30,000,000 Germans die so that the rest of the German population can survive on food production in the homeland."

The bishop is correct that no country in the world would permit such a volume of immigrants. There are still a few countries which welcome a few selected immigrants, but those countries are subject to pressure from dozens of countries that are far too full. For every person who actually manages to find a home in a new land there are five thousand persons who would like to follow.

Here is another way to look at it. Germany's *increase* since 1939 has been about one and a third million a year, a rate roughly equal to the total stream of immigrants from all lands into the U. S. in the years 1910-1914, which were the years of our heaviest influx. Even if the U. S. could open wide its doors again and absorb migrants at the rates it absorbed them before World War I, and even

if we shut out migrants from all other countries in order
to take Germans, still we could handle only the current
increase of Germans; we would not be *improving* starvation conditions of those remaining in Germany.

The English are in a slightly better position than the
Germans for emigration, since some of their colonies are
giving them special opportunities. A hundred thousand,
says John D. Leonard in a news story of June 15, 1948,
left in the preceding year and a half, and nine times that
many are waiting only for boats.

If that number of migrants were leaving Germany, the
effect would be hardly noticeable—because the increase
by births is so much greater. Even in England, with a
birth rate higher since the war than before, there is probably no improvement; the conditions merely get worse
less rapidly.

Bishop Dibelius thought that if German industry were
allowed to develop to a higher degree than ever before,
the Germans could take care of themselves. However,
American producers are not eager to have their German
competitors back in the field. They do what they can to
keep even the British from recovering their colonial markets. Thus, for instance, through our State Department
action, loans to Britain were conditioned on the reduction of colonial preferences.

American exporters have a tremendous public backing. With nine-tenths of the economists of the U. S.
building up a sentiment for reciprocal trade agreements,
anyone who advocates foreign sales as low as the average
of the years between the wars gets the stigma of an "isolationist" label.

So there is very little chance that German industry
would be permitted to revive to a degree even approaching its prewar output; the Bishop's dream of a degree of
development higher than ever before and increasing to

take care of the increasing population is a remote specu-
lation indeed.

The German churchman saw a third way of handling
the situation—letting about thirty million Germans die
so that there would be enough food for the rest.

There seems to be at least a fourth possibility. Margaret Sanger has been suggesting that the distressed countries of Asia and Europe have a ten-year moratorium on
reproduction. If that suggestion were followed, and if,
after that, reproduction were resumed in a measure suited
to the conditions, instead of in a wild orgy such as has
followed World War II, would not the Bishop's third
course of action be unnecessary?

When the Bishop spoke of the British paying for necessary imports with exports, he seems not to have realized
that the prospects for the British have suffered a setback
almost as severe as those for Germany. Mrs. Sanger had
the situation better in hand. Hungry countries should not
bring any more children into the world to starve, she said.
Does that include England? she was asked. "Definitely,"
she answered.

Chapter 2

It's a Small World

Figures of Colin Clark on real incomes, and of the International Labour Office on real wages, show that between the wars Americans fared more than four times as well as Italians. Richard A. Lester has expressed a general truth which helps explain that contrast in wages. I quote, in this section, from his *Economics of Labor*, copyright 1941 by the Macmillan Company, used with their permission: "Fundamentally, it is physical productivity per worker that explains national differentials in the level of real wages." And again, ". . . labor scarcity is largely determined by the population-resources ratio."

Lester showed that from colonial times on down, wages in America have been higher than in England, even though at first England's equipment was far superior to that of the colonies. His material factually demonstrates the wholesomeness of what some people have called our condition of "underpopulation."

As early as 1630, he reports, a Massachusetts governor stated that fewness of workers led them to demand excessively high wages, and in the 1630's the Massachusetts legislature set maximum wage rates for "Carpenters, Joyners, Brickelayers, Sawyers, Thatchers, Wheelewrights, Tylers, Mowers, Master and inferior taylors, and labourers." But demand for workers was so great that in spite of legislation of that sort, "excessive rates" of wages became "a general complaint."

Remember that there were no unions to raise wages; there was only the fact that workers were in demand because, working with abundant resources, their productivity was great.

In Virginia, too, wages were high, compared with those in England, a colonial treasurer there declaring that Virginia wages were much higher than those paid to comparable workers in England.

And from Maryland in the 1600's a colonial writer was urging impoverished Englishmen to come to his colony, where they could "live plenteously well."

Said Lester:

"In all the colonies at various dates, from 1633 to 1776, there were complaints that 'Labour is dear,' and, according to statements in 1651 and 1698, wages in the northern colonies were from two to three times as high as in England. A committee of the Pennsylvania legislature stated in 1752 that immigrating workers soon set up for themselves, which 'keeps up the Price of Labour, and makes it more difficult for the old Settler to procure working Hands.' This committee concluded: 'For so long as Land can be easily procured for Settlements between the Atlantic and Pacific Oceans, so long will Labour be dear in America.' "

The apprenticeship period in England was for seven years. In the colonies, other economic opportunities were so abundant, for anybody trained or untrained, that the seven-year training period was unattractive, and in order to induce young men to acquire skills the apprenticeship time was reduced. In New York City, for example, in 1680 an ordinance was passed providing that "coopers, carpenters and smiths &c., serve five years before being allowed to set up business."

The advantage of "underpopulation" has been evident from the time of Adam Smith. Said he in *The Wealth of Nations*:

"The plenty and cheapness of good land are such powerful causes of prosperity, that the very worst government is scarce capable of checking altogether the efficacy of their operation."

Time after time Adam Smith referred to the circumstances which made for high wages and all-around prosperity as "plenty of good land." Of course, the "plenty of good land" to which he so often referred as the cause of prosperity could be expressed as RELATIVELY FEW PEOPLE.

Ellsworth Huntington, in his *Principles of Economic Geography*, a John Wiley and Sons publication, reached the conclusion that the prosperity of present-day Australia is similarly a result of the fact that Australians are few. He found that prosperity prevails in spite of droughts "because the population is sparse and the farms therefore large enough so that the good years tide over the bad ones." And in industrial occupations the workers fare well because of their scarcity. "Hence," says Huntington, page 444, "there are few poor people in Australia, and a large percentage even of the poorer classes have homes of their own."

As Lester remarked on his page 216, "Undoubtedly the man-land or population-resources ratio plays a most important part in the determination of value productivity per worker in a country."

•

Resources of all sorts influence real wages. But the soil resources are the vital ones, because they are the sources of *food*. As a permissive and limiting factor for population numbers and levels of living, food is likely to be controlling.

The oil, ore, timber, etc., and the technology used in working them into useful products, have influenced the *distribution* of food. Manufacturing people work up tools, conveniences, and luxuries, sell them, and thus get purchasing power with which they buy wheat from afar. Europeans have done that for over a century. They thereby maintained for that time a superficial prosperity. That prosperity depended essentially on their ability to buy food from outside. The prosperity was only as reliable as the food supply—and the food supply was, and is, largely out of the control of the Europeans.

There seems to be a widespread illusion about the depth and stability of industrial prosperity. The industrial revolution has been a cause of confusion in many minds concerning the relation of men to earth. The reason is that while there has been surplus FOOD, anywhere, it could be drawn to the areas where the industrial revolution was most advanced. The people with extra food were glad to sell their surplus in order to get the purchasing power to buy the products of the machines. Actually the people working with the machines have often if not usually been better off than those who produced the food. But that advantage could apply only when food was in surplus. When food is scarce, those who produce it have the advantage. In the years of scarcity that lie ahead, the people who have come to depend on other lands for food have painted themselves into a corner. Assembly lines, power shovels, fast autos and airliners—those are toys and trinkets; a man must eat!

Fairfield Osborn on pages 42 and 43 of *Our Plundered Planet*, a 1948 book put out by Little, Brown and Company, tells us this:

"The industrial revolution in Europe, with its accompanying tremendous increase in population, was to a very considerable degree supported and fed by the United States and Canada, whose land resources were hastily developed and prodigally expended to help meet the pressing demands of a population that increased from 175,-000,000 to almost 400,000,000 in a little more than a century."

". . . The once apparently inexhaustible natural assets of this continent are now little more than sufficient to support its own increasing population, and the reserves in lands in the far corners of the earth are being drained through misuse."

Evidencing the fact that food producers hold fast to their food products where food is scarce is a little book by Frank A. Pearson and Floyd A. Harper, of Cornell University, entitled *The World's Hunger*. It was published by the Cornell University Press in 1945. The authors show that the Asiatics produce about 40 percent of the world's food, but export only 2 percent of the amount they produce! Where population is dense and food is hard to get, human energy must concentrate on that one objective, food.

Various wishful thinkers, and those among the economists who have been gambling on the industrial revolution as a cure for human hunger, are due for a tremendous jolt.

•

In our relations with the earth the fact of *diminishing returns* is fundamental. Two men working ten acres of farming land can produce more bushels of crop than one man working those ten acres, but they cannot produce so many bushels *per man*. That illustrates the Law of Diminishing Returns. If the farmers in Ohio were to double in numbers, the production on Ohio farms would not thereby double. *In probably every major region of the world, any substantial increase in number of persons working the soil brings about a smaller proportion of increase in amount of food.*

There is no more important law in any science than that law of diminishing returns. In the following table I illustrate its application. In all cases below the horizontal line that cuts through the table there are diminishing returns. They are shown in the column headed "Average production per man." If the 100 acres are divided into four farms, and each of the four farmers has three sons who take over the land, their level of living must be substantially less than if there had been only one son each. However, to avoid the confusing concept of decreasing fertility, let's not assume any passage of years. The table represents alternative situations in a single year. Thus *if* four men work the hundred acres the average production per man is 312.5 bushels, whereas *if* five men work the hundred acres the average production is 308 bushels.

Sometimes the law of diminishing returns is stated with an oozy indefiniteness: "With any one factor of production held constant. . . ." Let's not do that. That will serve as a start for the law of diminishing *productivity*, but the law of diminishing *returns* is historically and appropriately more specific. The economy as a whole can have only *land* as the constant factor. And there isn't a matter of "holding" it constant; it is constant in spite of us—not absolutely, but for most purposes practically constant. In the following table, for all cases land is 100 acres.

ILLUSTRATION OF THE LAW OF DIMINISHING RETURNS

Number of men working the land	Acres of land worked by the total number of men	Total production of the hundred acres, in equivalents of bushels of grain	Production in bushels of grain attributable to the man in the series who is now considered for the first time	Average production per man, in bushels	Average production per acre, in bushels
1	100	200	200	200	2
2	100	500	300	250	5.00
3	100	900	400	300	9.00
4	100	1250	350	312.5	12.50
5	100	1540	290	308	15.40
6	100	1780	240	296.67	17.80
7	100	1980	200	282.85	19.80
8	100	2150	170	268.75	21.50
9	100	2300	150	255.55	23.00
10	100	2440	140	244	24.40
11	100	2575	135	234.09	25.75
12	100	2705	130	225.42	27.05
13	100	2830	125	217.69	28.30
14	100	2950	120	210.71	29.50
15	100	3067	117	204.47	30.67
16	100	3181	114	198.81	31.81
17	100	3292	111	193.65	32.92
18	100	3400	108	188.88	34.00

For that illustration I chose soil that is not very good. Also, those farmers have only a little help from tools. The showing is simpler that way. The difference is that one man or a few men on those hundred acres would produce more with a lot of equipment, but the productivity of additional men would fall off more rapidly; and if as many men as 18 have to support themselves on the hundred acres, elaborate tools are not likely to increase their productivity, so they would not replace any but the simpler ones. The less ground a man has, the less advantage he has in the use of farming equipment.

Clearly there is less product per man if more men than four work the 100 acres. After four, the more the workers, the less is their per capita product. Actually there are diminishing returns after the third man, but the social significance of diminishing returns is more apparent after the fourth man, as can be seen in the column showing average production per man.

"Hold on," a critic might say, "that supposed law of diminishing returns doesn't take account of the fact that the soil can be improved, and that the crops can be improved, so that the hundred acres will yield more produce."

John Stuart Mill thought he had taken care of that, by the stipulation: "in any given state of agricultural skill and knowledge" by increasing the labor, the produce is not increased in an equal degree.

But the critic might protest that no "given state of skill and knowledge" lasts long enough to matter; the improvement of soil and of plants is frequent if not continuous, and for some periods in some countries the increase of product has exceeded the increase of people.

Nevertheless the law still stands. The improvement, and the occasional increase in per capita product, are *rarely if ever the result of the increase in workers.* In the predominant body of cases, if the men *do not* increase, the average agricultural productivity increases by the full average result of the effectiveness of the improvement. If the men *do* increase, they act as a downward force on average productivity, opposing the effect of the improvement.

Alvin Hansen might still object to that generalization. As indicated on page 218 of his *Economic Stabilization in an Unbalanced World*, he might think it "ignores the fact that a new technique may not be economically feasible without an increase in population." But Hansen was not centering his reasoning on *food*. He wrote of optimum population with *general* level of living as its measure, and he seems to have been dealing with short-time, transitory developments, unmindful that a new technique may lead merely to mining the soil, or may build up a country's temporary average income by drawing more heavily on the food production of other regions.

One should notice, in a world perspective, that skill and knowledge have not been able to increase world production sufficiently to meet the increasing need that arises from the world's expanding population. Ordinarily it is only one kind of product at a time that is improved. The total food supply is increased very little. Thus the increased yield of corn from hybrid seed, for example, and other improvements taking effect since 1940, have been no match for the 200,000,000 increase in world population since that date; in fact they have not even offset the destructive forces operating at the same time. The improvements have not yet been applied on a world scale, but by the time they can be so widely applied, the population will have increased still further.

The law of diminishing returns reports the result of a contact of people with physical environment. There is less product per worker from a large number of workers because the workers have, on an average, less to work with —less *earth* to work with. A given amount of land is limited as to the area in which plants can spread their leaves to the sun; and thus the cause of diminishing returns is physical. The land is limited as to the earth volume near the surface, in which plants can spread their roots; and in that way, too, the law of diminishing returns has a basis in physical facts. The land is limited as to the amount of water and other chemical substances available for the plants. And thus in that third way the cause of diminishing returns is physical. Scarcity of soil presents a resistance to the increase in the volume of plants, and thus a resistance to the increase in numbers of a population, or else a resistance to its level of eating, or both.

Of course many things that men use for other purposes are similarly subject to diminishing returns; cotton, wool, pulp wood, jute, for examples, and in some circumstances those may furnish a resistance to population numbers— but those circumstances are less likely, so keep the focus on food.

Except for diminishing returns, quantity of land in the world, or in one country, or on one farm, would have no relation to quantity of production. Except for diminishing returns a twenty-acre farm would produce as much as a thousand-acre farm. If additional volumes of crops could be had in proportion to capital and labor put on the land, a given outlay of capital and labor would produce as much on a small acreage as on a large acreage. But additional expenditures and additional labor on a given acreage bring less results per unit of expenditure or per unit of labor, so the amount of land available in the world, or in one country, or on one farm, is important in terms of per capita production, and in terms of population policies.

The fact of diminishing returns seems to have been first seen by the French statesman Turgot, in 1767, although it seems not to have been correlated with Turgot's physiocratic theories. The fact of diminishing returns was mentioned briefly and incidentally by Thomas Robert Malthus in the 2nd edition of his Essay on Population, which appeared in 1803. He formulated it more definitely in 1815. In the same year Sir Edward West independently expressed the law. According to F. Lester Patton in a little 1926 book, *Diminishing Returns in Agriculture*, two other economists, independent of Malthus and West and of each other, also formulated the Law of Diminishing Returns in 1815. They were David Ricardo and Robert Torrens. That 1815 rash of insight, according to Patton, was stimulated by two reports of parliamentary committees, which had dealt naïvely with the subject of intensive agriculture. The expressions of the Law of Diminishing Returns were in refutation of those reports. Of the 1815 statements, that of Edward West was probably clearest: "Each equal additional quantity of work bestowed on agriculture yields an actually diminishing return."

It is necessary to put a lot of emphasis on the law of diminishing returns. That law is essential to a clear understanding of the relationship of men to earth, and so to a living. Occasionally, even yet, a writer too lazy or biased to look up the facts completely misrepresents the population scholars; describes them as believing the earth furnishes a *fixed* amount of food. Thus the lazy writer dresses up a bugbear which he can easily overwhelm, but he leaves untouched the real facts and the population men's reasoning about them. Shadowboxing of such a sort was *Time's* disgrace in its discussion of William Vogt's *Road to Survival*, November 8, 1948.

Incidentally, that *Time* article, "Eat Hearty," left out of the reckoning many detailed human experiences which *Time* itself had reported.

The doctrine that "there are only so many slices in the cake," which the *Time* writer ridiculed — and used in smearing population scholars — is apparently an expression of the *wages fund* doctrine, in its mid-Nineteenth Century form. That was curious patter, generally accepted for a brief while, but inconsistent with facts, including the fact of diminishing returns. I doubt if any population man has taken the fixed fund doctrine seriously since 1869. John Stuart Mill had believed in it awhile, but in 1869 he acknowledged its fallacy. Francis A. Walker, Director of the U. S. Censuses of 1870 and

1880, first president of the American Economic Association, and president of the Massachusetts Institute of Technology, laid the very dead doctrine to rest in *The Wages Question* in 1876. If I am correct in thinking of the slice-of-cake expression as a reference to the fixed wage fund, then *Time* is at least 72 years out of date.

Time's statement that population men believe there are "only so many slices in the cake" is only one item of nonsense in the many of which its tirade against population men was composed. Other misleading concepts in *Time's* treatment of population have been exposed by G. I. Burch in his article "The Eat Hearty Hoax" in the *Population Bulletin* for January 1949, and by Bernard DeVoto in *Harper's Magazine* for May 1949. DeVoto tells that when the Great Issues course at Dartmouth College set up *Time's* "Eat Hearty" as an exhibit of slanted journalism it needed ten pressboard panels 28 inches by 11 inches to report the article's errors, distortions and misrepresentations.

The population analyzers, in their reports of the relations of men to earth, base their warnings on reproduction recklessness, on the destruction of resources, and on diminishing returns in agriculture. In evidence of diminishing returns they might call attention to an article on rural Japan in *Time*, February 21, 1949. *Time's* writer, Sam Welles, mentioned the high per-acre yields. He said that the 1948 food production of the Japanese islands was slightly above the 1931-1940 average. "But the population has grown still faster, so there was less food for each mouth."

The law of diminishing returns is keystone to an understanding of the colossal problems that now beset the statesmen of the world.

•

The people of some areas depend, in part, on the raw materials and food products from the resources of other areas. Thus the Netherlands have depended on cocoanut oil, rubber, and various other products from Java, which products they have sold for purchasing power with which to buy food for Dutchmen in the Netherlands. If those products become less available to the Netherlands, either the levels of living in the Netherlands must fall or their population numbers must decline. *Time,* December 23, 1946, quoted a Dutch businessman, Pieter DeJong:

"We've already lost our trade with Germany. If we lose Indonesia too, The Netherlands will become one of the poorest countries on the Continent."

According to Hague negotiations of November 1949 the Dutch have now relinquished their sovereignty over most of Indonesia, but Dutch citizens are to retain such property rights as are already established.

The Japanese, before World War II, came to depend on raw materials and food from Korea, Manchukuo, and Formosa. Hereafter, those products of other lands will be available to the Japanese under less favorable conditions if at all. The Japanese, then, must experience either a reduction in their numbers or in their level of living. Since their level of living is not far above subsistence, it is probable that their numbers must decline.

Thus far that has not taken place because the United States citizens at a cost of more than a million and a half dollars a day have been providing the Japanese with supplies which in part make up the difference between what they used to get from outside their islands, and what they can get now from outside their islands in trade relations which they can no longer dominate.

A country that comes to rely on an international market in which to sell its manufactured products, and in which to buy food, has its future dependent not alone on its own population conditions but also on the population conditions in the rest of the world. That dependence on a foreign market tends to end in disaster if the people in the customer countries are increasing in numbers; and in almost all countries they are.

Thus the "expanding economy" doctrine, insofar as it implies an international outlet for manufactured goods, is a delusion and a snare. England fell into the expanding economy trap a century ago; is squirming now in the aftermath as the jaws of the trap clamp tighter—higher food costs against narrowing markets for her industrial products.

The processes of exchange hid from too many Englishmen the realization that food from afar is insecure, that *food producers have a priority on what they produce.* Americans, with English mistakes to learn from, should know better than to follow the English pattern.

On that point that food producers have a priority on what they produce are some facts reported in the *United Nations Bulletin* for March 15, 1949. The population of the rice-eating areas has increased by nearly 100,000,000 people in the 1939-1949 decade—about 10 percent. World production of 145 million tons of rough rice during 1948-49 is 2 percent off the pre-war average, in spite of the fact that the 1948-49 crop was grown on 6.2 million acres more than the pre-war rice land. The surplus rice available for international movement in 1949 was less than half the annual quantity that was shipped before the war.

Thus, with production down 2 percent, shipments decreased more than 50 percent. That is a hunger-charged illustration of the principle that when food is scarce, food producers have a priority on the food.

I think I can make the tragic truth concerning an internationalized economy a little clearer.

To see how the disaster develops for the manufacturing country with foreign sales outlets, we have two varieties of prospective customer countries to consider:

1. those in which the inhabitants have little opportunity to get into manufacturing;

2. those in which the people do have an opportunity to get into manufacturing.

The Orient is not a very good outlet for manufactured goods because its people cannot afford them. The Asiatics must concentrate on producing food, but even when they do that they have little food to sell; they need it all themselves just to keep alive. I think we can say, concerning the customer countries with little opportunity to get into manufacturing, that if and *as their population becomes dense in relation to soil, the inhabitants have to give a larger and larger proportion of their energy to the production of food for themselves.* With the increase in their own numbers they become less dependable as a source of food for manufacturing countries, and a less active market for the manufacturing country's wares. Ellsworth Huntington illustrated, in paragraph 126 of his *Principles of Economic Geography*:

"A monsoon climate and great density of population, when taken together, make North China one of the smallest contributors to world trade in proportion to the number of people."

And again, "the density of the population and the small size of the farms, make it impossible for the people to buy much."

Now let us investigate the plight of a manufacturing country that depends on sales to people in a country which can develop its own manufacturing. For the first part of this analysis we go to W. Stanley Jevons, a brilliant English economist who made the basic causal sequences clear in *The Coal Question* in 1865.

"Jevons" is one of the most famous names in British economics, but it is famous primarily in connection with an analysis of demands for goods. Perhaps because Jevons himself centered his later efforts on *demands,* the economic principle that appeared in his first book—the principle with the greatest impact on England — was overlooked. That principle reports the TRANSFER OF THE EFFECTS OF THE SLOWING DOWN OF EXTENSIVE EXPANSION in the New World, the transfer to England of the effects of the end of free land in America. Let's call it Jevons' law. It has not even yet, at the time of this writing, been accorded its appropriate place in the world's thinking.

Yet anybody who claims to understand population problems cannot afford to be ignorant about that transfer —and in five minutes you will be master of the principle yourself.

Jevons told of the outgoing migration from England, which was attracted by the undeveloped resources of the far reaches of the world. Prosperity in England resulted (1) from the draining off of excess people, (2) from the stimulation of sales of English manufactured goods in new areas, and (3) from the flow of cheap food and raw materials to England. The prosperity encouraged early marriages in England.

"But now comes the most serious point of all," said Jevons on page 424 (3rd edition, revised in 1906 by A. W. Flux and published by Macmillan and Company).

"After a certain period emigration will begin to have a very different effect upon the destinies of this country from what it now exercises. Instead of extending across the seas an agricultural system, it will develop, or rather complete, abroad systems of iron and coal industries in direct competition with ours. . . ."

And now comes the heavyweight reasoning:

"It is well known that in spreading over a new country, settlers are naturally apt to exhaust the virgin soil they get so cheap, regardless of manures and agricultural arts by which its fertility might be maintained. . . . It must pay better to take the cream off the land when the farmer can freely select new farms of untouched richness. A gradual inland migration is the result. . . ."

He pointed out that with abundance of opportunities in America the population would continue to grow; and (page 427) "with such a growth of population, agriculture must soon be carried to its first limits. Within a century the choicest lands will have been taken up, and the second and third rate lands must be settled, or the old exhausted lands revived by more diligent culture. Agriculture will begin to lose its extremely easy and profitable character in the States."

Clearer than most men's hindsight, Jevons' prophecy continued. Coal, and manufacturing dependent on coal, would offer the more tempting opportunities, in the New World, in comparison with agriculture. The shift in America from agriculture to manufacturing would threaten England's commercial position.

"Corn," said Jevons, "will be growing dearer in the States, while coal and iron are growing dearer here."

The coal and iron would be growing dearer in England because of the increasing depth at which the coal would have to be mined. The English manufacturing industries depended and still depend on English coal.

So the English would lose the advantage of getting cheap grain in America, and would lose the American market, and eventually the world market for its manufactured goods. Gradually the might of Britannia, proud Mistress of the Seas, would fail. Englishmen would have to choose between wholesale emigration or "a change of habits"—by which Jevons seems to have implied a reduction of birth rates.

The other English economists of the time, and the government men, and the general public, gave too little heed. Birth control was practiced increasingly, it is true; but not enough (and by the wrong people) —and now, as Jevons foresaw, Englishmen face wholesale emigration, or a more drastic "change of habits." One thing that Jevons seems not to have foreseen is the fact that wholesale emigration is confronted with tremendous and increasing obstacles.

Jevons was foretelling the consequences to his country from the limit to new acres in the New World, and from the exhaustion of old acres in the New World. The declining yield of crops resulting from the exhaustion of fertility is not strictly diminishing returns. It can better be designated as depletion of resources. But the analysis has value to us partly because it helps directly to explain the fate of a country that cannot grow enough food for its people. It has value to us partly because the *mechanism of transfer* of effects of exhaustion of fertility does apply also to the *transfer of the effects of diminishing returns.*

The British once depended on beef from the U. S. West. Britain had no control over our beef production. When our population increased, our per capita beef production declined. Sixty years ago, said M. K. Wisehart in *Pathfinder* for March 9, 1949, for every 100 persons in the U. S. there were 97 cattle and calves. By 1949, even before the blizzards, there were 53 cattle and calves per 100 persons.

Land that would grow wheat became too valuable to be used as pasture. At the same time there was a greater demand for beef from our own enlarged population.

At higher prices, Britain now gets beef from Argentina, Mexico, and Canada. But populations in those lands are growing, too!

Is the law of diminishing returns involved in this story

of beef? Yes; as population grew in the United States, the requirement for grains and vegetables put well-watered lands into more intensive use. However, diminishing returns prevented the greater and greater intensification of use; in other words diminishing returns prevented the growing of indefinitely greater crops, *made "extensive" cultivation profitable* even on lands of lesser rainfall or irregular rainfall. So, *because of diminishing returns from the earlier vegetable and grain lands, some of the American grazing lands were plowed up*; and of our beef poor Britain got none.

•

A little more discussion of that transfer of the effects of diminishing returns may help. Let's pin it down with an example. Englishmen get part of their food from Canada. There is reason to believe that gradually the quantities of Canadian wheat available to Englishmen will be less. The reason is that the Canadian population is increasing, and will eat more of the food themselves.

But, you might say, twice as many people in Canada will grow twice as much wheat, and so have twice as much to ship to England.

No, you wouldn't say that; you would know that the law of diminishing returns would prevent a doubling of wheat with a doubling of the Canadian population, because each Canadian would have less land to work with.

E. Parmalee Prentice, in his 1944 book, *Food, War and the Future,* reported the presidential address of September 1898 by Sir William Crookes to the British Association for the Advancement of Science. Sir William said there had been expectations that the Canadian northwest would supply the world with wheat, but performance had lagged behind promise. As the wheatlands of the northwest increased, the wheat areas in eastern Canada exported less. The Dominion's added acres were little more than enough to meet the requirements of Canada's growing population.

But though you see that twice as many people growing wheat would not grow *twice* as much wheat, you might think that added people in Canada would grow as much more wheat as they themselves would eat, so that the surplus for export would remain as large.

The size of that surplus depends on the population total at which the Canadians will stop their own increase, if they will stop it anywhere. The chances are that Canadians will continue to increase in numbers far past the point at which there will be as much food to export as is now exported. If they multiply to a density like that in the Orient, they, like the Orientals, will have almost no food exports. But viewing the transition from today's stage, *because of diminishing returns, not many more people than the present number of wheat growers are likely to be attracted to wheat growing* until the Canadian level of living becomes much lower than now. Instead, Canadians will carry further their diversification from agriculture, to include more manufacturing. In that way they will avoid *for themselves* the bad effects of diminishing returns in agriculture.

The *U.S. News and World Report* is an independent weekly magazine on national and international affairs, published in Washington. This excerpt from its issue of April 30, 1948, is copyrighted and is used by permission:

"In Canada, industrial expansion is under way on a big scale. The growth of Canada's production, in fact, has paralleled that in the United States since the war. . . . Industry is turning out nearly 80 per cent more goods

than before the war. . . . More than 5000 new factories
have been built since 1939. Most of Canada's 25,000 pre-
war plants have been or are being enlarged."

Of course, Canadians have no realization that they, in
their increasing numbers, hold their high level of living
at the expense of Mother England. U. S. citizens do not
realize, either, that their own increase in numbers and
further industrialization register in harder times for the
older industrial countries.

Roland R. Renne, on page 57 of his *Land Economics,*
a 1947 book published by Harper, testifies to the drift to
the cities (though he does not relate it to diminishing
returns from the soil). He thinks of the cities growing to
numbers sufficient to absorb farmers' surpluses of food.

"Wherever the fertility of the soil or the state of the
agricultural arts has produced a surplus of food and raw
materials beyond the needs of the producers," he says,
"towns and cities have developed."

In getting into manufacturing to keep up their own
income as their numbers grow, Canadians will have less
wheat to send to England, and, becoming more and more
industrialized, they will take less of English manufactured goods. So, as a consequence of diminishing returns
in Canada, Englishmen must pay more for food and raw
materials, and must have a less eager market for their
exports.

That is an instance of *transfer of the effects of diminishing returns.* Any country that expands its population
beyond the support of its food production, as England
has done, risks, in the words of Malthus, "a long period of
retrograde movement and misery." It may be able for a
while, like England, to supplement its food production
by food imports, but when the population increases in
the lands from which it has received the supplementary
supplies, the food importation will be possible only with

rising costs. The levels of living may for a time continue high in the erstwhile food-*exporting* place, but they are bound to fall in the area that has been *importing* food.

Robert Scott Moffatt in 1885 dealt with the idea of England's risk, on pages 50 and 125 of *Henry George the Orthodox*. He pointed to the fact that as the population of America increases, using more food, her surpluses will ultimately diminish. And he asked, "Will England or Europe then be able to maintain such an exotic population?"

He discussed as a source of danger the English practice of importing raw materials, working them into finished products, then exporting the finished products and importing food. If England could thus double her manufacturing she would be in extreme peril: "America would sooner or later insist in organizing manufacturers for herself," leaving England in the lurch.

J. M. Keynes, in 1920, gave attention to Europe's risk on pages 23-25 of *The Economic Consequences of the Peace*. The prosperity of Europe, he said, was based on America's large exportable surplus of food, but "as a result of the growth of population overseas, chiefly in the United States," that basis of prosperity was not secure.

"Europe's claim on the resources of the New World was becoming precarious; the Law of Diminishing Returns was at last reasserting itself, and was making it necessary year by year for Europe to offer a greater quantity of other commodities to obtain the same amount of bread. . . ."

In a recent treatment of the subject, Rupert B. Vance in *Foreign Affairs* for July 1948 seemed to say that the risk has culminated in disaster. Vance said that by making food accessible by foreign trade the Industrial Revolution delayed the population crisis of England for a hundred years. But in multiplying up to the possibilities that the Industrial Revolution presented, he said, England created a denser population than England could reasonably be expected to support, "once industrialization had spread over the globe."

In the same vein Aldous Huxley presented "The Double Crisis" in *Science News Letter* for March 26, 1949:

"The manufactured articles which Western Europe exchanged for food and raw materials have tended to become less acceptable in proportion as the nations of the New World have developed their own industries. Europe will find it more and more difficult to pay for supplies which, as the population pressure on the New World's eroded soil increases, are bound to diminish."

Jevons and Moffatt and Keynes and Vance and Huxley were building on the foundation that Malthus had laid on pages 187 and 188 of *Additions to the Fourth and Former Editions of an Essay on the Principle of Population,* Book III, Chapter XII, published in 1817. Malthus had forecast that cheap food in America would be temporary, that America would eventually "manufacture for itself" and "withdraw its corn from Europe."

But the basic question is, WHY? *Why will not the larger number of Canadians have the same ratio of farmers to total population that the earlier number of Canadians had?* How can we be sure that the farmers will be a *smaller* proportion of the population?

So far as I know, that question had not been made explicit until I put it in a little mimeographed practice book copyrighted in 1930. In 1939 I formulated it thus:

"Why would the increasing number of people in the new countries not continue to specialize on the old crops rather than to diversify their energies and reach into occupations that once were England's exclusively?"

Jevons' material applies as part of the answer: the people in a new land turn to manufacturing as they strip away the fertility of the soil.

No doubt, too, there is partial answer in manufacturing itself, in the increasing effectiveness of its techniques, in the erstwhile new lands, the United States, and Canada.

But the rounded-out answer must include the law of diminishing returns in agriculture.

Diminishing returns make it seem to the young sons of farmers that their greater opportunities are in the factories. Farm wages, reflecting diminishing returns, are influential in the occupational choices.

Diminishing returns in a food-*growing* area register their effects in a distant food-*consuming* area, often much sooner than in the food-growing area itself. Diminishing returns in agriculture lead to the diversification of the people of the food-growing area to manufacturing.

Looking into the future with the aid of this addition to the law of diminishing returns, we must see that more people in the U.S. or in Australia or Canada or South America, either by births or migrations, will prevent so much shipment of foodstuffs to foreign lands. As our own increase in population stopped our exports of beef altogether, so our further increase will prevent a shipment of so much grain. A continuing increase of population would terminate our grain shipments completely.

The same principle applies in domestic trade too: if you fill Texas with more and more people, you will make beefsteak and grapefruit more costly to New Yorkers. For thirty years the increase in Southern population, experiencing diminishing returns in agriculture, has made laborers increasingly available for manufacturing. Now our cotton industry centers in the South; not in New England. In fact 75 percent of U. S. textiles are made south of the Mason and Dixon line, and a wide variety of other manufactured products are produced there: furniture, glassware, chemical products, newsprint, container board, masonite hardboard, for illustration. William H. Nicholas, in the *National Geographic Magazine* for March 1949, quoted the President of the Southern Railway System: "Along our lines new plants have averaged one a day for the last three years." Says Nicholas, "More and more, Dixie is converting its own raw materials into manufactured goods instead of shipping them north and buying them back as finished products."

•

In explaining the fact that diminishing returns are transferred, in their effects, from a maturing country like Canada to an industrialized country like England, I merely joined the older concept of diminishing returns to Jevons' analysis of the mechanism of transfer.

But now I shall set forth another economic principle. It is, I believe, completely new and original. And am I wrong in thinking it is so important that it should change the policies of nations?

This too, like the adaptation of Jevons' findings, is dependent on the law of diminishing returns. One begins to think of that law of diminishing returns as a "mother lode" with several veins and placer deposits not far away.

Turn back a few pages to the table entitled "Illustration of the Law of Diminishing Returns." Observe that with 18 men working the 100 acres, though they produce relatively little per man, they have a relatively high average productivity *per acre,* and a high total production. Now take nine of the 18 men off from the hundred acres. The average productivity of the nine that you leave there is high. If those nine are the only ones to consider, it is a great advantage to them to get rid of the others. But note well that the total production and the average production per *acre* are now only about 68 percent of what they were with 18 men working those 100 acres.

Multiply the men and the acres and the total production by a million, and assume that they constitute a universe. If nine million of the 18 million men leave their hundred million acres, and establish manufacturing enterprises in cities, they nevertheless have to be fed from the same old hundred million acres. But when we thus reverse the usual direction of scrutiny of the scale of diminishing returns—when we *reduce* the number of men per unit of land—we find that, though the per capita productivity of the remaining farmers increases, the total product *decreases*. The half of the population who go to the cities are still in need of food. The average amount of food available for the 18,000,000 men (and their families) is reduced to about 68 percent of what it would be if all the men had stayed on the soil.

If the 68 percent is an ample supply, then, since the men in town will make useful manufactured goods, the diversification of occupations to include manufacturing seems to be appropriate adjustment.

Before we go further in this discourse, let's get this much down as a principle, applying everywhere except where crowding is extreme: *Fewer workers produce a smaller total of food than many workers.* You saw that on our diminishing returns scale. It is a simple generalization, and you may think disgustingly simple; but it shows why not many countries can go far with manufacturing (except as they gamble on an outside source of food).

That generalization has meaning in connection with another economic generalization which is better established in economic parlance, namely, Engel's law. Ernst Engel, nearly a hundred years ago, found that the lower the income of a family the larger is the percentage of that income which is spent for food, and the smaller is the percentage spent for education, recreation and luxuries. Those findings have been verified by the budget studies of the U. S. Bureau of Labor Statistics.

Engel's report of the comparative persistence of the demand for food is really just another way of saying that food is a prime necessity. We may be sure that in a country in which real incomes are low a very large proportion of effort must be used in the production of food.

In densely populated countries the land must be worked intensively—must be worked far down the scale of diminishing returns—in order to provide enough food. Except for intensive cultivation, food prices would be still higher and poverty would be still greater.

As we proceed down a scale of diminishing returns per worker, as workers increase we must watch results in our correlated columns showing *total* production and the *per acre average* production. We eventually arrive at an absolute maximum total and an absolute maximum per acre average. The total production will go up no further with further increases of manpower, and will actually go down instead—further and further down.

What happens to returns *per worker* when the maximum per acre average is reached and passed? No change occurs in the trend. Those returns per worker keep on going down with increases in workers.

We get valuable light on the whole problem by taking a look at China.

John Lossing Buck, in *Land Utilization in China*, a 1937 book published by the University of Chicago Press, reported the results of an extensive study of Chinese farms. He classified the farms by size into five groups. Simplifying the data on his page 283, we get this:

PRODUCTION ON CHINESE FARMS

Farm group	Men equivalent per 100 crop acres	Crop acres per man-equivalent	Production per man-equivalent in equivalents of bushels of grain	Production per acre in equivalents of bushels of grain
A	25.	4.0	76.1	19.0
B	31.25	3.2	62.0	19.4
C	38.46	2.6	53.5	20.6
D	47.62	2.1	43.1	20.5
E	66.67	1.5	30.6	20.4

(On American farms for comparison: 746.0)

There we have a striking statistical showing of diminishing returns. It is something like our other table except that this one shows a condition at a subsistence level, and an arrival at an actually declining yield *per acre*. As to the diminishing returns, where one man cultivates four acres, as in Group A, he produces the equivalent of 76 bushels of grain per year. But where two men cultivate four acres, as in Group D, they produce only the equivalent of 43 bushels of grain each. Since they have less land per worker with which to work, their efforts are less fruitful.

As to the men in Group E and their families, the total food production would be about as great if they went to the cities or jumped in the ocean, and left their land to the people in the other groups. Actually the acre production would be greater by about the extent of the productivity of the scraps of land under their hovels and in the pathways to their doors. But if only that many people left the farms, a Chinese farmer's life would still be a miserable struggle for a bare survival, with famine threatening in the bad years.

Above C, on the scale—possibly even above D—a reduction of people working the soil would *reduce total food production*.

Now with these food facts before us, consider what are the prospects for prosperity for the Chinese *by way of industrialization.*

Concentrate on the fact that food is the prime necessity. Most of the Chinese get not much more than enough to keep them alive now. If the people in Group E go to the cities, the change in total food will be insignificant. If they could get into factory production, and if they could keep alive, they might make for a higher level of living of somebody insofar as the level of living depends on commodities other than food. But *their factory production would not increase the amount of food.*

As to market for their manufactured goods, the people remaining on China's farms would be not far above subsistence level, and would not constitute a very active market for the manufactured goods, especially in poor crop years.

And what about the food prospects of those people who go to the cities? To the extent that their food must be grown in China, they are worse off than if they stay on the land. One reason is that those who produce more food than enough to keep alive, eat a little more. Also, in case of shortages, those who produce the food have a priority on it. Additionally, as some of the farmers move off the land, the survival rate of persons who remain will be slightly higher, and, even as the exodus proceeds, the population on the farms will be kept about as high as before. All in all there will not be so much food available to those who go to town as there would be if they stayed on the land.

So incentives in China in *normal* times are about as incentives in America have been in *depression* times. There is little demand for industrial workers because employers have a poor market for industrial products. There has been a "back to the farm" movement. In China it isn't a movement; it is, instead, a constant pres-

sure landward—because people are in less danger of
death by starvation if they are close to the sources of food.

We learned that in a new area with an abundance of
food supplies, diminishing returns in agriculture *stimulate* manufacturing—because of diminishing incentives
for agricultural production. Diminishing returns, there,
are accompanied by diminishing incentives. Now we
find that in a crowded land the scantiness of food—which
results from diminishing returns in agriculture—tends
to *prevent* manufacturing. Where food is scarce the incentive is great to keep close to the source of supply.

If the people in the E group leave the farms, and the
land they have had is worked by the D group, then the
D group, because of their larger acreages, would become
an addition to the C group.

But at any rate, if as many people as those in the E,
D, and C groups were to go to the cities there would be
less total food produced in China.

Isn't it clear from following diminishing returns to its
implications in total food production that there is no
reasonable hope of adequate food for Chinamen by way
of industrialization?

•

To show the futility of manufacturing, as a means of
meeting a crowded country's greatest need—the need for
food—is not to condemn *all* manufacturing in China, or
other crowded lands. It is to say that *misery that stems
from food shortages* has no cure in industrialization (and
most misery in crowded lands does stem from food shortages).

To the extent that the people of crowded lands buy manufactured goods, they may have advantage in making them instead of importing them. In order to import them they would have to yield up food in payment. If they manufacture the goods which they would buy, the man power thus used does not reduce the total food supply.

There might even be some advantage in manufacturing for *export,* since the labor, at that Group E level, would add no food to the total, no matter how employed.

But the point that must be stressed is that *there is no improvement in the food situation from the industrialization.*

In India there has been a rather substantial development of manufacturing, but its hoped-for benefit is a will-o'-the-wisp. The appalling conditions in such factory areas as have developed there indicate that factory production has not resulted in the slightest improvement of the level of living of the masses.

Yet President Truman in "Point Four" of his 1949 inaugural address, and Secretary of State Dean Acheson in his first press conference, made it a major objective of the Administration to industrialize the "underdeveloped areas," assisting native capital with U. S. investments. Following their lead, Secretary of Commerce Charles Sawyer, on April 24, 1949, proposed that the U. S. Government guarantee convertibility of profits received by U. S. private investors in backward countries into dollars. By June 1, 1949, United Nations officials were discussing the "Point Four" plan in terms of many billions of dollars. Carried in the newspapers of 1950's All Fools' Day was the story that the U. S. House of Representatives had passed the Foreign Aid Bill with its inclusion of $25,000,-000 to be used in launching the Point Four program.

The government of India itself refuses to believe the evidence in Bombay and Karachi, for example. In the former the 1931 census showed 74 percent of the total population living in one-room tenements, an increase from 69 percent in 1911. In Karachi, almost a third of the population existed at the rate of six to nine persons per room. Nevertheless Premier Nehru is attempting to encourage both foreign and native investment in enterprises for the manufacture of automobiles, tractors, heavy machinery, machine tools, rubber, textiles, and paper.

In a crowded country, can the factory products of those who go to the cities be sold abroad, and can food be brought in from abroad? Can the prospective manufacturing population anticipate a steady other-country market for their manufactured goods, coupled with a reliable other-country source for food? They will have to have *both*, in order to come out with even a subsistence.

The other countries are resistant to additional manufactured goods. Only a relatively prosperous land can finance the purchase of manufactured goods—and even in a prosperous land there is pressure for the increase of people of that land to get into manufacturing too, as has already been shown by the Jevons analysis, and by my exposition of the influence of diminishing returns in getting people off the farms.

There is, then, no reasonable hope for China, or for India, Java, or Korea, to improve their conditions by shifting to manufacturing, because there is too little market anywhere in the world for the things they might manufacture.

If China could conceivably make the shift of two-thirds of its population to manufacturing, and could find a market for its manufactured products, could it *buy* FOOD? China's own food production would be much less than it is now—with the relaxation from diminishing returns which I have just discussed. There would be more food produced per farmer, but less per acre and less *as a total*. In order to maintain as much food per person as its pres-

ent subsistence level, China would have to absorb
tically all of the food from the New World that ha
viously been going to European countries. Euro
would have to go hungry. Yet I have dealt with only
China, in this example of a shift to manufacturing.

Imagine the rest of the Orient as food buyers too, and
what happens to the glib sophistry that manufacturing
is the way out for the crowded countries?

Here, stated briefly, is the new economic principle:
For an area in which the population is so dense that because of diminishing returns a large proportion of its
people can produce only enough food to keep alive, a
shift of workers to manufacturing has little chance of
improving its economic conditions.

Narrowed to its food meaning the law is this: Relaxation from diminishing returns, that is, withdrawal of
some of the pressure against the resisting soil, reduces
total food production.

In a world perspective: abatement of agricultural effort
anywhere would increase starvation.

And now, combining Jevons' law and my two exten-
sions of the law of diminishing returns, we get this: A
country in which the population increases beyond the
carrying capacity of its own soil can have only temporary
relief, if any, from manufacturing. Thus stated, the rule
is broad enough to include England, which did get a
century of grace from its population malfeasance, and
India, China, and Java, which can get no grace at all.
England had its postponement of punishment because it
was early in manufacturing. But England is going to bed
without its supper now, and will go without breakfast too
when the United States stops the dole.

The *emphasis* in the law of diminishing returns is
usually on the *decreasing* production *per man* that results
from increasing the number of men cultivating the land.
An aspect which is usually incidental is that as more men

cultivate the land there is an *increase* (though a diminishing increase) in product *per acre*. My new principle could be based entirely on that usually incidental aspect of the law of diminishing returns: more men result in more product per acre and more total product; *fewer men result in less product per acre and less total product*.

Suppose, in a crowded country, a government were to carry on a policy which would relax the pressure on the soil. It would thereby proceed backward on the scale of diminishing returns. If it did that without reducing its total population it would nevertheless be reducing the number of people in agriculture and reducing the proportion of its people in agriculture. Though the per capita production of food per farmer would be increased, the per capita production of food averaged over the total population would be reduced—and the per capita production of food for the world's population would be reduced.

That conclusion could be arrived at by the use of reason from the law of diminishing returns, without additional facts. So it is really a corollary of the law of diminishing returns.

The new principle clarifies the resistance of a crowded land to manufacturing. I have used it in connection with evidence from India and China. The evidence, together with the principle which makes the evidence cohere, ought to put an abrupt stop to the recurrent proposal that the overcrowded countries undertake manufacturing as a cure for their poverty, and it ought to take the haze away from the truth that it is necessary to meet population facts with population measures.

•

Surpluses of farm food production above farmers' consumption have been prerequisite to the development of cities. That is the other side of the same coin that Roland R. Renne gave us, reported earlier in this chapter. Where the surpluses do exist, the villages tend to become cities, said Renne. And now I point out that where food surpluses are not present or are not easily available, villages must remain villages, and the cities must remain few.

Huntington mentioned that in paragraph 119 of his *Principles of Economic Geography,* published by John Wiley and Sons, where he wrote of India:

"cities are neither numerous nor large in proportion to the population. A subsistence economy is so widespread that there is not much opportunity for cities."

There has not been much *opportunity* for cities because there has not been much chance of cities getting food.

Huntington was prospecting close to pure gold in that economic geography text, and some of the ore he turned up on the subject of surpluses is valuable indeed. In paragraph 24 he reminded us that Java is one of the most densely populated countries in the world, with more than 800 people per square mile, and with farms of from 1 to 3 acres. It is impossible for farmers with so little land to raise much of a surplus of food. They have to eat almost all they produce. So Java's farmers have too little food to sell, to feed the Island's city people. The city people have to import food from other countries.

"If good rice land were taken for rubber plantations," said Huntington, "the necessity of depending on imported food would be still greater. Moreover, some of the farmers would be thrown out of work, for an acre of rubber demands far fewer hours of labor than an acre of rice. Such conditions have caused the Dutch, who govern Java, to limit the use of rice land for rubber. Even without this legal restriction the high price of the good land would drive the rubber planters into the rougher, more remote, or less densely populated regions."

Over in paragraphs 985 and 986 he compares Java and Siam. Siam's 14 million people produce about 4½ million tons of rice, which is about 643 pounds per capita. Java's 45 million people produce about 5½ million tons of rice, which is about 244 pounds per capita. The main reason for the difference is that the population of Java is so dense that there is only half as much land per farmer as in Siam. Siam

"not only feeds its own townspeople, who are more numerous proportionally than those of Java, but in addition exports about 1,400,000 tons of rice per year."

But Huntington didn't find the vein of truth which carries with it a warning: a shift to the cities of a large enough part of the rural population to permit a substantially larger per capita income for the remaining farmers, would nevertheless reduce the per capita food production of the total population, since those who moved to the cities would still be a part of the total population.

Now let me summarize our Chapter 2 findings thus far:

1. An increase of workers on a fixed land area increases the product in less proportion than the proportion by which the workers increase.
2. (a) In a land where food is plentiful, diminishing returns direct people away from farming.
   (b) Hardship results in manufacturing areas.
3. Where food is scarce and not readily imported, diminishing returns keep people in farming, make resistance to manufacturing; diminishing returns in crowded lands keep people near starvation level with or without manufacturing.

•

In the preceding chapter, I relayed some distressing facts about Korean conditions from Andrew J. Grajdanzev's *Modern Korea*, a John Day Company book of 1944. But when Grajdanzev wrote, my corollary of the law of diminishing returns, detailing the dependence of a manufacturing population on agriculture, had not yet been formulated. He followed along where many others had gone, and at the end of the trail he, like the others, made a leap in the dark. He pointed to the low net value of product per day per worker in Korean agriculture: .59 yen in 1937, as compared with 8.22 yen in Korean industry. Then he made the jump to this:

"It is not Korea that is 'over-populated'; it is the agriculture of Korea that is 'over-crowded.' Far more extensive industrialization would seem to be the only solution for this extreme poverty."

And again, he said on page 89:

"In Japan and Korea, the same or almost the same amount of foodstuffs could be produced with the help of machinery, with a fraction of the labor that is now being spent, and thus free a tremendous amount of human energy to raise the standard of living. It is not overpopulation that lies at the root of Korean and Japanese poverty, it is low productivity coupled with oppressive social conditions and often caused by them."

Grajdanzev would have manufacturing started in Korea, and have Korean farmers become factory workers. He would have a *correlated shift to machinery on the farms, which he thinks would hold the total food production as high as before.* That is doubtful but conceivable. Assume the same food total. It would temporarily offset some of my formulations. However, the people who remain on the farms, now in some years eating only enough to keep alive, since they would be producing more per capita after the change would probably eat more. They would still have some food to sell, but, averaged over those who left for the factory jobs, that which would be for sale would be less per capita for those factory workers than the subsistence they got when they too were on the farms.

Also, the higher level of living of the farmers who remain on the farms would not instantaneously lower their birth rates. Their death rate would be reduced; their survival rate would rise. The population *on the farms* would soon be as numerous as it was before. There would then be as little food as before left over to send to the cities. The factory workers in Korean cities would have to look elsewhere than to Korea for food.

We have seen that the outside market for Korean manufactured goods would be problematic. Now we see that the demand they would have for food from outside Korea would be an increase of the world's demand for the world's food.

In connection with that outside market for Korean manufactured goods there is this consideration: Manufacturing is a kind of production that cannot be maintained everywhere—on any but a very small scale. Large-scale production in *one* place requires, or results in, an entire absence of that sort of production in many places. So if some of the factories which Grajdanzev imagines in Korea were successful, they would have a market only by taking away the market of other manufacturers, presumably those in Japan. Thus, if industrialization occurs in Korea, the poverty of the Japanese in Japan will be made more stringent.

●

In the crowded world of today there are not many places where food surpluses are possible. In the *Survey Graphic* for March 1948, J. W. Evans of the U. N. Food and Agriculture Organization says:

"The United States and Canada together have been the source of 75 percent or more of the total grain shipments.

"This dependence of importing countries on one region for their subsistence is a disquieting aspect of the postwar food situation, since it places supplies so completely at the mercy of the weather. Thus the increase in the United States has been made possible by a run of good seasons. A cycle of poor seasons would reduce the exportable surplus to small proportions. . . ."

Aldous Huxley, commenting on the weather cycles, has shown how perilous it is for population to increase to the extent that would be permitted by the years of plenty. To limit the load to the low productivity of the years of scarcity would make more sense.

And for Europe it isn't altogether a matter of lean years spacing the years of good crops. There is also the long time trend to allow for. Pearson and Harper, in *The World's Hunger,* already referred to, show that Europeans produce 28 percent of the world's food, and import a fourth as much as they produce. *If Europe were not to increase her population at all, she would nevertheless be due for a future of suffering as the populations increase in the exporting areas—the Americas, Africa, and Oceania.* Says *Life,* April 26, 1948, "Millions in Europe would be starving today were the farmers of the U. S., Canada and South America not in the export business." True, and it is equally true that, in reference to food, those people will be in the export business in less measure 25 years from now if their own population trends continue. European countries have the alternative of *reducing* their populations or sinking to lower levels of food consumption. The industrial revolution can work wonders in making kitchen ranges, but it is almost futile in providing what is cooked on them, and extending the industrial revolution into agriculture helps but little. As Pearson and Harper report on page 56, "Mechanized equipment does not overcome the most important conditions limiting yields, the natural fertility of the soil and climatic conditions."

The Pearson and Harper book clarifies the conditions that make for food productivity. Land area as such is of little use. For its productivity there must be

> favorable temperature
> sufficient rainfall but not too much
> reliable rainfall
> slopes not very steep
> fertile soil.

"Few persons recognize the veto power of any one factor." Consider "reliable rainfall" for instance.

"The agriculture of an area is largely determined by the low rainfall years," say Pearson and Harper. "Large areas in South Africa and Australia have enough rainfall during some years but it is too unreliable for crop production."

On page 48 of *The World's Hunger,* they have presented a volume of information in a single table. Their method of analysis is similar to that used for wheat by Ellsworth Huntington on page 28 of his 1940 book, *Principles of Economic Geography*. Pearson and Harper compute 35.7 billion acres as the world's total. They show that elements of productivity must necessarily be in combination, that the essential combination is present in few places, and that the proportion of earth that is thus useable for food production is very small. Of the world's total land surface:

43% of it has *adequate rainfall*. (I am surpris
how low they set their sights for "adequ
inches of rain a year!)
34% has enough rainfall and *reliable rainfall*.
32% has enough rain, reliable rainfall, and *enough heat*.
21% has enough rain, reliable rainfall, enough heat, and
suitable topography.
Only 7% has enough rain, dependable rain, enough heat,
sufficient flatness, and *fertile soil*.

Europe has the highest proportion of its land adapted
to food production: 37 percent; "North America is a
poor second with only 10 percent." Asia has 6%; South
America 5%; Africa and Oceania (Australia and New
Zealand) 3%.

Pearson and Harper think there are not many more
acres that can be brought into use than are now in use.
They see possibilities for some increases in productivity
per acre of lands now in use, but not a great deal—by
fertilizers, by use of more machinery, by new and improved varieties of crops, and by livestock improvement.

They think the population-resources ratio is most significantly measured by the amount of grain produced per
capita, since grain is three-fourths of man's food. By that
test, the density of population for the different areas compares inversely as the pounds of grain produced per person compare; thus Asia, with fewest pounds of grain produced per person, has greatest density of population.

	Pounds of grain produced annually per person
Asia	592
Africa	605
Europe	788
Oceania	1545
North America	1859

If everybody would accept the Asiatic level of living,
the world would support almost three billion people, but

at North America's level of living the present world production would maintain fewer than a billion persons—
fewer than half the present world population.

Animal products are only 6% of the world's food.
They are only 3% of consumption in Asia, but 25% in
America and 36% in Oceania. People in the lands of
plenty have choices among foods; others take what they
can get.

"Animal products comprise over two-thirds of the diet
of the people with high incomes," say Pearson and Harper, page 17. "On this basis it would appear that the
world would like to increase its consumption of animal
foods about four or five times."

There are well-intentioned persons who advocate increasing the health-giving "protective" foods and providing them to undernourished people everywhere. Pearson
and Harper, on page 71, show how fantastic the idea is.
To give a quart of milk a day to those not now so supplied would require extra acreage equivalent to that now
required for grain to feed the whole of the present world
population.

And that assumes that the population remain stationary; whereas actually, with a quart of milk a day, the
survival rate would be much higher and the population
would grow faster than ever.

Clearly our efforts at amelioration must be in the direction of reproduction correctives.

Any level of living above a subsistence level is a result
of civilization, but civilization is a complex accumulation
of artificialities which have been invented item by item,
many of them with the intention of improving the level
of living of individuals or groups. The whole structure
is threatened by human reproduction, which for the most
part has remained a force as uncivilized as fire in a factory
or water in a surging flood.

Chapter 3

Expansion Fever

Difficulties have arisen in Britain under the new government planning as a consequence of lack of reserves. If an objective is not reached in one area of operations, related objectives are unattained too. As John Jewkes has illustrated the point, a shortage of steel prevents the making of machine tools, and a failure of the machine tool program results in low production of finished goods. He thinks that a way out of the dilemma is to maintain large supplies all along the line, as precaution against unforeseen shortages in the flows of materials.

Excess capacity has a function comparable to the function of large supplies of materials.

Government planners in our state governments, in our national government, and in foreign governments have looked upon unused capacity as *waste,* and to eliminate unused capacity has been one of their announced objectives. But wherever unused capacity is eliminated, tie-ups increase and productivity declines, for unused capacity is insurance.

Earth resources are part, a major part, of the necessary

reserves for a smooth-running economy. But since these resources are exhaustible, and since some of their products are available under conditions of diminishing returns, there is need to avoid the population expansion that would overload the resources.

I think you have seen that as to *India*. If there were fewer people in India by 200,000,000, the remaining inhabitants would have more land per capita with which to work, and consequently a greater average productivity. If *England* had only half her present population, Englishmen would be better off than they are now, too.

In the existing circumstances there can be no significant "shortage of labor." Rare indeed in these times would be a case in which the average productivity of labor in general, anywhere in the world, would be increased by an increase in number of laborers. Certainly in England, where the resources have to be gleaned from the very bottom of the barrel, there has been no general shortage of labor for a century. That means that *at no time in the past century would a widespread increase in the number of laborers have resulted in an increased average productivity*—and that is more emphatically true now than ever before. People, then, are the one category of which there must be no reserves—and of which a shortage can occur only in those exceptional cases where more people would be good for the people already present by raising average productivity.

By that same criterion, welfare of the people does require reserves of everything else.

It is normal in the handling of businesses to provide that there are surpluses—reserves—all along the line. Good judgment requires it. Oftentimes actual reserves are not thought of as such, however. For example, an engineer plans a bridge. He estimates the probable load, but does he make his bridge just strong enough to bear that load? No; he builds for a strength far in excess of the immediate and apparent need.

And for a bridge already built, a sign is posted: "Load limit: 10 tons." Does that mean that the bridge will collapse if a load crosses which weighs 5 percent more than that? No; there is still a reserve strength. Before the bridge would actually collapse it would probably take a load four times that which is posted, though there would be an increasing risk, and the bridge itself would deteriorate under loads of twice the posted figure. But notice that good engineering policy calls for a very substantial reserve strength.

The principle of reserves is in use all around us, and makes our levels of living as high as they are. A few more examples: Tires are made to hold a load several times as great as that to which they would normally be subjected. Their extra strength is a safety factor, a form of insurance. You drive a motor, perhaps of 80 horsepower. It gives excess power, which puts less strain on it for its usual work than if it were pushed to its absolute capacity; and additionally, that power is available for a quick pickup.

In general, Americans believe in surpluses—believe in reserves. Those provide security against unpredictable possibilities.

Oddly, in the matter of the relation of men to earth's resources, many Americans partition off their usual reasoning about the helpfulness of reserves. They make no allowances at all for clumsy organization, bad judgments, weather upsets. They know that a large proportion of human arrangements *are* inefficient; that most people do need some insurance against bad judgment; that the weather is only loosely predictable; yet such realities are out of mind when they think of population. They expect perfect timing of production, a delicate allocation of men on the various phases of production, ideal weather, maximum production year after year. They're unrealistic;

unreasonable. The logic of the bridge fits but they don't apply it. They argue for crowding the resources of their state or their country harder and harder. They don't think of the case quite in those words, but it amounts to that. They say, for instance, "There is enough land in America for twice as many citizens as are here."

Of course that is true—but with a doubled population there would be sharply diminishing returns from agriculture, probably depleted soil reserves too, and diminished resources as basis for manufactures; and increasing costs not only for manufacturing but for sewers, water systems, city transportation, etc., and for crime control; altogether a lowering of levels of living.

Even if the world, or a country, were not yet in a condition in which doubling its people would lower the average productivity, there would be good reason to recommend that it stabilize its numbers.

If people had the same unrealistic attitude toward their daily life as many have toward their relation to earth resources, they would not realize that a stenographer has to be able to write a hundred or more words by spurts in order to be able to take 80 words *reliably*. They wouldn't think of a bracket of increasing risk for the load *and the bridge* under loads above 10 tons. If they captained a steamer they would accept additional shipments or passengers till the water lapped the portholes—gambling that there would be no storm. On land, they would push every production factor to the breaking point; they would drive workmen to collapse; they would crowd every agricultural area till there were no state parks, and no brush land growing up to new timber.

Durability is a kind of reserve—so, if one can, one gets asphalt tile or inlaid linoleum rather than printed linoleum. A rope company advertises its product as "unsurpassed for durable strength" under tough punishment; the rope which men trust "wherever safety counts." Men want a rope with reserve strength; if they are wise they will want a land that can meet an emergency too.

And since geographic resources are not readily expansible, that means that adaptation requires attention to the number of people. Excess of population reduces all our reserves. People who are poor from overpopulation not only jeopardize their future income through depleting geographic resources; they must buy poor grade rope, less durable floor covering, tires less safe. When men are too plentiful, they have to take more risks; their own worth is in an inverse ratio with their numbers.

Extra freight cars and busses, extra coal in the ground, extra unused waterpower, are elastic elements, ready for us and our children in case of unpredictable need. They are money in the bank. They are an insurance for high levels of living.

•

Education is a form of reserve. From an economic standpoint one doesn't need much education to make a living in boom times. But when the going gets rough an education makes for readier adaptation.

In a sense education is a luxury. It is one of the first things to be slighted in depression. And always illiteracy is high in lands where population presses hard on the resources. Some people think of the ignorance as a cause of poverty—and it does work that way; but also, poverty is a cause of ignorance. And poverty may be hard to overcome if the geographic resources are scanty.

•

Here, about halfway from the equator to the north pole, the earth yields up practically nothing in winter. But the winters are regular in their unfruitfulness, and close enough together so that a large proportion of people readily make arrangements for them. If productivity is insufficient in the lush months to provide for the lean months, the condition of overpopulation is not hard to see, though even under such conditions many people are likely to blame their lack of reserves on some item out of their control. Fathers are reluctant to accept responsibility for becoming fathers. If they can get away with it they conjure up the rationalization that their misery is "an act of God or the public enemy."

Famine, in contrast with the annual barrenness of earth, is irregular, and the intervals between famines are longer. More foresight is necessary to avoid famines than to avoid the impact of winter's scarcities. Actually, famine is the result of lack of reserves, and lack of reserves is usually the result of too many people: too much reproduction. A nation that has no reserves is only as well off as its poorest year permits, but to a nation which is well above subsistence and with ample reserves, a poor year is not serious.

If a nation has reserves of resources sufficient to yield on a permanent basis enough income for healthy living, protection against weather cycles, and as much education as its citizens want, what a tragedy of shortsightedness it would be if they were to sacrifice that prospect for themselves and their descendants in exchange for a larger population of miserable and illiterate beings harassed by malnutrition and recurrent famine!

A country's transition to poverty is concealed by the complexity of environment. Housing shortages, for example, are caused in large part by building restrictions, rent regulations, and labor rules. The persistent additional cause—greater cost of getting lumber out of

smaller forests and smaller trees, is likely to be overlooked. And even an increasing demand for housing may
not be associated, as it logically should be, in the public
mind, with increasing population. The population basis
for rising food costs and other living costs is likewise ob-
scured by complexity.

•

Australia is often thought of as a land of opportunity
for excess people from other parts of the world. What
are the facts? Australia is one of the rare spots on the
earth where men have not yet crowded so hard as to eliminate all reserves of food resources. And yet it has no
great abundance of reserves. Its area is 3,947,581 square
miles, which is about the area of continental U. S. with
Mexico added. But the eastern rim is all that has a suitable amount of rainfall for crops. That totals an area
about the size of South Carolina. There is an additional
belt of land which totals about the area of Texas that is
suitable for grazing. That's all. That band of grazing
land shimmers into desert which, for 40% of the continent, is as dry as the Sahara. On that rim and that band
are Australia's 7½ million inhabitants.

The desert is spreading, says William Douglass Forsyth,
in *The Myth of Open Spaces,* partly as a consequence of
close nibbling of vegetation by sheep in times of drought.
Forsyth is a member of the Population Commission of
the United Nations. Formerly he was research secretary
of the Australian Institute of International Affairs and a
research fellow of the School of Commerce at the University of Melbourne. As to how many more people Australia could support, Forysth calls attention to the fact

that the best land is already under cultivation. The lands that remain are, for the most part, inferior.

And yet Australia's Minister of Immigration, Arthur A. Calwell, with the attitude of most government administrations, is eager to increase his country's inhabitants. In his 1945 booklet entitled *How Many Australians Tomorrow?* he formulated his problem in part as how many inhabitants Australia should have, "—or more realistically how many *can* she have because it does amount to that."

Just why he thinks it does amount to that is not clear. If defense is the objective, it must be remembered that effectiveness in war depends largely on equipment, and that equipment depends on surpluses of income above consumption needs.

In the same tone as that of Minister of Immigration Calwell, Marc T. Greene, in the *United Nations World* for March 1949, advocates for Australia a lower level of living, though he doesn't put it in those words and probably doesn't realize it. There is disorganization in production—and so Mr. Greene would increase the immigration. Some of the agricultural workers have gone to town—because, in part, of the weather uncertainties—and so Mr. Greene would increase the immigration. Two-thirds of the Australian population live in the cities—and so Mr. Greene would increase the immigration. There are slum conditions and lawlessness in Sidney—and so Mr. Greene would increase the immigration.

The crux of Australia's problem is productiveness, he says, but apparently he speaks of total, and not of per capita productiveness. And of course he has not seen how city productivity is geared to diminishing returns and irregular returns in agriculture.

Mr. Greene remarked that "much of Australia's empty land gets plenty of rain"—but he did not tell that the

average of "plenty" includes for large areas som
of scorching droughts. If population were de
drought would result in famine; in the absence of population congestion the drought is not much more serious
than inconvenience. Irrigation schemes for drought areas
require more regularity of rainfall than exists.

Statisticians sometimes deal with the concept, OPTI-
MUM POPULATION, the *best* number of people. In
thinking of Australia's population prospects in terms of
optimum population, we must realize that the belt of
grazing land that thins down to the central desert feeds
approximately 112,000,000 sheep which constitute a large
part of the mutton and wool for the world. We must
think of Australia's population in connection with the
transfer of the effects of diminishing returns to the people
of other lands. To the extent that the Australian population grows, it will do so at the expense of people in other
parts of the world who have been depending on Australian mutton and wool.

Another necessary part of our thinking in connection
with optimum population for Australia is the concept of
a reserve of resources to serve as insurance. A phase of
that insurance is enough grazing area per thousand head
of sheep so that there will not be too close cropping and
a consequent invitation to erosion. In other words what
may be optimum population for 5 or 6 years may be a
disastrous excess of population when the 10-year or 500-
year view is basis for judgment. In the use of the concept
of optimum population there has sometimes been too
little consideration of destructive land practices.

And of course we must not make the blunder of considering Australia as a cure for the world's overcrowd-
edness. Two or three years of *India's* excess births would
plunge the whole of Australia to an Asiatic level of living,
and would put such pressure on the sparse pasture lands

that wind erosion would rapidly reduce even their present carrying capacity.

•

The Americas to the south from the U. S. ought to be, many would think, classifiable with Australia, Canada, Northern Europe, and the United States, as lands of great possibilities for favorable living conditions. But such a classification is not tenable. South America, Central America, and Mexico are already far down the muddy road of erosion and soil leaching. In most of the Latin American countries the populations are too numerous for the resources, and conservation of the resources will therefore be difficult. Not only that, but practically no conservation measures have been started. And from the population side of the ratio, the Catholic hierarchy wields tremendous power. With its other-worldly assumptions about birth control and sterilization, it is likely to block any attempt at adaptation. Altogether, South America, in its present trend, has a slim chance for any future other than that of Asia and Italy, with gnawing hunger as its outstanding characteristic.

There is only a small proportion of level or near level land in the Latin American republics, and the rainfall in most areas is either too scanty or too great. Overpopulation is already almost as extreme as in Puerto Rico, and for most of the land south of the Rio Grande the carrying capacity was never so great per square mile as in Puerto Rico, and the soil has suffered even greater damage at the hands of the forest vandals and the plowmen.

Of the 20 Latin American nations, all except three or four are overpopulated. That conclusion is reached by

William Vogt in *The Road to Survival,* published in 1948 by William Sloane Associates. Vogt continues,

"They are able to feed and shelter their citizens, and supply water for their many needs, only by a progressive and accelerating destruction of natural resources; biological bankruptcy hangs over their heads like a shaking avalanche. It has already fallen on Haiti and El Salvador, where hundreds of thousands of people are slowly starving to death."

Even with the soil sluicing down the rivers, the South American who has any concern about it is rare, and practically nothing has been done to stem the loss. Says Vogt, speaking of Chile, where he had traveled some 10,000 miles:

"I saw soil erosion on well over 90 percent of the cultivated slopes and in the central part of the country on *all* the slopes where cattle were grazed. In this entire distance I saw only one field plowed on the contour."

Robert J. Alexander, writing in *Land Economics* for May 1949, in discussing the housing scarcity in Chile showed that the low level of living in the cities there correlates with the poverty on the mistreated farms. In the seven years ending in 1944, he said, only 7,300 houses were built, as an annual average, though 12,800 per year were necessary to keep up with the population increase. A study of working class conditions in Ovalle revealed that of 564 bedrooms, more than 80% of them accommodated three or more persons; more than 22% slept five or more persons. A 1942 sample survey of working-class houses from various parts of Chile had indicated an average number of occupants per bedroom of 3.6.

Corn, which, at least in the United States, ought to be grown only on land that is almost flat, and nowhere on steep land, in the countries south of us is grown on steeper and steeper hillsides as the population grows, its open row cultivation inviting rapid erosion. There is little coal on the continent; wood and charcoal are the usual fuels, and trees for these have been used as wantonly as in the U. S., and watershed areas left unprotected. The South American governments are even less conscious of the future needs of their countries than are the state and national governments of North America. In 1944, Vogt tells us, forest fires ravaged a quarter million acres of Chile's timber. The Chilean government had not one fire warden or forester in its employ. Graft in many of the countries to the south of us is even worse than that of our cities. Mexico has a timber law with a rare and farsighted requirement that three trees be planted for each tree that is cut—but lumber companies pay graft instead of complying.

J. Russell Smith, well known geographer, in the *Geographical Review* for January 1949 had a review of some Pan-American studies by William Vogt. Smith commented that the people of Salvador, in Central America, get only 1500 calories a day as an average, the poorer people consuming even less. If they are told to "quit pasturing, quit chopping, quit plowing land with 75 percent slope, what can the poor Salvadorians do? What do we do in this country? We are chopping wood 50 percent faster than it grows and sending topsoil to the sea by billions of tons a year, and our situation is infinitely easier than that in which the Salvadorians find themselves."

The statement of Paul B. Sears in *Deserts on the March,* published by the University of Oklahoma Press, applies to both Salvador and the U. S.: "The inexorable laws of cause and effect operate in the production of food from the soil just as in every other realm of physical experience. No man, no nation, can spend resources faster than they are built and escape the inevitable reckoning."

In the *Wall Street Journal* for August 24, 1949, David O. Ives reported a Salvadorian program in agricultural education which has been under direction of a few U. S. farm experts and for which the U. S. has contributed part of the expenses. First fruit of the program is a 1949 crop of graduates who are intended to be key men in the improvement of the country's methods of cultivation. The hope is that changes of methods will stop the waste of resources, and at the same time produce enough more food to meet the needs of the population.

But it is like trying to mop up the floor without turning off the faucet that is overflowing the bathtub. Salvador's population has increased by 50 percent in the last twenty years; 26 percent in the last decade.

In evaluation of El Salvador's predicament, a few general truths may be helpful: (a) Food supply is produced on a finite earth surface, a surface that is not expanding. (b) An increase of the food supply, then, must be produced with an increasing resistance. (c) Reproductively, in contrast, the population is infinitely expansible. (d) Thus, population *tends to* increase to the limits of the food supply. (e) Population *does* increase to the limits of the food supply when and where (as in El Salvador) population is not controlled. Putting "d" in money terms we get (f) : Supply of labor *tends to* increase to such an extent that wages will be at a subsistence level. And putting "e" in money terms we get (g) : Supply of labor *does* increase to an extent that puts wages at a subsistence level when and where birth control, or some other sort of population control, is not practiced.

"Subsistence level" requires a little clarification. Some people say it can be modified by custom; and it can. It means just enough income to keep alive. Are cigarettes included in a subsistence level? Only if many workers die rather than go without them—spending their money for those instead of for nourishment, and eating too little bread to keep alive. The point is that if wages are extremely low, people die, and thus cease to be a part of the labor supply. In "g" I have intended to say that if there is no population control, *wages will become that low!*

I agree, with a bow to Wilbert E. Moore for his article in *Population Index* for April 1949, that some element in the environment which has not been usable may become usable as a consequence of the development of new techniques. In that case it adds to resources. But even considering that possibility, resources are finite; logically as well as historically mankind arrives at stages in which food is available only with increasing resistance. It has been said that in various circumstances mankind may fittingly control *either* technical organization for increase of food supplies, *or* resources conservation, *or* reproduction. Perhaps so, but control of the technical organization, and the resources, since those are finite, must inevitably be insufficient if reproduction is wild. Even with improving techniques and with conservation of resources, men are sure to eat themselves out of surpluses above subsistence if their numbers are not somehow kept down. Only control of population can *keep* men above a subsistence level.

And in El Salvador, only control of population can *get* them above a subsistence level.

Mexico lies just across the river from the U. S., and for much of the border there isn't even any river. But what a difference in level of living! The 17 million acres on which the 23 million people get an average of 1900 calories a day are gradually washing to the oceans in spite of a well-designed conservation service. Said Vogt:

"Between Mexico City and Morelia, a distance of approximately 200 miles, I counted kilometer posts from which it was possible to see erosion. There was active gullying visible about every two miles."

And he tells also of another trip, an airplane trip, in which he flew low over the area north and west of Mexico City. More than 90% of the cultivated land which he observed was heavily damaged by erosion. "Many of the cornfields were perched precariously between deep gullies that were surely devouring them."

"One may see stone walls balanced four or five feet in the air, on narrow plinths of earth from which the adjacent soil was washed away many years ago."

The State of Oaxaca, unfit for agriculture, is nevertheless being cultivated, and will be a desert within 50 years. The water runs off so directly now, with practically no cover and little remaining soil, that many peasants have to walk 5 miles to their cornfields, 5 miles to water. Little wonder that the average Mexican income is only one-eleventh that of the U. S.

Ominously, the corn is planted higher and higher on the slopes. Miss Mary Snodgrass tells me that in her travels in Mexico she herself in more than one instance has seen a man hoeing corn on a slope so steep that he had tied himself to a tree by a rope. Additional millions of Mexican acres are available for cultivation, but apparently not much of the virgin land is even so good as that which is now being worn out. Mexico's poverty is partly a consequence of its customs, but given the customs there are too many people for the amount of good land. Changes of customs — changes which might encourage greater efficiency — will be cancelled by the high birth rate except as the changes are such as to reduce the birth rate directly.

•

Haiti, island republic in the Caribbean, is the size of Vermont, but with its 3,000,000 inhabitants is desperately overpopulated. Max Eastman said of it in *Reader's Digest* for December 1947:

"Haiti has the climate, soil and growing conditions of an earthly paradise. Yet for over 100 years Haiti has been going steadily downward until today the average per capita income is $20 per year. In no other country are individual holdings so small—or more inappropriate, for sugar, coffee, bananas, sisal and citrus fruits — Haiti's most profitable crops — can be managed best on large plantations."

For those persons who try to explain poverty in terms of maldistribution, and particularly for those devotees of Henry George who, following literally his every detail, think that withholding of land by the rich is the fundamental cause of poverty, Haiti should be an eye-opener. For Haiti has a wide distribution of land, yet because its reproduction is uncontrolled, its general condition is poverty as abysmal as any in the world.

In a consideration of the population end of the man-land ratio in Latin America, we may well notice an item from *Time,* June 7, 1948:

"In Medellin, Colombia, Candido Zapata, 81, veteran of four marital ventures, attended the christening of his 54th child."

And I quote Kingsley Davis, "Latin America's Multiplying Peoples," in *Foreign Affairs,* July 1947:

"the population of the entire region to the south of the United States is growing faster than that of any other major region in the world. . . . During the 20 years from 1920 to 1940 it added approximately 40,000,000 or about 41 percent to its number."

Its rate of increase was more than double that of the world as a whole.

"One of the great myths about Latin America," says Davis, "is that it contains huge open spaces and can easily absorb mass migration from a crowded world."

•

The areas that have a capacity to produce extra food are few, and *there is not a single large area in all the world whose trends point to a continuing ability to supply food to the crowded lands.* Many of the South American countries are increasing their own numbers even beyond their own long-time carrying capacity.

I am not giving space to every region of the world; only to a few problem-packed ones, and a few to which men have looked with special optimism. Even in the latter the optimism is inconsistent with a population policy of laissez faire.

In general our spotlight has been moving closer and closer to the United States. In the next chapter I put the focus on our hapless ward, Puerto Rico, and one chapter later on the United States itself, the hope of the world.

Chapter 4

Nightmare in the Isle of Dreams

The migrations from Puerto Rico are so matter-of-fact in 1950 that they no longer hit the newspaper headlines. Actually they have far-reaching meanings of which the news items never did give more than a hint.

For a sample of the facts themselves let us go back to *Time* of August 11, 1947:

"More than 1,500 Puerto Ricans arrived in the U. S. last week . . . the 1947 version of the Okies."

The article pointed to the expanding population of the island as reason for the migration. Suddenly, after World War II, Puerto Ricans started an exodus to the New York City area, and in a few months there were 350,000 of them in Manhattan, Brooklyn, and the Bronx, and their worst congestion was in Harlem.

"Unemployment in Spanish Harlem has risen with each packed plane's arrival," said the *Time* writer, "and New York's state and city authorities have begun to worry about the area's rising relief costs, crime, the swift rise in tuberculosis and venereal disease. . . ."

Time for June 12, 1950, reported that the Puerto Rican jobless are costing New York City over $15,000,000 a year.

Puerto Ricans are migrating to other places than New York City. The *Cleveland Press* for February 12, 1948, reported that the problem of importation of Puerto Rican unskilled labor into Cleveland industry "has the CIO on a spot." National CIO policy, said the writer, does not discriminate in employment because of race or color, and the Puerto Ricans coming to the Cleveland area to work in the Lorain plants of the National Tube Company are coming with approval of the CIO United Steelworkers.

Yet local CIO members were apprehensive about the migrations. They had expressed their feelings at a meeting of the Cleveland Industrial Union Council the night before. Several delegates had thought the Council should take action on the problem.

Cleveland's WTAM on June 10, 1950, informed its hearers that Pan American Airways was expecting soon to transport 3,500 Puerto Ricans to Michigan for work in sugar beet fields. You might keep that in mind as you read in the next chapter about unemployment in the San Joaquin Valley.

The U. S. Congress should take a lesson. The Congress of 50 years ago tried to solve a population problem by calling it something else — and now the problem has grown to much larger proportions. Millions of dollars were spent to overcome the "ignorance," and improve the "bad health conditions." But there wasn't a whisper about birth rates. The only effect of all the gush and money has been a doubling of the population. Said *Time*, May 2, 1949, "The hardest fact of the island's life is that it has too many people and too little land."

Whenever a Congressional committee makes an investigation of Puerto Rico its members try hard not to see what is really wrong—and they succeed wonderfully.

What *could* Congress do about the real problem of Puerto Rico: the population problem?

Could it condition its grants for education on the teaching of birth control? Could it provide that relief payments and sugar bounties, and tariffs against competitors' sugar, be legislated only if there is agreement on the part of the beneficiary territory that its people have not more than two children per family? Could it condition our sugar purchases on a Puerto Rican marriage law and its enforcement, which would permit marriage or reproduction only for those who have jobs, and who pass a variety of other tests?

Franklin wrote in 1751, "there is supposed to be now upward of one million English souls in North America (though scarcely eighty thousand have been brought over by sea) . . ."

More than four times as many Puerto Ricans have migrated to New York City alone in the past ten years as the number of Englishmen who came to all America in the 140 years preceding Franklin's writing. It becomes clear that if Americans will not handle the population problem as a population problem in Puerto Rico, they will face its derivatives on the mainland. But of course many Americans may still refuse to interpret either the Puerto Rican poverty or its derivatives as *population* problems.

•

Farthest east of the West Indies islands, Puerto Rico is about a thousand miles southeast from Miami, Florida. It is 95 miles from east to west and 35 miles from north to south. Its shape, like that of Kansas, is a rectangle, but it totals only 3,435 square miles, whereas Kansas contains *twenty-three* times that much land—82,276 square miles. Yet this little Eden gone wrong, this miniature of Kansas, 1/23 the size of Kansas, has more inhabitants than Kansas has.

Puerto Rico's 2,200,000 people constitute a thousandth part of the world's population, but the island's area, far from being a thousandth part of the world's land, is actually less than a thousandth part of the area of the U. S. and its possessions. If all of the U. S. and its other possessions were as thickly populated as Puerto Rico is, they would contain as many people as are in the whole world. But they couldn't all keep alive unless, like the Puerto Ricans, they were fed, in part, from outside.

The birth rate of Puerto Rico, according to José L. Janer, has remained practically unchanged throughout the administration by the United States—about 40 per 1000 per year, to compare with half that for continental U. S. It was 42.4 in 1946, says *News Exchange*. There were fewer than a million inhabitants on the island when the U. S. took over in 1899, but how they do increase! Compare percentage rates of natural increase per decade as reported by Clarence Senior, in the *Journal of Heredity* for May, 1947:

Russia	23.2
Puerto Rico	21
Egypt	16
Jamaica	15.7
Philippines	15.4
Japan	12.5
India	11.5
Italy	9.3
Germany	7.5
U. S.	6.1

After a while we shall have troubles of crowding in some of our other possessions too, so we should make a further comparison. However, the following figures are not only for births over deaths, but for percent increase per decade from all sources.

Panama Canal Zone	31.3
American Samoa	28.4
Alaska	23.2
Puerto Rico	21.1
Guam	20.4
Hawaii	14.9
Virgin Islands	13

Mr. Senior argues for birth control. He thinks that to keep the poor people from getting knowledge of birth control methods is as undemocratic as to deny them any other type of useful knowledge. And birth control information becomes essential education in Puerto Rico.

Puerto Rico is the American extreme of population disaster. Luis Muñoz Marin is governor now—the first elected governor. He was preceded by Jesus T. Pinero, first native-born governor, and preceding Pinero was Rexford Guy Tugwell. In *The Stricken Land,* a Doubleday & Company book of 1947, Tugwell told Puerto Rico's story. Passages from *The Stricken Land* are quoted by permission of Doubleday & Co., Inc.

But Tugwell seems never to have seen the real problem—never to have churned its population phases about in his mind. Even so early as his inaugural address he announced, in effect, that he intended to keep away from the real heart of the Puerto Rican misery, and thus in his first decision he made his failure inevitable.

On page 154 of *The Stricken Land* we read this concerning that inaugural speech:

"I didn't think, I said, as some people did, that birth

control would reduce poverty; I thought it was more reasonable to intensify the exploitation of the island's resources and so enlarge the sources of employment and income. An educated people enjoying reasonable living standards would make their own accommodation to environment. An ignorant, poverty-ridden and disease-stricken people were naturally reckless about their own or their children's future."

The utter impossibility of transforming these hordes to "an educated people enjoying reasonable living standards" without approaching the problem through population control seems never to have occurred to him. And so, in that speech on the day he became governor, Tugwell gave assurance that he would maintain the laissez faire policy with regard to reproduction.

He was shocked, but not enough, it seems, by an appendage to the inaugural parade. It constituted a demonstration of faith in him, but also it was a demonstration of appalling poverty. Thousands of workers from the sugar plantations, many in rags, barefoot, and hatless, slowly shuffled up the avenue, flinging their arms and shouting, and carrying sloganed banners: "Tugwell will do for us what Roosevelt did for America."

Governor Tugwell's attitude about population control was not the attitude of the man who had appointed him. On page 35 is this account of Roosevelt's position:

"There was one other matter on which the President was clear: the frightening increase of the population had to be stopped. He was inclined in this matter to follow the prevalent line of thought among social workers and others who came into close contact with poor people: there were too many of them and it was better to stop them at the source than to connive at the high death rate which is nature's way of keeping a workable balance between numbers and resources."

But the birth control substitute for starvation as a means of keeping a balance between men and resources was the social workers' idea, not Tugwell's.

Tugwell based his opposition to birth control on heredity. He thought that birth control would be practiced in proportion to intelligence and other good qualities, that the worst human stock would go on breeding while the better stock reduces its numbers in the future population; and that because of the differences in birth rates the result of a birth control policy would be dysgenic.

There *is* a risk of a dysgenic result, and it is a probability if nothing is done about it. But Tugwell's policy amplifies that probability, as I plan to show soon.

•

Tugwell thought the Puerto Ricans might manufacture something, and swap it for food. He has been more optimistic, he says, than most of those with whom he has discussed the matter. He mentions our war experience in stepping up the flow of goods, and he thinks industrial and political reorganization will yield the same results. If so, he says, "there would certainly be enough of everything for everybody."

But, Doctor Tugwell, how many people are "everybody"?—if you keep them all alive and their children and their grandchildren, and if they don't have any population control? Let us remember too that the flows of wartime goods drew on raw materials and those drew on geographic resources.

But Tugwell's illusion that there would be enough of everything for everybody made him cold to birth control.

"The President thought it ought to be tried and so did others. During General Winship's time the legislature was to act in the matter, legitimizing the dissemination of contraceptive information. Puerto Rico being predominantly Catholic, this would require a good deal of courage on everyone's part. Somehow or other General Winship would be absent when it came time to sign or veto the bill: and Mr. Menendez Ramos, as Acting Governor, would sign it. In my time as Governor the rather surprising results—negative—would begin to be apparent as data accumulated. The futility of the measure, taken by itself, would be quite apparent."

Surprising that the results were negative? Why should one be surprised that, under an administrator opposed to the law, the law got negative results?

•

Though Tugwell subscribes to the myth that in the world as a whole there is "enough for everybody," he knows that in Puerto Rico there is not enough. On page 19 we find this:

"The soil and the climate would not bear the burden of feeding two million people. The people themselves had outrun their food supply if not their other resources."

We must conclude that Tugwell saw the importance of the man-land ratio in Puerto Rico. What an opportunity would have been his if he could have seen that the man-member of the ratio is sometimes subject to reason, whereas the land-member is comparatively inflexible.

The dismal present and the still darker future for the

island are reflected in passages on pages 53 and 55 of *The Stricken Land*, where Tugwell tells first of the slums of the cities. He describes one view encompassing a thousand houses made of picked-up boards eked out with flattened oil cans, where people lived at subhuman levels, on a diet of rice, beans, and dried fish "and never enough of these." They were hosts of innumerable parasites, subject always to disease.

Then we are told of the helpless rural areas, from which some of the slum dwellers had come:

"Many an old coffee stand was now mere brush from which the workers had dragged themselves away. 'Where,' I asked, 'could they go?' 'You saw El Fanguito, La Perla, and the other slums,' said Menéndez. Silcox and I looked at each other. Here it was, that nexus between soil destruction and the impoverishment of people which we could talk about in the States but which no research had yet tied down to fact. This was an island. Migrations were short enough to be seen. The people had washed down out of the hills along with their soil and come to rest in the slums. It was even clearer in the tobacco country. For there the process was quicker. A hillside was cleared and cropped for two or three years, then had to be abandoned, a gutted ruin of a field, filling the streams and reservoirs, moreover, with useless subsoil silt."

Those slums that Tugwell described were such as he had seen on his first trip to the Island, in 1934. Seven years passed, and he returned in 1941, not yet as governor. The President had asked him to report whether or not the slums were gone.

Tugwell was shocked, he said (page 73), that the slums had spread and seemed about to overwhelm San Juan. Nearby El Fanguito, which had consisted of a few hundred squatters' shacks in 1934, had grown to a seemingly

endless expanse of squalor. The shacks were in rows; the
piles of garbage and filth accumulated in the open spaces
between, and were regularly lifted and set down again by
the tides. These slums were startling evidence, Tugwell
thought, of the failure of efforts to outpace the forces of
disintegration with schemes of housing and public works.
But if he saw that the "forces of disintegration" were *human beings* whose members were out of balance with
earth, at any rate he never saw that re-integration could
come only by stopping the increase of human beings.

The slums came up again for discussion with Roosevelt
after Tugwell was governor. He was after funds for
Puerto Rican rehabilitation, and he could get the funds
only with the President's help. He went to the White
House with pictures of the still-growing slums. Tugwell's account continues, page 126, with Roosevelt's reaction:

"He said that, damn it, he had told every Governor
since he had been President that it was his business to
clean up that disgrace to the flag—and now, eight years
after he had begun to talk about it, I was showing him
that it was many times worse than at the beginning. What
was the matter? To that I made the best answer I could,
not really knowing. I thought it was because there were
about 6,000 new families founded every year, of whom
about 5,500 settled in the slums where they had no rent
to pay, or at least very little, since most of them were
squatters."

Since Tugwell's time, the government has improved
the "streets" of El Fanguito, and in the nearby San José
Housing Project the government is financing the con-
struction of 5-room concrete houses for sale at $4000 each.
Life for January 1949 reported that 3,500 of the dwellings are now occupied; that contractor L. D. Long of

South Carolina is completing 3,500 others, and can turn out 37 per day. At that rate he can just about match the current increase in San Juan's slum families.

Time, May 2, 1949, reported that the San José Housing Project was then almost complete, with shelter for 6,200 families, but remarked that few families had moved out of El Fanguito, "and officials privately admit that it may be necessary to ring the slum with barbed wire to prevent new squatters from moving in."

But though the facts pointed unmistakably to over-population as the dynamic cause of the slums, could Tugwell see slums as a population problem—a problem to be approached with hypotheses for influence on quantity or quality of people? No; he still had eyes that saw not. And Roosevelt himself did not press his view that "the frightening increase of the population had to be stopped." He let his Governor proceed along a path of illusion, with golden teasers scattered here and there. On that path, beyond the gold lurks famine.

On page 213 the ex-Governor wrote of a "problem of population density," but he seems to have thought of handling the problem in terms of its cause only via an unworkable indirection. Repeatedly the cruel facts were acknowldged; repeatedly Tugwell's mind went to palliatives, never to a direct discouragement of reckless breeding. On pages 253 and 254 industrialization is his emphasis. As to agricultural improvement, he thought that advances might yet be made, although he acknowledged that it seemed more likely that the trend would be the other way because of soil exhaustion and erosion. And he says, "even if agricultural possibilities did enlarge, there still would not be enough wealth to go around."

•

The health problems of Puerto Rico are mostly economic. Malnutrition and poor housing make for a high T. B. rate, said Tugwell. Poverty makes prostitutes and prostitutes increase the venereal disease rates; absence of shoes and latrines preserve the hookworm evil. Bathing and laundering in contaminated streams induce bilharziasis. And contaminated water supplies and lack of sanitary disposal of sewage cause dysentery and enteritis.

Tugwell expressed the belief that improving those conditions would reduce the birth rate:

"A people which overbreeds is a people in despair, like a sick tree which flowers desperately out of season in the attempt to perpetuate its race when its own individual survival seems unlikely. People relatively secure and hopeful for their children are careful for their future. Not only is their number regulated by love and foresight, but training in vocations and careers are opened to each of them. Thus economic improvement transforms a vicious downward spiral into an upward one."

In that passage we get the same theory that Governor Tugwell had expressed in his inaugural address: raise their level of living, and people will somehow reduce their birth rates. Does he mean that they and their children will reduce their birth rates sufficiently to make a stationary population *without birth control?* or *with* birth control? or hasn't he thought about that? It really is important.

If he means *with* birth control, then why not give them, and all of them, birth-control knowledge in regularized channels instead of depending on the information getting around by grapevine?

If he means without birth control, what then? late marriages? twin beds? monasteries? There is little chance that they would work. I don't think they ever have worked anywhere yet. Ireland? No. Even Ireland has some birth control, and reproduces about 25 percent too many for a stationary population.

Probably Tugwell hadn't thought about whether there would be birth control or not. Probably he merely recalled vaguely that in Northern Europe and the United States, somehow, prosperity has been coincident, for the last century, with declining birth rates, and that in the families with relatively great prosperity the decline in birth rate has been very pronounced.

But there has been a gradually spreading circle of people among whom birth-control methods are known, and the birth control has been part of the explanation both for the decline in rate of reproduction and for the difference in birth rates—which Tugwell himself, on pages 35 and 36, deplored. The people who are especially alert get the birth-control information first, just as they are likely to get any information first.

And thus it comes clear that Puerto Rico's choice is population control or starvation; and Tugwell himself, though expressly repudiating birth control, unconsciously depends on it for his hope.

I mentioned, in connection with India and China, the impossibility there of reducing the birth rate significantly by way of the attitude changes that grow out of prosperity. There is reason to be sure that even in Puerto Rico the prosperity cannot come first. Can we commit ourselves to take on an increasing burden of support for increasing numbers of Puerto Ricans in excess of self-support? Can we agree to such subsidizing for several decades, while the population grows from the present 2,200,000 to perhaps six million or ten million? Can we, thereafter, take care of five million to nine million and more above what the Island will support—take care of them at that comfortable level of living which would eventually develop interests in conflict with reproduction? Obviously not!

Even if by sacrifice and suffering on the mainland we could carry that financial burden, to what end would Tugwell expect it to lead? The fact must be recognized that if the Puerto Ricans ever reach the stage of prosperity at which they limit their reproduction, their main means of doing so will be BIRTH CONTROL or STERILIZATION, the very processes that Tugwell refuses to face.

And if the development of birth-control knowledge is by the haphazard and gradual method that Tugwell's approach implies, it will be accompanied by the differential birth rate in much more accentuated degree than if everyone is informed of contraceptive techniques at once. The differential birth rate is the one and only logical excuse Tugwell had for refusing to get behind the 1937 law establishing birth-control clinics. Birth control is slowly spreading in Puerto Rico, but at the present rate it is the handmaiden of the differential birth rate.

If the Tugwellian plan for prosperity by doles could be maintained for a period long enough to develop the psychological interests which would interfere with reproduction, the population would increase, as we have seen, presumably to three or more times its present total. Could we then, with continued doles in amounts which would be equivalent to prosperity, expect a sufficient practice of contraception to *reduce* the population from that high point back down to the present 2,200,000, or to the 1,000,000 that the Island could support? That is not likely. It would be like trying to pump out the sea after it had flooded the farm land. Better keep it out.

In summary, if and when the Puerto Ricans could become self-supporting by way of the Tugwellian indirect method, the active, though hidden, element in the process would be birth control. So there would be more sense

in applying birth control now—and I mean really—by
exposing 100 percent of the adults to it.

•

Was Spain less helpful to Puerto Ricans than the U. S.
is? Tugwell shows that the American influence in Puerto
Rico, in spite of the spending of what now amounts to
over a billion dollars of U. S. money there, has gotten
nowhere. "Indeed," he says, on page 299:

"the situation had worsened rather than improved.
Somewhere along the line the vicious downward spiral
had begun which, unless checked, would, from the forces
generated within itself, gather momentum."

"Forces generated within itself." Yes; sex. Why be so
mystical in reporting it?

•

In *The Stricken Land* there are other items relating
to population. Tugwell tells of a $14,000,000 subsidy for
food growing. A large proportion of Puerto Rican acreage
had been used for growing sugar cane. With that specialization, dollar productivity was greater partly because of
the absence of the U. S. tariff against Puerto Rican sugar
while sugar from many areas was kept out of competition
by the tariff. If the Puerto Rican population had depended on other agricultural crops, at world prices, the
returns to workers would have been even less. But now
Tugwell was trying to shift some of the producers to food

crops. That move was probably appropriate, especially as a war measure, with shipping facilities scarce. But whether the Puerto Ricans produce sugar or food crops, it appears that the two million and more of them can get enough wages to keep alive only if part of the expense is borne by the citizens of the mainland.

As Tugwell stated it on page 481:

"Her population had increased until only the most generous subsidy from her rich Northern associate could keep her alive."

Whether or not she, Puerto Rico, as a governmental and economic unit would remain alive without U. S. help, it seems clear that hundreds of thousands of individual Puerto Ricans would not be able to survive.

And of course the people rather than the governmental unit was what Tugwell had reference to. He had said on page 165:

"How, outside our tariff and preference system, and without our assistance, however whimsical and spasmodic, were half the people of Puerto Rico going to live at all? I thought they could not, even if the levels of life were reduced to those, say, of Haiti."

But as to remedy—a remedy directed toward the cause of the distress—Governor Tugwell had expressed his decision in his inaugural address, and on that subject his mind never opened. Through the President he could almost surely have gotten the U. S. Congress to relax the restrictive Federal legislation that stymied the Puerto Rican law of 1937, and could thereby have gotten contraceptive and sterilization facilities to every adult on the island. But with the local law crippled by an ancient Congressional act, and opposed by Governor Tugwell himself, reason never had a chance. The best claim the Puerto Ricans have to our present doles is that the U. S.

Congress, and the Governor appointed by the U. S. President, acted as their enemies, and blocked their own self-help that could have come from their law of 1937.

The program of *industrialization,* which Tugwell favored, and for which in 1942 he set up the Puerto Rico Industrial Development Corporation, must have hard going in an area in which there are practically no minerals. *Something* can be done toward industrialization—is being done now—though with adverse effect on the U. S. mainland. Tugwell's Puerto Rico Industrial Development Corporation has spent many millions of dollars; has started factories for making cement, glass, paperboard, shoes, and clay products. Also, glove materials are flown from Miami, Florida, a thousand miles away, worked up in Puerto Rico and returned by plane. Puerto Rican belts, sandals, and sisal bags are hand-worked and sent to the states. A cigar factory is in operation. By March of 1950 the government-operated Puerto Rico Industrial Development Company had encouraged the coming of 119 new businesses, of which 54 had gotten into action. They make yeast, dolls, dinnerware, frozen food, glue, rugs, and a great variety of other goods, mostly of a "light manufacturing" sort.

The low wages are the chief inducement, but also, new enterprises are tax exempt for 12 years.

A *New York Times* story of May 1, 1949, told that a School of Industrial Arts, one of the largest and best-equipped in the world, with machinery and equipment valued at $15,000,000, is operating in Puerto Rico at Rio Piedras. It is part of a veterans' training program. It would soon be ready for 3,500 day students, and an equal number in night classes. There was a waiting list of 22,000. Other industrial schools were under construction in seven other towns.

The adverse effect on the mainland, of such industrialization as actually takes root on the Island, is in unemployment. *Time* for September 27, 1948, reported that Royal Little closed his textile plants in four New England towns, wiping out 5,000 jobs. He was about to close a New Hampshire sheet and blanket factory, and thus displace 3,500 more workers. The reason? A transfer of operations to Puerto Rico. The Puerto Rico government had offered him buildings on credit, tax free for twelve years. And Puerto Rican laborers could be had at less than half the New England wages.

The Puerto Rican program is parasitic in two ways: it requires the use of savings of mainland citizens to finance it, and to the extent of its success it displaces workers in other lands. Even if an enterprise is completely new, instead of transferred, if it sells its products on the mainland it must have a similar influence on mainland unemployment.

And though, in a small measure, industrialization will give purchasing power by which Puerto Ricans can supplement their scanty supply of home-grown groceries, the possibilities in that direction are a drop in the bucket compared with the food need of today; and the food needs of next week will be greater because of the intervening births.

According to the head of the Puerto Rico Industrial Development Company, as reported by T. A. Wise in the *Wall Street Journal* for March 4, 1950, the industrialization program by that date had created 8,000 new jobs for Puerto Ricans. The ridiculousness of putting very much dependence on such a program is made graphic by the fact that there are 8,000 more Puerto Ricans *every two months!* In the eight years that the Industrial Development Corporation had been maneuvering to provide those 8,000 jobs the Puerto Rican excess of births over deaths was approximately 370,000!

The idea that industrialization can solve Puerto Rico's

population problem is a fallacy, as we have seen. There is a related idea that *agricultural* machinery can solve or partly solve the problem. That too is an illusion. Tugwell has not fallen for that one, but some other Americans have, so the proposition should be reported.

Machines are cutting sugar cane in Hawaii now—machines with rotating knives. One operator on one machine cuts 70 to 80 tons of cane per hour, doing the work previously done by large numbers of men. Suppose those machines are installed on the third of Puerto Rico's arable acres that constitute the sugar plantations. The people who have thought of machines as a cure for hunger would find that the basic problem—food—is not solved, not even ameliorated, by the machines. Agricultural machinery frees men for "other production." But will that other production make more *food* available? Since the food production depends on the soil, and the soil is in small amount per capita, the displaced workers can add little to total food production. Otherwise said, total food production and average food production would be almost as much without the machines, and would probably be more. And because of the scarcity of other types of resources, "the release of men for manufacturing" is likely to become merely an increase in unemployment.

John Lossing Buck, who made the important study which I presented in Chapter 2 of production from various sized Chinese farms, had an article in *Foreign Affairs* for October 1949. Writing further about China, he analyzed the illusion that an overcrowded land can save itself by mechanizing agriculture.

"A Chinese farmer with a tractor and its accompanying instruments would find that his work would be done quickly," said Buck, "but he would have nothing to do when it was over, and his expenses would be so much greater that he would be bankrupt in the first year."

". . . General mechanization is impracticable," he continued, "until favorable changes occur in the man-land ratio. . . ."

And again, "it is the number of people in relation to the amount of land that determines the possibility of farming with machinery. Putting farms in large 'cooperative' or 'collective' units in order to mechanize agriculture would not alter the fundamental ratio of men to land, except for the worse."

Buck's observations concerning China would be fully applicable to Puerto Rico except that, being smaller, and being pampered by the Federal Government, Puerto Rico may be able to market an increasing manufactured output in the U. S. — at the expense of small business establishments here.

As to *emigration,* as a means of meeting the Puerto Rican need, it bodes no good for the mainland. It is getting under way now, as our opening quotation in this chapter shows. But though the outflow is substantial, it is not entirely offsetting the new births. So, at present rates, the burden on mainland citizens—subsidizing reproduction on the island — must become increasingly severe.

However, my concern is not limited to the harsh conditions for Puerto Ricans on the island, nor to the financial burden on the citizens of the mainland. We should think also of the welfare of the places to which the migrants go, making for unsocial differences in birth rates there—under the principles which will be discussed in a later chapter. There is no implication that the Puerto Ricans have a lower average hereditary basis for intelligence—I don't know anything about that—but the point is that the Puerto Rican *average,* migrating to an area, puts more pressure on that area's *best* for further reduction of its birth rate.

And here is another consideration. If they come to the United States, what will make them more prosperous in the United States? Their greater opportunities will result from the fact that a large proportion of Americans have practiced birth control in the past. And the chances are too, that, where other people have low birth rates, they will in some measure trim their own birth rate.

But *somebody's* RESTRAINT IN REPRODUCTION in the past is basis for the prospect of greater prosperity for Puerto Ricans on the mainland than on the Island. Isn't it reasonable to encourage their staying in Puerto Rico—and making possible their prosperity there by facilitating population control there?

Chapter 5

Crowding? Who?—Me?

We have seen plenty of evidence, in the earlier chapters, of a general tendency for population to outrun the food supply. But are you still of the view concerning the occurrence of actual suffering through population causes, that "it can't happen here"? Is enough being done to prevent it?

Population problems, though social in their results, are separate in their causation. Reproduction is something that can easily be overdone.

A few months ago the newspapers carried an Acme picture of Mrs. James Robinson of Pottstown, Pennsylvania. Of eleven children, seven of them were yet too young for school, being between the ages of four months and five years. It is unlikely that Mrs. Robinson thinks of her troubles as a population problem, and it is not likely that very many people who saw the picture of her brood thought in terms of population problems either; and yet, here is a definite example of the cause of famine and wars that grow out of the upset ratio of men to resources. By making a living more difficult for others of the same generation as Mrs. Robinson's children, Mrs. Robinson also prevents some other of the nation's children from having a college education. In the Robinson family we have population problems at their source.

News stories of October 4 and 5, 1949, reported the birth of triplets to Mrs. Irma Griser of Pitcairn, Pennsylvania. Perhaps her husband, Arthur, can feed and clothe the Griser couple's total of 17 children on his $160 a month, but as they grow up they will make the economic struggle harder for others of their generation.

The *Cleveland Plain Dealer* for June 14, 1948, told of 81-year-old Salvatore Arsena, former bricklayer, who lived in New York in the early 1890's, then returned to his native Sicily. In March 1948 he came to Cleveland with his 77-year-old wife to live with two daughters. They have had 19 children. Four sons live in Sicily; 2 sons and 2 daughters in Cleveland. Good average folks, apparently; but 8 living children could not be made a rule for good average folks in America without making it a hell —as Italy already is.

Anthony Dupré, 68-year-old former circus trapeze performer and trick bicyclist, has 35 children. He was born a Frenchman, had 22 brothers and sisters; was first married in Argentina. His first wife died in 1914 after having had 14 children. Then he went to New Orleans and married again. His second wife bore 11 children; his third had 6. He married his fourth wife in New York in 1945 where he is a dishwasher in the Waldorf Astoria. Soon they had a daughter; and in May 1948 the 34-year-old wife gave birth to triplets. A good average man, apparently—nevertheless he is your enemy, grasping for the food from the plates of your own children.

Some parents are more capable than average; more adaptable. In such cases, more than a replacement number of children seems suitable—but in those cases there ought to be *some* restraint. Mrs. John Funk, Jr., age 35, of Cincinnati, was reported by the *Cleveland Press,* May 8, 1948, as having 14 children, no twins. The husband, age 38, owns a radio business, and they have no financial worries. On September 13, 1949, the Sun Oil Company's "3-Star Extra" radio newscast told of Mr. and Mrs. Harry Bailey, of Troy, N. Y. They too have 14 children. Mr. Bailey, to keep the family supplied, holds down four jobs, and works 18 hours a day. But the Funks and the Baileys are appropriating too many of the world's limited opportunities.

A United Press news item of June 16, 1948, from Atlanta, Georgia, tells of Mrs. Maude Ethel Pope, age 38, who was married at 11 to a boy who was 12. When she hit the headlines she had had 21 children. Accounts differ as to whether 9 or 13 of them were still living. She got tired of receiving eviction notices. She and her husband had saved a nestegg, so they bought a lot and some building material. She dug a big basement with pick and shovel. Husband Bill helped with the foundation of a new house; then she did the rest of the building; wouldn't let him do any more—he has enough to do making a living. After she finished the house she dug a 30-foot well, then slowed up to wait the two months to her 22nd birthing.

I think Mrs. Pope has something worth while, in considerably greater measure than the average woman; yet I question if her special merit is sufficient to justify *ten* seats at the world's dinner table.

For hundreds of thousands of instances of reproduction there is still less justification.

A *Cleveland Press* story of May 24, 1948, pictures James Peattie, age 37, keeping house for 8 of his 9 children, and holding down a job as repairman with Republic Steel Company by which he earns between $55 and $70 a week. Mrs. Pearl Peattie, age 33, after a nervous breakdown and a serious operation, went to live with her mother, and is suing for divorce. She has the 9th and youngest child. It seems that the Peattie family must be added to the list of those in which paternity has been in excess.

Mr. William W. Harvey and his wife advertised their seven children, age 9 months to 8 years, and, one by one, gave them away. An Associated Press news item from Lake Worth, Florida, June 21, 1948, told of the bitter experience. Husband, age 36, radio announcer; wife with a heart condition—two years to live, started from Binghamton, N. Y., and went from city to city, job to job. Finances dwindled. Came an eviction notice. They thought giving the children away was better than any other prospect. Another population item, isn't it?

News Exchange of the Planned Parenthood Federation reported in February 1949 that the court in Brooklyn sent for the father of three juvenile delinquents. The father told the policeman he couldn't come; was too busy taking care of his eight other small children—and his wife was in the hospital giving birth to their 12th baby. The family was on relief.

Lavern J. Ryel, age 34, was born in Berea, Ohio; and so was his wife Alice, age 25. Lavern had dropped out of school after the 7th grade; Alice after the 8th grade. Both are dishwashers in Cleveland. They met in a tavern and were married in 1944. Both drank; and Lavern's father didn't like Alice because of her fondness for beer. On June 23, 1948, they were arrested for abandoning their two children. They had paid $12 a week for a single room. That was too high, and besides, they had had trouble with the landlady. They got another room at $5, but the landlord wanted no children, so those were left with Mr. Ryel's father, but he was unable to keep them long, so they took them to their $5 room. That caused their eviction. They started, in the rain, with the sleep-

ing babies in a tattered baby carriage to the policewom-
en's bureau, but on the way decided to leave the babies,
one age 2½ years, the other 10 months, in a hallway,
hoping somebody "would give them what we couldn't—
a home."

The babies were found, after several hours, along with
two empty beer bottles in the carriage, and two pop
bottles containing the babies' milk, which had soured.
Alice, at the jail, asked for another chance to try to find
a home.

There were only two children in this case, yet under
the circumstances I think Cleveland, the country, and
the world, would be better off if there hadn't been any.
And as to *additional* children, could anybody reasonably
advise this couple to "let nature take its course"?

•

The housing shortage is a population problem. It is
impressive as a population problem because its impact is
so often on the very families that have been indulging in
parenthood to excess. The *Cleveland Press* for June 19,
1948, reported that for the previous six weeks George
Gilgallen, age 33, and Mrs. Edna Gilgallen, age 30, and
their five children, had lived with no home except a
battered 1937 Ford. George works for a storage battery
company, averaging $48 a week. They were evicted be-
cause the landlord had six children and needed the home
himself. The Gilgallens went in debt to buy the Ford.

James and Doris McDaniels were in a still worse plight.
They had been living in Kirtland Park with six of their
ten children, the *Press* reported, for the previous six
weeks. Evicted from their previous home, they had

stayed with friends a few days, but "running out of welcome" they had moved to the park at the foot of East 49th Street.

Time for March 15, 1948, told that Landlord Oren W. Breidenthal of Kansas City was brought to court by building inspectors, who had found four families living in the basement of his house, five families on the first floor, five on the second, six in the attic, six in the barn, and one in a trailer on the lawn.

The large families are not the only ones who are cramped for room; they have put pressure on all of us, and we are all a little apprehensive of the prospects if and when we have to find another place to live.

The *Cleveland Press* for July 16, 1948, told of evicted families drifting downtown. These items were included:

"Many relief families lived at Hotel Morrison, 1308 Huron Rd., until recently, when demolition of the building began. A number of the families were moved to upper Prospect.

"Vincenzo Sidoti, 61, his wife Mary, 41, and their eight children were moved to 5115 Euclid Ave., where relief officials pay $9 a day for three rooms. A ninth child, Paul, 17, is in the Army.

"The Sidoti family paid their own way on the father's earnings until early this year, when the home they had lived in for 18 years was sold.

"Another family, with eight children, lives in a hotel at 4709 Euclid Ave. They have told relief authorities they would like to use about three months' rent as a down payment on a home. Then they could go off relief."

At least 2,500,000 families in the country were living doubled up when the Federal Housing Act of 1949 was passed. That initiated the Government building of 810,-000 dwelling units over a 6-year period. And in April 1950, Congressmen considered it necessary to provide 4 billion dollars worth of Federal funds as guarantees on mortgages, and other forms of housing credit. Government aid for housing was coming to be of considerable magnitude. Among the causes for this increase of functions of the Federal Government is the fact that our numbers are expanding in such measure that they constitute a population problem.

•

I started the chapter with illustrations of the fact that *population problems, though social in their results, stem from separate pairs of individuals.* We must not lose sight of that fact, for therein is the possibility of the solution of the problems.

Now, keeping the separateness of sources in mind, let us observe other instances—in America—in which the extent of reproduction seems to point in the direction of sizeable problems.

The plight of the Navajo Indians which first came to public attention in the fall of 1947 was primarily a case of population expansion. Their reservation, taking in parts of Arizona, Utah, New Mexico, and Colorado, is about six times the size of Puerto Rico. It is mostly barren waste, but it supported the earlier Navajo numbers by furnishing pasture for their sheep. As their population increased from 8,000 to 56,000, however, they increased their flocks. The sheep became too numerous for the sparse vegetation. The area was overgrazed, and erosion by wind and rain became acute. The United States Government ordered the gradual discontinuance of sheep raising. That left the tribe with practically no means of support—as they would have been in a few years even without the Government order as a consequence of the destruction of the soil. They were reduced to an average daily diet of 1200 calories—about 40% of what is supposed to be a minimum for health.

News disclosures, particularly reports by *Time,* brought: various personal gifts, $100,000 from the American Red Cross, an order from the Social Security Board that state agencies accept Indian cases, and, for the Navajos and the Hopi tribe (on another arid Arizona reservation) a $2,000,000 relief fund from the other American people via Congress.

Were the one-time "vanishing Americans" given any birth-control information? Apparently not; so may we expect history to repeat with an amplifier when the present relief funds run out? The Bureau of Indian Affairs has taken one step which is supposed to be a partial measure to avoid that. With a whopping appropriation for the purpose, it has initiated a school program for the Navajo children, designed to educate them to do their wholesale breeding away from the reservation.

•

Roland M. Harper, in an article in *Eugenical News,* tells of the Croatans, a people of mixed ancestry, mostly Negro and Indian, who have been living since colonial times in the Carolinas. It is probable, thinks Harper, that the census reports of 252 Croatans in 1890 and 14,833 in 1930 show, primarily, improved census techniques in classification. However, a North Carolina Board of Health report of 1933 contains an estimated birth rate for the Croatans of 35.4, and Harper computes their birth rate in 1935 to have been over 40—which is about twice that of the U. S. whites in that year.

Life for October 27, 1947, featured the reunion of a Mormon family, the descendants of Charles C. Rich and his six wives. Of the 2,000 descendants of Apostle Rich, 401 had gathered to celebrate the 100th anniversary of the arrival of their ancestor in Salt Lake City. He had been a Kentucky farmer. By the time he died at age 74 in 1908, he had 326 grandchildren.

Forget Rich, with his polygamy; to get a per capita concept, put the 2,000 descendants in terms of those six wives. They averaged 333 descendants apiece in a hundred years. In another century at that rate the Rich tribe would number a third of a million. Apparently many of the Riches are practicing birth control now, so such a continued expansion is not likely. Yet even a far lower rate of increase, if generalized to other groups, would be enough to crowd the land in a very few years.

Take a look into Canada—which seems now to have plenty of room. In the *Scientific Monthly* for May 1947 English Geographer C. B. Fawcett stated:

"The French Canadians now number about 4 millions. Practically all of them are descended from the 5,800 immigrants who reached Canada before A.D. 1680, when immigration from France ceased. This gives a six-hundred-fold increase in 250 years."

At such a rate of increase, give them another 250 years and the total number of French Canadians will be 2,400,-000,000, which is just about the present population of the whole world.

True, there is no possibility that such a rate of increase will continue. The French Canadians will come to a practice of contraception or their death rate will rise by way of starvation and the other positive checks to population increase. Long before that, however, they may crowd the rest of the Canadians to virtual extinction.

A United Press report of March 9, 1950, from Phoenix,

Arizona, told of several families in a farm camp nearby. They live in one-room tin shacks without electricity or running water. The children have no shoes and the shacks have no furniture. The families had been living on biscuits and lard—but some had not eaten anything for ten days.

The group is made up of about a hundred families—cotton pickers, who usually pick citrus fruit in March, but in early 1950 a freeze had ruined the citrus crop. They had lived in the state too briefly to qualify for state relief, and local relief was exhausted.

The plight of these people illustrates several things: (1) a failure of social organization; (2) the desirability of surpluses; (3) the sensibleness of keeping the children few in an environment of such uncertainties.

Lester Velie, in *Collier's,* dated April 8, 1950, tells of comparable poverty conditions, affecting more people. They are farm laborers in California's San Joaquin Valley. There are 200,000 of them, and with their families they must number nearly a million—nearly 10 percent of all Californians.

Those San Joaquin Valley folk constitute several times the total population of the neighboring state of Nevada. They are seasonal farm workers who pick cotton or fruit at piece rates or at hourly wages—when there is work; who live in labor camps and shantytowns; and whose children, in considerable proportion, are plagued by typhoid, skin diseases, lice, and malnutrition.

In part these unfortunates are victims of the transition to large-scale farming. But also they are the victims of the ignorance and superstition and carelessness that permit many of them to reproduce far beyond reason. Many of them have six, eight, and even more, children.

Americans are too intelligent, thought my friend, Dr. Chandrasekhar, to let a quantitative population problem arise here. Could it be that a quantitative population problem *is* arising here? Are those conditions in the San Joaquin Valley very much different from the conditions in India itself?

American recklessness in reproduction is general. One more illustration: *Life,* in its issue dated December 26, 1949, reported the primitive reproduction of the Kentucky mountaineers. In Leslie County there are 48.5 births per year per 1000 people—even more than the birth rate of some of the "backward" areas of Asia (and headed for the same subsistence level of living). Yet the Leslie County birth rate was reported as characteristic of that of the whole six million people in the Southern Appalachian hill country! Those, our enemies, are robbing your own posterity of opportunities that should be available to every human being.

•

The most serious aspect of our population problem in the United States, as in most of the world, is the *attitudes* that prevail in some groups about reproduction. The conditions themselves can be corrected when, where, and if the attitudes can be realistic.

In the Western Hemisphere, the most difficult obstacle to reasonableness in the appraisal, as well as in the correction, of population troubles is the attitude of the Catholic priesthood.

In Old Testament times the government itself was under the Church, and in fact practically all living was under the direction of the priests. As education increased, the people themselves participated more and more in analyzing environment, and adapting their behavior to it, especially after the invention of the printing press. The

Catholic hierarchy has retained dogmatic control over larger segments of living than any other clergy—in the Western World, at least. They claim that reproduction is within the scope of their authority, and rationalize about it in opposing birth control and sterilization, just as the clergy of some sects a few years ago opposed vaccination against smallpox. It seems to me that the hierarchy is as weak in its population analysis as it was in its astronomy when it condemned Galileo for reporting that the sun rather than the earth was the center of our planetary system. However, as will be shown later herein, a large proportion of Catholic laymen are doing independent thinking about reproduction, and fewer than half of the Catholics follow the twaddle of the clergy in that phase of living.

It is possible that the cardinals can, in time, stimulate a breeding program which will give them political control in the U.S., and then, joining Church and State, collect Church revenues by levies against all taxpayers. But there are two points I wish to call to their attention in this connection—one later in the book, and one here.

The U.S. is the largest source of funds for the Roman Catholic central organization. If, in the hierarchy's objective of breeding for control, they pauperize the U.S. to the extent that Italy is pauperized—and, if the trends continue, that is likely—the revenues for Rome will have to be reduced, in spite of the larger personnel from which the revenues will be drawn. Funds for the Church, like funds for an army, are ordinarily from surpluses of income above daily needs. People who breed to a subsistence level are impotent in war except as their government presses some of them below subsistence in its collections—as Louis XIV of France did. And a church among poverty-stricken people is in a disadvantageous position compared with a church in a land where there are surpluses above daily needs.

The Catholic clergy is not the only group which is building population attitudes inconsistent with human welfare. The General Electric Company is doing harm in a similar way. In a "General Electric Houseparty" at 3:30 daily, at the time of this writing, a prize is offered for the woman in the Hollywood audience with the largest number of children and grandchildren, there being also a grand prize for the week. I was listening on July 8, 1948, over WGAR at 1220 when a ten-inch oscillating electric fan was presented to a Mrs. Troutman, who had 17 living children, 45 grandchildren, and 37 great-grandchildren. Thus the General Electric Company is glorifying the poverty-makers of America's tomorrows, leading other couples to the idea that there is merit in reckless reproduction.

Chambers of Commerce used to put on campaigns to increase the size of their towns. To some extent that antisocial practice continues. No matter what happens to *average* incomes, the incomes of proprietors with corner stores usually go up as numbers of customers increase. But many Chamber of Commerce members have recently awakened to the long-time prospects for decrease of average incomes from population growth and are refraining from their erstwhile naïve boosting. The attitude of utter abandon in reproduction is not universal, of course, but the indiscriminate approval of reproduction has been sufficiently widespread to make for disturbing facts and prospects.

•

The overall picture shows an appalling U.S. recklessness concerning population. Babies born in the U.S. in the single year 1949 were 3,581,000—a number about the same as the total population of the country at the time of the adoption of the Constitution. By 1790, when the first census was taken, the U.S. population totaled 3,929,214. It took 183 years—from 1607 to 1790—for population growth to reach that figure; but now the *net increase* is that many every *two years*. In 1949 the population of the U.S. passed 150,000,000. That is an increase of more than 18,000,000 from 1940's 131,669,275.

The significance of such a number is not easy to grasp. The increase *since 1940* is more than twice the 1940 population of all of New England. We make a big to-do about Greece and her problems, but our own population has increased *since 1940* by more than twice the total population of Greece. You have some idea of Iceland? It would take about 135 Icelands to reach the numerical magnitude of the people added to the U.S. between 1940 and 1950. Yet the acreage from which we draw our living has not increased at all, and the fertility of our soil has decreased.

The added numbers of people are a dynamic force that will work in several directions. There will be strong demands for athletic goods, schoolbooks, housing, movie theaters. Some businesses will flourish for a time; some will sag. The *land,* which is the non-increasable factor of production, will be subject to greater strain. Food prices will take a larger proportion of income—especially for animal products—as intensive cultivation claims pasture land for products which will yield more dollars per acre.

A news item of June 15, 1948, is clarifying: Milk cows had declined in number by 2.6 millions in the previous three years to 25.1 millions—had declined while the baby crop was reaching an all-time record. Meat prices are likely to stay high too. More acreage is required for beef than for any other widely used food, and as M. K. Wisehart confirmed in the *Pathfinder*, March 9, 1949, the population was increasing more rapidly than its meat supply.

One reason for the larger *increase* in the U.S. population in the 1940's is the fact that we *started* the decade with a larger population than we started any previous decade. Even the same *percentage* of increase would have resulted in a larger absolute increase. That consideration of the size of the population in the base year, simple though it is, has great importance. The increase since 1940 has been about 14 percent. When the country was new, a 14 percent increase in the population wouldn't have meant much. With or without the increase, the people rattled around like a half-dozen marbles in a chalk box. There was plenty of room. But now a 14 percent increase is as much in absolute numbers as a 460 percent increase would have been from the 1790 base.

The tremendous population increases in America, and the prospects of further increases, should not blind us to the fact that it isn't as bad as it might have been. Birth control has been practiced in increasing measure for the past century and is practiced now by *a large majority* of married people. Except for that fact we should have had a rate of increase presumably not far from that which prevailed before 1860: 35 percent per decade. With that rate of increase the population by 1950 would have been 450,000,000. That is approximately the population of India. With that many people, of course we should be sending no food to Europe, and there would be no Marshall Plan; we should have very little meat or milk in our diet; very few people could get a college education; illiteracy would be high; automobiles would be rare; few people could have more than one room per family. The levels of living now experienced in the United States would be impossible except for the fact that there has been a widespread practice of birth control.

Various statisticians have predicted that the population of the United States will level off with a total of 160,000,000 to 190,000,000. But *in making those guesses they have assumed that the use of contraception will increase at about the same rate as in past decades and that contraception will be practiced by a much larger majority of the population than now.* If contraception, or some other form of birth control, is not adopted by the larger proportion of people, the numbers will not level off as expected, and we can be sure that the conditions of Asia will before long be matched by the conditions of America. And this is important: *people who resist population control are in effect advocating Asiatic living conditions for the United States.*

•

But is there any possibility that contraception, in the country as a whole, will be carried too far? Yes, there is! Some people already carry it too far, and the people of a country as a whole may do so. This possibility will be discussed in later chapters. Suffice it to say, at this point, that in America as a whole, and throughout most of the world, the quantitative trouble is that there is *too little* practice of contraception, and *too many* babies are born.

•

The growth of population makes demands for more products, and so makes for more rapid use of metals and oil. There have lately been some studies which show a disconcerting depletion of our supplies of graphite, tungsten, lead, zinc, and various other mineral products. For some purposes that depletion is important. It is well to recognize that population may be in excess in ratio with housing, and in ratio with fuel and in ratio with metals. But I don't think we should go into much detail about them here, because we must not for a moment get out of sight of the fact that the most important ratios relating to number of people are the ratios with *food*—and the soil sources of food. If we go into much detail concerning the metals and oils, there is danger of getting sidetracked on controversial issues. For example: Can shale oil be produced cheaply enough to substitute for pool oil when the deposits are in lower supply? Can atomic energy be made practical for heating, and power, and so compensate our rapid using of some kinds of fuel?

Those and similar problems are arresting, but they are schoolgirls' piffle compared with the vibrant question, WILL THERE BE ENOUGH TO EAT?

I have pointed out earlier herein that the soil itself, through erosion and cropping, is regressing to a less fertile condition, and that crop production in the future must be at higher cost. *We are losing our economy of reserves;* and to the extent that it thins out, the American levels of living must also decline.

One might think of this generation of people as holding the earth in a trusteeship, maintaining its abundance for the generations to come. That is not the prevailing attitude. There seems to be a frenzy to use everything up as soon as possible, stripping the earth to barrenness. What reason could there be for crowding more people here? Even if there were merit in mere numbers without the attributes that differentiate the species as human, such a course seems shortsighted. It is very unlikely that the total numbers over the long eons can be increased by increasing the present inhabitants.

•

America's past has been a history of destruction. And the destruction continues! We have been, and we are, living far beyond our income of timber as well as soil and other geographic resources. Our supply of timber has dwindled to one-fifth of its earlier figure. We are taking out mature trees one and a half times as fast as they are replaced. Wisdom involves plenty of attention to the conservation problem. American life becomes slightly more costly if we adopt a thoroughgoing conservation policy, but much more costly within a few years if we do not engage in a conservation program now.

Rarely now is timber burned just to clear the ground, yet a tremendous amount of it is burned through carelessness. Kenneth Scheibel quotes one forest-fire fighter thus: "The three main causes of fire are men, women, and children." The annual average number of forest fires in the United States on Federal lands is approximately 9,500; in State and private forests, 160,000; total 169,500. You will find those almost unbelievable figures supported in the *Statistical Abstract,* in which data from various sources are consolidated. The areas burned over on Federal lands average, per year, about half a million acres. The areas burned over in State and private forests average, per year, an appalling 23,000,000 acres. That is seven times the area of the state of Connecticut. As an average we burn that much out every year.

Probably no cigarette smoker who starts one of the fires, to say nothing of the millions of other men and

women in the same fraternity, thinks of changing his
ways in the interests of conservation. I suppose we might
charge each smoker for about a third of an acre of timber
each year as part of the cost of his habit, but actually the
seriousness of those fires reaches far beyond the money
value of the destroyed timber as such.

I have often been asked why I don't smoke.

If you had spent hours, as I have, flying in a gray
smudge, while the Douglas fir monarchs flared and
crashed, and the very soil itself was burning beneath you
—and if you had realized what the holocaust meant in
terms of America's prospects; and if you felt as I do that
participation in a practice is a vote for its consequences,
I think you wouldn't smoke either.

The Forest Service maintains over 3,000 lookout towers
and a fleet of airplanes for spotting fires, and a group of
fire jumpers who parachute to the area of new fires to
catch them early. In 1948 seven thousand fire fighters
were added to the 1,200 on the permanent staff in an
effort to keep the fire damage as low as possible.

In some areas flying fire patrols are maintained on
regular schedules. I was one of the men employed by the
Forest Service in its first year of that work, 1920. At that
time the flights were in Army planes with Army pilots
and Forest Service observers. The Army had, however,
done the same work without Forest Service men the year
before. Fire jumping came later. And helicopters in
forest-fire service are very recent.

Though Wisconsin's forest fire of 1871 took more lives,
I suspect that the North American conflagration that destroyed most timber occurred in Ontario, Canada, in
early June of 1948. It licked up the big trees on an 80-
mile front and continued out of control for weeks. California was a trouble spot too, in that year. In 1949 we
suffered most in Montana.

But what has the vanishing forest to do with population? Take it in connection with our vanishing minerals, and the vanishing surface of our farm land. We have been living on our fat—at an average level of living higher than was warranted by the long-range condition. Fewer people constitute less of a drain on resources; they can afford to live in a more happy-go-lucky way. Our population is denser now and we've got to be good—or we'll hurt. And the more people we get, the more frugally we'll have to live. Good sense will lead us to conserve our resources, to live more frugally, and also to put the brakes on our reproduction recklessness.

•

There is a very serious misconception in the mind of the average citizen that forests are lumber, cordwood, and a source of paper, and nothing more. Those uses, important as they are, cannot compare with the forest function of *holding back rainwater* and releasing it gradually. Forests are necessary to the prevention of floods and droughts.

The drought in California in the early months of 1948 contains a warning of population limitations. Complexity cloaks over the population cause of misfortune. Lester Velie had an article in the *Reader's Digest* for August 1948, condensed from *Collier's,* in which he pointed out that California dairy cows were slaughtered and steers sent out of the state because of drought in Central Valley.

The Federal Government has planned to spend 3 billion dollars for Central Valley within the next ten years; to alter the courses of rivers, build reservoirs, and cut canals in order to open up 50,000 new farms. But, on the strength of that reclamation plan, speculators have already bought and sold land far in excess of the acreage that the new project can supply with water.

In the seven-year period, mid-1940 to mid-1947, California's population increased by 42.1 percent to 9,812,-000, and by 1950 is over ten millions. Earl Warren, Governor of California, in an article in the *Saturday Evening Post* for August 14, 1948, with the usual political philosophy that "bigger equals better" tried to rationalize to the effect that the state's growth is O.K. But he did point out that south of San Francisco, where three-fourths of the Californians live, there is not a single river flowing all year around to the sea, that Southern Californians drink water from Owens Valley, 175 miles to the north, or from the Colorado River, more than 200 miles to the east, that "water is life itself in California," and that "the final limit to California's growth is going to be water."

William Vogt in *Road to Survival* reports the experience of California's Santa Clara Valley. Originally there was such an abundance of underground water that if one dug for water he was very likely to get a flowing well. By 1910 there were thousands of these artesian wells, but the underground water was being drawn off more rapidly that it was replaced from the storm-fed mountain streams. Pumping became necessary, and the volume of water pumped up expanded from 25,000 acre feet in 1915 to 134,000 acre feet in 1933. The water table had been lowering about 5 feet per year, and dropped 21 feet in 1933. The last artesian well stopped flowing in 1930; the usual lift in 1934 was 165 feet. With absence of water in the earth's body the land surface itself sank 5 feet in 20 years, permanently reducing the underground storage capacity. Yet so dim has been the average citizen's comprehension of his relation to the earth that Californians in 1922 voted down by 7 to 1 a conservation plan that would have cost $4,000,000. Within the next 20 years farmers spent over $16,000,000 for new wells and more powerful pumping equipment.

Seven states and Mexico have claims, to the extent of 17,500,000 acre-feet of water annually, from the Colorado River, but that much water is a million more acre-feet than the river supplies. So, in the Southwest, where the flow, though not yet the forest source of the flow, is in consciousness, the river has become a bone of contention.

Though the Southwest is most parched, and most water-conscious, yet in several other parts of the country we are lowering the water tables too. Industry uses vast amounts of water—and air conditioning puts a new demand on the reserves.

Partly our trouble stems from wasteful practices, partly from high levels of living, which include air conditioning, partly from increasing swarms of human beings. Each of these three developments is antagonistic to the other two.

Velie, in his *Reader's Digest* article, stated that we are using up our underground water supply faster than it collects and we are thereby lowering the water tables, in some areas as much as 55 feet in six years. In the panhandle of Texas the ground stores up about 50,000 acre-feet of rainwater per year, but recent wheat prices have induced a pillaging of the water reserves, and with 6,100 new wells added to the 1,100 wells of the 1930's, the farmers pumped up 750,000 acre-feet of water in the single year 1947. They are using the ground water reserve 15 times as fast as it accumulates.

In the *Reader's Digest* for October 1947, taken from the *Country Gentleman,* is an article by Clinton P. Anderson, then Secretary of Agriculture, entitled "Soil Murder on the Plains."

Anderson reported that from Mexico to our northern border huge tractors, pulling the world's largest plows, were gambling with land that should never have been taken from the herdsmen. The plow-up boom, he was convinced, would result in destruction of soil, and in economic harm.

History seems likely to repeat the experience that followed World War I: a wheat boom, then a bankrupting excess of wheat; then a horrifying Dust Bowl.

Better weather settled the soil in 1941, and since then the raiders of the plans have cashed in on the most favorable growing conditions prairie history has ever recorded.

But there is a weather cycle in the grasslands, and their long-time average rainfall is near the minimum at which crops can grow. And nowhere else in the United States do the unfettered winds lash so mercilessly. The packed earth, bound by grasses, can take it, but plowed, if it is dry, it becomes fine and loose; and a drifting desert results.

In a series of years of phenomenal rainfall we have grown tremendous crops, and have shipped nearly half our wheat to a war-torn world. But we can't keep it up. Secretary Anderson reported that of 123,000,000 acres of cropland in use on the plains, 22,000,000 acres are worked with a large element of risk. They should be taken out of cultivation and put in pasture. That applies particularly to some of the lands most recently brought into use. There is another large portion of the 123 million acres on which the risk is considerable, and on that, too, our cropping has gone beyond reason.

At about the same time that the *Reader's Digest* carried the worried Secretary's report to the nation, *Time* announced that drought was leering in the grain states; in Kansas a dust haze filled the air, and little sand dunes began to pile around the fences. The rains came! and that immediate danger was over.

The 1949-1950 winter was somewhat on the dry side, and on March 24, 1950, there were dust clouds over Texas choking the airways as high as three miles; and for days, 40-mile winds, punctuated with 80-mile gusts, swept over Texas, Oklahoma, and Kansas, with a gritty threat of catastrophe. Again on April 10, 1950, the winds sped at 60 miles per hour, and again earth was torn loose and deposited in far places. *Life,* dated April 10, 1950, showed pictures of the drifting dust at Lamesa, Texas, and near Wichita, Kansas.

And still we are taking foolhardy risks—plowing land that should be in permanent grass. We are sending forty-ton loads over the bridge with the ten-ton limit. If we keep it up, let's not pretend to be surprised when the crash comes!

The men who make the tractors are not favorable to the brief boom that can be theirs with the plowing up of cattle lands. An enlightened ad of the Caterpillar Tractor Company reads in part as follows:

"Nature worked double-shift for thousands of years to build the rich layer of topsoil that produces our wheat and corn and cotton. The standard of living that makes America the best fed, best clothed nation in history is *only six inches deep.*

"That's why soil erosion is a national calamity. Ancient civilizations, now buried beneath deserts, tell what happens when topsoil goes. So does China, where erosion has made starvation commonplace. The 'good earth' that muddies our own streams is beefsteak, milk, bread, dresses and shoes—lost forever.

"Nearly two-thirds of our crop and grazing land has already lost part or all of its topsoil. We have left some 460 million acres of good farm land—enough to maintain our present standard of living *if we keep it.*

"One effective method of fighting erosion is terracing, which forces storm water to run off so slowly it can't carry away soil."

A salute to the gentlemen of the Caterpillar Tractor Company! In the long run there is more bread as well as beef for us all in terracing the rolling land that regularly gets enough rain, than in ripping up the dryer cattle lands for exposure to the eroding winds.

The lands that have remained in pasture, some of them, are overgrazed. There is a struggle right now by the U.S. Forest Service to reduce animal feeding on about half the ranges in the National Forests, mostly those on watersheds. Grazing on the public ranges is under a permit system, the government selling the right to pasture at an average payment of 40 cents per cow-month and 10 cents per sheep-month. Permits average about 6,000,000 cow-months and 10,000,000 sheep-months per year.

Opposing the Forest Service is a subcommittee of the Public Lands Committee of the House of Representatives, which is being pressurized by cattle barons and sheepherders.

Though overgrazing is widespread on privately owned

lands too, the controversy concerns only part of the open spaces under mangement of the Forest Service—is limited to about half of 1% of the pasture area of the country—but since it is on watersheds and at headwaters, overgrazing there is particularly serious.

•

Considering food production in terms of immediate conditions, there are some marvelous developments which tend, fortunately, to offset—and, unfortunately, to obscure—the underlying wastage of American soil. Improved seeds and breeds and hybrids are the most spectacular of the developments. They also include a wide advance of knowledge: for instance, knowledge as to what planting time for wheat is best to avoid damage by the larva of the Hessian fly; knowledge that the yield of fish ponds can be increased by putting in minerals; knowledge of feeding practices that increase the production of milk.

Results have been greater yields both per acre and per man. Both can be important.

In *Life* for August 23, 1948, John Dos Passos reported developments which he thought constitute an "answer" to the thinning of the soil and the increasing of the human hordes that depend on it—an answer to "the increasing needs of this country and of the world." The use of corncobs as cattle feed may be more productive than their earlier use as fuel or fertilizer. The development of hybrid plants and hens makes for a larger food total. The sprays that decrease the insects leave a larger total of food for human beings. The grain dryers and efficient cultivating machinery and harvester machinery have advantages too, of a sort, but seem not likely to increase *total food*.

And this gaunt fact still grins over the horizon: All the improved yields per acre are cancelled out if population continues to increase.

•

Imaginative people like to think of various other romantic possibilities for increasing, on an enduring basis, the world's food—and gladly I join them. Processing the algae of the oceans into edible products is one alluring plan. Hydroponics—that is, raising food plants by rooting them in chemically treated water—is another. Perhaps there is a future for them. We may well continue experimenting. But it would be folly to place any dependence on them. At the present time those processes are submarginal; that is to say, labor and investment in those directions yield less product than they yield when used in land agriculture.

•

The need for reserves cannot be thought of meaningfully in a one-sided way. A reserve of fuel in the ground is much or little according to the number of people it must serve and the length of time it must serve them. And so it is with soil productivity. In a consideration of soil reserves the world as a whole is in a desperate plight;

those reserves are too scanty; in other words, its population is too numerous. The people of the United States, in consequence of their recently adopted role of brother's keeper for all nations, have reason to worry. Even our own near prospects are not too good—there are too many people even here. If we look to the long future, unless our population growth is promptly checked and our waste and extravagance curtailed we must recognize the probability of a miserable existence for our own descendants.

E. Parmalee Prentice, in his appraisal of surpluses and reserves of resources, puts population in its appropriate setting. His book, *Food, War and the Future,* was published in 1944 by Harper & Brothers. The following gems from his pages 2, 20, 30, 31, and 66 flash crystal clear:

"There is no progress when man works for existence only, or works on a maintenance ration. Progress came when the surplus came."

"Abundance can never be permanent in a world where there is a constantly increasing population, since, as the population grows, even the greatest supplies become inadequate."

"Sooner or later, if population continues to grow, we must expect to see in the western world the conditions which we see in other lands, where the numbers are beyond those for whom adequate provision is possible. There is nothing in Asiatic geography which makes misery unavoidable in that continent, and there is nothing in the geography of Europe and America, nothing in our history, or in the character of our inhabitants, which ensures for us the standard of living which we are sometimes told is the birthright of every human being.

"The great problem of Europe and America is the

problem of population—the question whether the tide of Asiatic conditions will roll over the western continents. Europe is already partly submerged. Whether it can save itself, we do not yet know."

"Of course, the first requirement for safety and comfort is that population shall not be excessive. Europe and America would be better off were numbers smaller. Our western world was happier, the possibilities before every person and, therefore, the inducements to effort were greater, and there was more dignity in life when population was less than it is now. It is most desirable that growth of population be deliberately checked and that numbers in every country be no greater than those which the country can happily support."

•

We took a tremendous bite when we set up the European Recovery Program. And when its four-year term is about to close we shall be called on to renew the program. Few Americans have given a thought to the population setting in which the Marshall Plan must be carried out. The foregoing chapters have sketched the conditions. One sees similar evidence on every side. The International Children's Emergency Fund established by the United Nations has reported, for instance, that 14-year-old boys in several European countries are 3 inches shorter on an average than 14-year-old boys were a few years ago. Infant mortality has jumped in some countries to eight times the U.S. level; diseases relating to malnutrition have greatly increased.

The United States has lately shipped abroad approximately 20 million tons of foodstuffs per year. That amount of food exports has depended on bumper-crop weather, yet it would support only 80,000,000 people, whereas at least 600,000,000 are close to starvation.

J. W. Evans is quoted in the March 1948 *Survey Graphic* as saying that the world has a "chronic insufficiency." He sees as one of the fundamental causes of it the persistent growth of population. Mr. Evans is a member of the staff of the Economics Division of the Food and Agriculture Organization of the United Nations. He reported an actual decrease in food supplies since 1939, whereas the population had increased about 10 percent. He pointed out—what you would expect after reading the chapter "It's A Small World"—that the volume of foodstuffs *moving in international trade* had been reduced more than the decline in food production. Of course. People who produce the food have a priority on it, and tend to take care of their own population increase.

The fact that there are *too many people* is a harsh reality, even when it is stated in the comparatively gentle reverse order: "There is too little food." Said *Time* on November 3, 1947, page 19: "The fact of economic life which Harry Truman refused to face is that there is not enough of everything in the world to go around."

Most people recognize that there is not enough *now*, but many think there *can* be. Robert M. Salter, of the Department of Agriculture, thinks it is possible to meet world food needs by using 8 times the present consumption of phosphate and nearly 18 times the present consumption of potash. But apparently he and the other people who argue that enough can be produced for everyone are also assuming (1) an impossibly smooth functioning of all economic institutions, (2) an even more intensive destruction of resources than we have had, and (3) ideal

Only those wishful thinkers who are not very good in arithmetic can believe that our finite country should commit itself to feed an infinitely expansible world population.

growing conditions. Also, and this is most important, they have neglected the fact that the population is continuing to increase, and that if, with exceptionally fine weather, universal philanthropy, flawless management, and complete efficiency, we were able to work up a production and distribution machinery which would feed the present 2.3 billion people, by the time the details were functioning, the population would have gone on to a new high.

•

A rapidly increasing number of Americans see the importance of the ratio of men to geographic resources. They worry about the haphazard use of the resources— the waste—and the rapid using up of scanty supplies. Many of them put all their attention on the ways in which the timber is cut, the oil wells drilled, the natural gas wasted or conserved, the coal mines propped, the hills contour-plowed. Some of them also see that things must be done about the *man* side of the man-land ratio.

A. J. Carlson, in the *Scientific Monthly* for December 1947, called attention to the expression of Sir John Boyd Orr, then Director General of the Food and Agriculture Organization of the United Nations, that we must double the world's food production in order to give the present population of the world an adequate diet. And Carlson comments:

"If we could do that—if we did that—what then? According to past records, increasing the food supply by better agriculture merely yields a parallel human population increase. . . . Why not give understanding and intelligence a trial?"

In this man-food ratio it becomes necessary to face the

fact that we have no chance to keep the food supply increasing to keep up with an unrestrained population expansion. The only hope that men can reasonably have of preventing starvation is by way of influencing the *man* side of the man-food ratio. Men must cease to expand their numbers. Men must reduce birth rates.

And that goes for us of the U.S. Too long, with a feeling of American self-righteousness, we have talked of population problems as if they were problems only in India but not in the Western hemisphere, or as if they applied to our sharecroppers of the South but not to anybody in Cleveland. These points we must ponder:

1. In order to keep up the levels of living to which we have been accustomed, we have been digging deep into our geographic reserves.

2. To have faith that our population will "automatically" cease to increase at a figure short of 200,000,000 is to have faith in birth control without having the clarity of analysis to realize it.

3. To increase the U.S. population by ten millions beyond its present figure, or even by one million, we make life harder for miserable people in other lands, and more risky for our own descendants.

Chapter 6

Joe Martin Is a Bachelor

The birth rates in most countries are considerably lower than they might be. In the United States they declined from an estimated 55 births per year per thousand of the population in 1800 to 17 births per year per thousand in the 1930-1940 decade. They rose to a recent high of more than 28 per year during part of 1946, and had subsided by 1949 to a rate of about 24. Since our death rate is only about 10, the population increase is still enormous, as the previous chapter has shown.

Whenever a birth rate is *low* it means that a substantial proportion of the population are exercising restraints in matters of sex. At least they are going to the trouble of using contraceptives; they are not allowing their desires to have uncontrolled sway.

The birth rate in a country is really a composite of many birth rates, or differently expressed, it can be broken down into a number of different rates. Not everybody reduces his reproduction in conformity with the average. *Who* among a population have the high birth rates and who have the low ones? Who use restraint? In what comparative measures do different classifications of people use restraint? We shall do well to think of the *decline* of the birth rate in connection with the *differences* in birth rates.

Time of March 17, 1948, carried a news report that Joe Martin, then Speaker of the U.S. House of Representatives, in less than three months had received five marriage proposals. His marriage proposals concern our present inquiry only as a reminder that Minority Leader Joe Martin is a bachelor—and that there is loss to the country in his childlessness.

In contrast, *Time,* in its issue of December 29, 1947, had reminded us that in early September,

"In Bell Gardens, Calif., Joseph Bray, 37, left his wife and 13 children and eloped with the 16-year-old baby sitter."

California's eternal sunshine has brought specimens of every level of humanity to the state. *Time* for July 28, 1947, told us that Mrs. Jesse Brink stormed into a county welfare office in Los Angeles, and threatened to go back to Oklahoma with her husband and nine of her eleven children because the relief check had been cut from $278 to $126. That amount "won't pay for our gasoline." California authorities held her to her word; bought her four new tires, deposited expense checks ahead at Phoenix, El Paso, and Abilene to be sure she lived up to her statement.

A news item of January 15, 1948, reported that the Brinks were back in California again, but that the county charities superintendent was not planning to accept them on the relief rolls.

But why don't Mr. Bray and the Brinks come on to

Cleveland? There might be an ambassador's suite left for them here. In the *Cleveland Press* for November 20, 1947, was a front page story reporting that William Wagasky with his wife and most of his family of eight children were living in Hotel Clarendon at a cost of $500 a month, paid from the city relief fund. They had been evicted nearly a year before. Mr. Wagasky, age 34, had a lung infection and asthma, and was incapable of working. I wonder if very many of those who saw the story of the Wagasky family in the *Cleveland Press* thought about it as a *population* problem.

We can be sure that the Wagasky family poses a problem of population *quantity*. From the skimpy facts reported in the news item, we cannot be sure whether or not the problem also directly involves *quality* considerations. Quality problems may involve either physical health or mentality.

Mental quality, at a time, is measured by tests the results of which are expressed in terms of intelligence quotients, usually abbreviated to "IQ." The tests most in use in America are arranged in such a way that the average IQ score for the general public is 100. A higher score reports more than average intelligence.

•

The significance of a high IQ score can be shown by reference to a study conducted by Lewis M. Terman and his associates, of Stanford University. A quarter of a century ago, among California children these investigators selected a thousand for study, solely on a basis of their high IQ's. The thousand subjects have been repeatedly restudied, and in December 1947 the Stanford University Press published *The Gifted Child Grows Up,* by Lewis M. Terman and Melita H. Oden. Nearly 90 percent of the gifted subjects entered college, and nearly 70 percent of the thousand are college graduates. The latter figure is about ten times as high as for the general California citizens of corresponding age. "Probably not more than one in a hundred of the general population graduates from a college with Phi Beta Kappa or Sigma Xi honors," the authors tell us, "as compared with about 16 percent of the total gifted group." Almost half of all the men in the study, and more than half of the fully employed women, are engaged in one or another of the professional occupations. In the case of men this is almost nine times the proportion so classifiable in the California population of employed adults.

In the general U.S. population, incomes from wages and salaries of urban residents, ages 25-34, who were employed 12 months in 1939, averaged $1,389 "compared with $2,373 for all gifted men (ages 20-39) with full-time employment. The corresponding medians for women are $916 for the census group and $1,660 for gifted students."

The proportion of Terman's group who receive high incomes is high:

Income levels:	Generality of United States Families (1946) (Percent)	Civilian Gifted Men (1944) (Percent)
$7,500 or over	2.6	20.5
$5,000 or over	7.4	45.4

The Terman group, selected in childhood entirely on a basis of childhood IQ, have a significant employment record. The proportion of the gifted men unemployed in 1940 was less than 1 percent. "In contrast, the 1940 census shows that approximately 11 percent of experienced male workers between the ages of twenty and thirty-four, employable and seeking work, were unemployed in California at this same period."

The IQ of offspring of the gifted group averages 127.7. That figure is about 24 points below the average childhood IQ of the gifted group members themselves. Since selection was in only one generation, a considerable regression could be expected. However, the proportion of offspring with IQ's of 150 or higher is approximately 15.4 percent, whereas in an unselected group the proportion with such high IQ's is only slightly more than half of 1 percent. Thus, IQ's above 150 occurred about 28 times as often among the children of the selected group as among the general public. There were instances of offspring of gifted group members having IQ's below 80, but the proportion was less than half the proportion of such IQ's in the general public.

•

The same issue of *Time* that reminded us of Joe Martin's childlessness quoted Ernest William Barnes, Lord Bishop of Birmingham, as saying: "Statistics show that the proportion of dullards and feeble-minded is definitely greater than a generation ago."

Studies are accumulating which re-enforce that truth and give it tremendous importance. *News Exchange,* of the Planned Parenthood Federation, in its issue of December 1948, correlated the sizes of families of which children are members with their intelligence scores. The study had been conducted by Professor Godfrey Thompson, an English psychologist who had recently tested the intelligence of 70,000 eleven-year-old residents of a Scottish city.

Professor Thompson found that the 7,284 children who had no brothers or sisters scored an average of 46 points in a possible 76 points. The 15,971 children from families of two children averaged almost that high. Children from three-children families scored less; those from families of four children averaged 35.3; children with seven brothers and sisters averaged 28.8. For families of 18 children the score was 7, and for families of 19, the score was zero.

Summarizing: in that city in Scotland, parents who had a stupid eleven-year-old child, as a general thing had many children; parents who had a bright eleven-year-old child had few children.

That is a different approach to birth-rate differences than the usual approach. Generally, people are classified according to some sort of achievement, and then the investigation is conducted to see how many children are born per thousand people in each of the classifications. Almost everywhere that studies have been made, the truth is impressive that dull couples average more births than bright couples. In general, as Dr. H. Curtis Wood observes, fertility varies inversely with intelligence.

The conclusion is inescapable that each generation is predominantly the offspring of the least accomplished people of the preceding generation.

The 1940 census of the United States correlated birth rates with various other social data. It costs more money that way but it has been a big help in analyzing what goes on. In studying birth rate differences, and what they mean to the future of the United States, we shall want to know what the Census Bureau found. Here is one disclosure:

In the volume *Differential Fertility 1940 and 1910: Women by Number of Children Under 5 Years Old,* page 25 shows that 2½ percent of women who never completed the first grade have three or more children each, under 5 years of age, whereas less than a half of 1 percent of college graduates have that many children. In other words, among the least accomplished of our people, five times as large a proportion have three or more young children, as the proportion of college grads who have that many.

Education is a real accomplishment which paves the way for other accomplishment. In the educational system there is a sorting-out process as well as training. Those who are sorted out, for the most part, just haven't got what it takes.

In the census volume *Women by Number of Children Ever Born,* there is this revelation in table 47: Of high school graduates only one woman in 500 has ten children or more, and only one college graduate in a thousand has ten children or more; whereas among the women with no years of education completed, one woman in every eleven has ten children or more.

Table 49 on page 155 shows that women who had completed one to four grades of school had 3,561 children per 1000 women, whereas college graduates had 776 children per 1000 women. Since these are averages, many of the women in those groups have not completed their childbearing. For completed families we should have somewhat larger figures. But the really significant aspect of the table is the comparison, of course, of the number of offspring of ignorant women with the number of offspring of educated women. The women who never got beyond the fourth grade have more than four times as many children per thousand as the college graduates have.

Here it is in a table:

NUMBER OF CHILDREN PER 1000 NATIVE WHITE WOMEN
CLASSIFIED BY EDUCATION OF MOTHER

School years completed by mothers	Number of children per 1000 women
Not any	3145
1-4	3561
5 and 6	2999
7 and 8	2141
High School 1-3	1155
High School 4	928
College 1-3	996
College 4 or more	776

That represents what is happening in America.

•

Birth-rate differences are not limited to one race or religion. The Census Bureau tables show that the "differential birthrate," that is the birth rate differences, apply among the Negroes as demonstrably as among the whites —even a little more demonstrably, at both ends of the scale. Our table showed that a thousand native white women with no education have 3,145 children, whereas a thousand of them with 4 or more years of college have only 776 children. Now compare the figures for the colored women. A thousand of them who have not completed any grades of school have 3,445 children, whereas a thousand of them who are college graduates have only 701 children. And as with the whites, the number of children goes by steps—practically in inverse correlation with amount of education: *the more the education, the fewer the children.*

Rev. Thomas Francis Coogan made a careful study entitled *Catholic Fertility in Florida,* which was published by The Catholic University of America Press in 1946. The Catholics are subject to the same sort of differences as are the rest of the population. The more rent they can afford, the fewer children they have; the more responsibility there is in their jobs, the fewer children they have; the more education they have, the fewer children they have.

Rev. Mr. Coogan found that for families practically completed—with wives of ages 40-49—in which both husbands and wives were Catholic, the numbers of births per 100 wives were as follows:

Education of Husband and Wife	Births per 100 Wives
3 or more years of college	216
1 and 2 years of college	262
4 years of high school	244
3 years of high school	324
2 years of high school	247
1 year of high school	289
8 years of grade school	291
7 or fewer years of grade school	416

There was not a very smooth working out of the rule, but unmistakably it is there; observe especially the contrast between the number of children of the parents with three or more years of college, and the parents with seven years of grade school or less.

As to occupations, too, 100 wives of managers and professional people had 158 births, whereas 100 wives of unskilled laborers had 302 births.

One significant aspect of the fact that birth rates differ in the same antisocial direction among Negroes as among whites, and among Catholics as among Protestants, is that if our present civilization cracks up because of lack of brains, the people of the most numerous minorities will not be able to do any better, because their brains are decreasing too.

If the minorities were to outbreed numerically the rest of the people, and thus to take over, they would make a fizzle of things too, because by that time the offspring of their unaccomplished members would be such a huge proportion of their total membership.

•

Why does the number of children of people correlate inversely with their achievement? Why is it that the people who reach goals are the ones who have few children? We shall do well to continue to consider the lowering birth rate and the differential birth rate together.

Frequently one hears a statement that the reason for a declining birth rate is the increasing cost of bringing up children. Let's not say that expression is wrong, but observe that it seems inconsistent with the fact that people with money have fewer children than those who are poverty-stricken. One might expect fewest children in families least able to bear the cost of children. But it doesn't work out that way.

Cost has to be considered in connection with the psychological quality of *restraint*. In the year 1819 the French economist Sismondi published an observation that restraint in reproduction is correlated with size of income: roughly, the more the income, the greater the restraint. He said it this way:

"While sympathy or the affections urge to marriage,

egoism or calculation defer, and through the interplay of
these forces population would naturally be regulated according to revenue. The natural limits to population are
always respected by those who have, while they are exceeded by those who have not."

Thus Sismondi made a start in explaining birth rates.
He reported that prudence is opposed to the sex urge,
and the wealthy are prudent. They keep the number of
their children within the bounds of their purses. Among
those who are prudent, cost of bringing up children *can*
have a part in decisions as to how many children to have.

Sismondi gave prominence to *attitudes* towards cost of
children, not to the cost. In that he was realistic.

Cost seems to be one cause of the decline in the birth
rate, through causing a portion of the population—the
prudent members (those of the prudent members who
know how)—to limit their reproduction.

One modern scholar (of several) who puts emphasis
on prudence is the Reverend Gordon Smee of Sydney,
Australia. He was quoted in the *Times-Herald* of Washington, D. C., on November 21, 1947, as saying that

"The birth rate of more intelligent people is declining
through their desire to ensure successful careers for their
children. They achieve this by limiting the size of their
families."

But it seems to work the concept of prudence too hard,
and surely it overstresses cost, to think of prudence in
relation to cost as the main cause of the decline in birth
rate or of the differences of birth rates.

One other money consideration should be mentioned,
however. J. C. Flugel presented it in *Men and Their
Motives*. That was published in London in 1934. International Universities Press, 227 W. 13th Street, New

York 11, seems to have it now. Flugel reminds us that the people who limit their reproduction in order to provide better for the children they do have must pay taxes in order to support the more reckless people with larger families. So the people who aim to protect their own children against poverty must have fewer children still, as a consequence of thoughtless people having more. Flugel thinks that if family limitation were practiced by more families there would be less tax burden, so the foresighted people would not have to limit their numbers of offspring so rigorously.

But the money considerations, (1) cost of children among the prudent, and (2) the partial transfer of the money burden from the reckless to the prudent, fall far short of explaining birth rate differences.

As it turns out, accomplishment of almost any sort— that is, achievement *beyond* the average—is coincident with a birth rate of *less* than average. The rule applies not alone to successful money-makers as such, but to successful athletes and successful dancers, and successful business men, successful scientists, successful farmers: probably successful people in any classification.

From any angle then, the reproduction restraint, necessary though it is in preserving a level of living above mere subsistence, is effectively practiced by the wrong people. The irresponsible, the foggy-minded, the ne'er-do-wells, and the helpless are the ones who should have few children if any. But those are the people who have the large families. And partly because of baby-kissing politicians of the past the scantwits think they are doing something commendable when they put another social burden on the relief roll.

•

I discussed causes of birth rate *decline* and birth rate *differences* in some measure in *Society Under Analysis*. That is a 700-page sociology textbook written by several sociologists including me, published in 1942, and now out of print. For the following list of eight considerations I draw on the findings first reported in that book.

1. Economic cost of children.
2. Decreasing use of children in fulfilling one's wish for recognition.
3. Declining security for children.
4. Decline in psychological value of children, as population increases.
5. Increasing difficulty in having one's merits recognized by the world.
6. Competition of other things with children in one's attention.
7. Belief that heredity is unimportant.
8. A favorable attitude toward smallness of families.

Now, second movement; same symphony:

1. There is some importance in the economic cost of children as a reason for not having a child nine months from now; and so birth rates decline. The comments of Economist Sismondi, Churchman Smee, and Psychologist Flugel apply.

2. The youngsters do not make a parent feel important any more. Their out-of-home influences are likely to give them attitudes that make Pop feel pretty small. He isn't boss of the ranch, or "master of all he surveys," as his grandfather was. If by some chance he feels important it is not because his children look up to him; they don't. And so the birth rates decline.

3. (a) What is the outlook for a child born nine months from now, as to the *character-forming* influences over which his parents will have little control? The out-

look is worse than it used to be when the city was smaller. And so the birth rates decline.

(b) What about the *political future* of the country in which a youngster will grow up? The drift to more centralized government isn't very hope-inspiring. Every decade the prospects look darker. And so the birth rates decline.

(c) How about the *economic opportunities* for a child born nine months from now? Nothing significant has been done to guard against business cycles and chronic unemployment. Those mean more now, too, than they did when, in case of unemployment, one could "go west, young man, go west," and get some land of his own. And so the birth rates decline.

4. Most people don't have much consciousness about what other people are worth to them, yet there is an influence. The more shoes you have, the less desire you have for another pair; the more dollars you have, the less a dollar means to you; the more of anything there is, the less you value a unit of it.—The more people there are around, the less prospective importance another one has for you. So an increasing population makes a prospective child less to be desired. Improved transportation puts one in touch with more people too—has the same effect as more people: a diminishing utility per person. And so the birth rates decline.

5. One likes to be somebody, to have influence. In a city of 100,000 people it is harder to be noticed, or even "to belong," than in a village of 1,000. One has to struggle more in the bigger place for recognition; so he is more likely to begrudge the time and money that raising a family would take. The denser the population, then, the more incentive there is *not* to have a child.

There is in most people a positive desire for children, but the numbered points, knee-deep in which we are now, indicate that the psychological resistances are stronger than they used to be, and the competing interests are stronger, because the world has changed.

6. The items which come to a person's attention these days are more numerous than they used to be. Radio, movies, lodges, clubs, make one wonder—how will I ever get through all that if I have a child nine months from now? The jumble of things to do is more impelling than it used to be. And so the birth rates decline.

7. The belief that heredity is not important had an increasing vogue in the 1920's and in the early 1930's. I think the country is regaining its balance on this point now, as the next chapter will show, but while the illusion of biological equality lasted, and still effective for those who still have it, the reasonable conclusion is, why go through the trouble of having babies; let somebody else have them.

8. When "it isn't being done" by the VanWhosWhos, there is a tendency not to do. Especially as a population grows denser, to have few if any children becomes fashionable.

•

A study of the decline of birth rates is included in the *Report of the Royal Commission on Population,* presented to the British Parliament in June 1949. There were ten men and six women on that Commission. The expenses of their various population surveys and their 272-page report were about $800,000. The report (Cmd 7695) is available at $1.45 from British Information Services, 30 Rockefeller Plaza, New York 20, N. Y. Though later herein I must take exception to the Commission's recommendations, their chapter on "Causes of Family Limitation," among other analytical chapters, is good.

One cause of family limitation, they said, is that Britain's increase from 10½ million inhabitants to 26 million in the years from 1800 to 1871 revived fears of overpopulation, and many saw in population pressure one of the most serious obstacles to social progress. There is no implication that a couple deliberated about the influence of their own reproduction on their country's overpopulation, but the concept of overpopulation turned public opinion against stairstep families, and provided a rational basis for propaganda for birth control.

Birth-control propaganda is reported by the Royal Commission as a separate reason for the decline in the birth rate—along with a burst of publicity that grew out of the trial of Mrs. Annie Besant and Charles Bradlaugh in 1877. Those two had sponsored the sale of *The Fruits of Philosophy,* a birth-control book written by one Dr. Charles Knowlton, an American.

The improvement of birth-control methods, and recently the establishment of clinics, private and government, giving advice on contraception, and supplying cheap and reliable contraceptives, are noted as causes of the decline in the birth rate.

The Commission discussed, as further causes, the desire of women to avoid the burdens of excessive childbearing, the influence of social example, the increasing importance of education, higher standards of parental care, the independence of women.

Decay of small-scale handicrafts that had been carried on in the family circle, the rise of factory organization, the loss of security, the decline of agriculture, and the shift of people to the cities,—these and other changes operate in a complex web of cause and effect. The decline of economic importance of the family made children an economic liability rather than an asset, and that "must have altered momentously the ordinary man's thinking about having children." It made a conspicuous contrast between the prosperity of the small family and the poverty of the large one. And the reduction of hours of labor, with increased importance of leisure, made children seem more burdensome.

At the same time, publications on evolution led to a questioning of man's need to accept his previous lot, loosened the taboos about the discussion of sex, opened the way for knowledge of means of controlling conception.

Incidentally, the Royal Commission commended the control of conception. Said the report, the

"gradual permeation of the small family system through nearly all classes has to be regarded, we think, as a fundamental adjustment to modern conditions. The most significant feature of this adjustment, in our view, is the gradual acceptance of control over the size of one's family particularly by means of contraception as a normal part of personal responsibility."

"We agree with the view that there is nothing inherently wrong in the use of mechanical methods of contraception." "The spread of contraceptive knowledge . . . has been one of the conditions of the great social advances that have been made since the 19th Century." "Control by men and women over the numbers of their children is one of the first conditions of their own and the community's welfare."

•

In *Society Under Analysis* I had worked out reasons why people do not *want* so many children as people used to want. The Royal Commission has covered some of that ground, and more thoroughly than I; and it has dealt more broadly with the subject.

Now the 64-dollar question is, why are there *differences* in birth rates? Why do great men have few children, while men who need an excuse for living have many chips off the old blocks?

The reasons for the *declines* in birth rates apply with different force to different folks. Those reasons for the *decline* in the general birth rate are reasons for the *differences* in birth rates too, *because they don't take effect on people equally*.

The degree of sensitiveness to the cost of a child, for instance, at least sensitiveness in advance of the child's birth, is quite different in different people. Sensitiveness to cost, and to the pressures named in both the Commission's analysis and my own, reflects the degree to which one is alive, alert, educated, and intelligent. People who are most sensitive to the various influences in their environment are most likely to master that environment and be successful. But in so saying we have said that they are more likely to be affected by the considerations listed than are uneducated or unintelligent or unsuccessful people. The alert person is more likely to sense a declining security for children than a slow-brained one is. The alert person is more likely to feel a lessened favorable influence of children on himself. He is more likely to see that there are difficulties between himself and his goals which may leave him little time or money for children. He is more likely to come in contact with a multiplicity of other items that compete with children. He is more likely even to have had contact with and been influenced by that vogue of belittling heredity; and more likely to be sensitive to a favorable attitude toward smallness of families.

The alert, educated, intelligent person is quickest to generalize on, and to see a lesson for himself in, the prosperity of the small family and the poverty of the large one. He is first to see an importance of education for his children, and most likely to develop a high standard of parental care. He is first to see the dangers of overpopulation, and quickest to reason away from assumptions and taboos that prevent adaptation.

And of course the alert, educated, intelligent people are the ones most likely to know about contraceptives and to be able to use them effectively.

•

One time, when Wallace P. Smith asked what I thought was the *most important* reason for accomplished people having a lower birth rate than unaccomplished people, I centered on the fact that accomplished people have *more interests, and more intense interests* than unaccomplished people have. That is number 6 in my original list.

Interests are the most influential cause of birth-rate *decline* because they are the most dynamic cause. Interests are the fighting line of one's mental army, the pioneer rim of one's habit patterns, the part of the self that is growing. Besides, they constitute the conscious phase of other reasons, some of which I mentioned and some of which were given by the Royal Commission.

Douglas Fryer, in his book *The Measurement of Interests,* tells us in effect that you can hang the word "interests" onto either the dogfight that attracts your attention, or the kick you get out of watching it.

Interests may be classified under innumerable headings. You may be interested in sports, music, literature, science, travel, social reconstruction, religion, personalities. Let's start again. Your major interests may relate to a hobby or to an occupation. They are the vast array of tiny details to which you give willing attention.

George A. Coe said applicable things in a Charles

Scribner's Sons book entitled *The Motives of Men.*
Speaking of occupational interests, he commented that
the chief output of mines is miners. "Hunting makes a
hunter; fishing a fisherman," he said; "when man
achieved the domestication of animals, he achieved likewise some taming of himself. When seeds began to be
planted, and fixed dwellings to be built, then seed
thoughts were sown in the mind, and he who erected a
roof 'built better than he knew,' for an advance took
place in the structure of domestic society. . . . The economic process and its economic product . . . makes the
man as truly as the man makes the product."

And he points out, p. 144, that "work has been done
upon the primitive drives, not merely by them, for there
is organization of selves and organization of society that
are not at all predictable from any scrutiny of raw
drives."

Edward L. Thorndike, on this theme, tells us in *The
Psychology of Wants, Interests and Attitudes,* D. Apple-
ton-Century, 1935, that the interest itself may change the
animal from what it was before. The wants, interests,
and attitudes which belong to the human species as products of its genes, says Thorndike, "would differ enormously from inventories of similar facts for living adults
in the present world."

Thus we change our original selves, and we build interests on interests. And having built up an interest in
movies, we are less likely to be lured by a church social—
or by the prospect of baby-sitting. Having developed an
interest in the Joneses and what you will have to do to
keep up with them, you are willing to let the janitor's
wife have the babies.

Situations evoke interests and interests create wants,
and wants in repetition. They occupy time and attention, and they take money. Crowds, neon ads, shouting

newsboys, theaters, operas, books, use up much of life. Given alertness and education, at least in Western cultures, the denser the population, the greater seems to be the variety of interests that compete with courting.

Interests—occupational interests, recreational interests, interests in the kaleidoscopic changes of a fast-moving world; these and our variety of values, make us over.

The number and intensity of your interests differ from the number and intensity of your neighbor's interests. You feel a little self-righteous that you have a broad field of interests. That, you think, stamps you as "cultured." You have a favorable attitude toward persons who know their way around in the 20th Century culture of the United States, and coincidentally a favorable attitude toward yourself.

What groups have the wide spread of interests, and the very intense interests; the interests which interfere with reproduction? You know the answer. The more alert a person is, the more complex are his interests. The educated person, the person who excels in this, that, or something, is the one who has the impelling interests. That is why there is an upside-down correlation between occupational success and offspring.

The uneducated have relatively few interests, and their interests are closer to the primitive drives. There is less "sublimation" by the uneducated, fewer branchings off from the surge of the urges.

There have been many commendations and many criticisms for the study *Sexual Behavior in the Human Male,* a recent W. B. Saunders Company publication written by Professors A. C. Kinsey, W. B. Pomeroy, and C. E. Martin, of Indiana University. Statistician Clyde V. Kiser, in the book *Problems of Sexual Behavior,* published by the American Social Hygiene Association, 1790 Broadway, New York 19, calls attention to the considerable differences in the size of samples in the different classifications of men. Yet Kiser considers the Kinsey report important, and believes that "It establishes beyond much doubt the reality of wide differences in patterns of sex behavior along socio-economic lines." Kinsey, Pomeroy, and Martin had reported that 98 percent of males whose education ended with the grade school have sexual intercourse before marriage; 84 percent of males of high school level, and 67 percent of college men have premarital sex relations.

Whether or not those percentages accurately reflect the facts, the study seems convincing that educated men have premarital sex relations in smaller proportion than the proportion of uneducated men of similar behavior; and the differences exist in spite of the fact that the less educated men marry earlier.

The same direction of differences in attention to sex was found by Dr. Kinsey to apply to girls, as reported by Dr. Clifford R. Adams, Director of the Marriage Counseling Service of Pennsylvania State College in *Pageant* for May, 1946. One-third of college girls had had sex relations by the time of graduation. Of girls who did not go to college, half had had sex relations by the time they reached the same age.

In a negative way these differences in sex experience between educated and less educated people are evidence of the influence of interests on differences in birth rates. The educated people probably have as much of sex hormones in their blood streams as uneducated people have, but they have other things to interest them, too.

There is a sensitiveness in an educated man's mind to the various factors in his environment. The greater he is, the greater is his sensitiveness. That sensitiveness is reason for his greatness, and is also the reason for his having few children, because in conformity with that sensitiveness he builds up his other interests.

In precivilization days, when the devil took the hindermost, the biological implication of success was survival of one's self and one's kin. The wage of insensitiveness was death. But now we save the unsuccessful, and they have most of the babies. Now the biological implication of success is extermination. Thus we have a reversal of the process of evolution of which Darwin wrote. Now, as Mrs. Marian S. Olden expresses the fact in the title of a pamphlet, there is *The Survival of the Unfittest.* The pamphlet is a publication of the Human Betterment Association of America.

Do not *interests* substantially explain why the 7,851 prominent women, with 5,037 college degrees, reported in *American Women* for 1937-38, have only 5,024 children?

Mary R. Beard tells us in the preface of her 1946 book, *Women as a Force in History,* that "Women have done far more than exist and bear and rear children." But the important question for the long pull is, *to what extent were they the same women?* These women who were doing something else than bearing and rearing children, were they bearing and rearing children too? No; not many of them were, and they bore and reared not many children. Mrs. Beard herself has been a notable force in history. She has been sole author of at least five books; has edited others. She and her distinguished husband together, besides having remarkably active additional careers, have authored, coauthored, or edited more than 30 books. And they are not ordinary books. They have had a large influence on American thought and government. The Beards had two children. I think our future would be better assured if they had had six more children, even at the sacrifice of a dozen books.

•

Characteristics of women in *Who's Who in America*
have been studied by Clyde V. Kiser and Nathalie L.
Schacter. Their findings were published in the October
1949 *Quarterly* of the Milbank Memorial Fund. The
study included the 2,409 distinguished women whose
biographical sketches appear in the 1948-1949 *Who's
Who.* 43% of those of ages 55 to 64 have never been married, whereas only 9% of women in the same age group
in the general population are still single. Of the *Who's
Who* women with masters' degrees, 66% never married,
and of those with doctors' degrees, 63% never married.

Even the married ones contribute little to the heredity
of future America. *Who's Who* women of ages 40-74
who were married or had been married averaged 1.3
children, whereas the average for women of that age
group in the general population of the same marital
status was 3.2.

For heredity insights we have to average the children
over all the *Who's Who* women, whether married or not.
They average three-fourths of a child apiece.

•

The Royal Commission believes that a major cause
of birth-rate differences is differences in the *know-how
of contraception.* That may be even more important
than interest differences, although in itself it may reflect comparative intensity of interests. Many people
have children because they don't know how to avoid having them—and the interests that compete with their sex
interests are not intense enough to stimulate them to find
out about contraception.

A study of "Social and Psychological Factors Affecting
Fertility," by the same Clyde V. Kiser, and P. K. Whelpton, is highly illuminating. Their findings are published

in the Milbank Memorial *Quarterly* for April 1949. Among the Indianapolis people they analyzed, the numbers of children that were *planned* in the less accomplished groups were no greater than the numbers planned in the more accomplished groups, but the planning was *less effectively carried out* in the less accomplished groups.

As I interpret the data, Kiser and Whelpton say that as to people who actually *plan* a family, the couples who are less successful in meeting the general problems of life are also less successful in carrying out their family limitation plans. They are less painstaking; more impulsive. If a more reliable, less bothersome contraceptive—like sterilization—were easily available to them, they would have as few children as the accomplished people.

The Kiser and Whelpton study includes only persons who had completed the 8th grade, and had lived in a large city most of the time since their marriage. They all have interests which compete with children. Practically all of them want to limit their families to few children; but those who are unsuccessful in their other objectives are also unsuccessful in keeping the stork away.

I think the nonsuccess of contraception among people who are relatively unsuccessful in life in general does not cancel the interest analysis. Perhaps an intensity of interest can be referred to as a determination. People who are usually unsuccessful in meeting their objectives may plan in a wishy way for a this-big house and a so-small family, but I suspect that they lack sometimes the sense, or usually the determination to carry out their plans.

•

The uneven success of family planning seems to make

untenable a recently developed definition of *standard of living*. In John Ise's *Economics* it is said that standard of living is "the standard of comforts and luxuries which men and women insist upon in preference to marriage or the rearing of children." To the extent that the rearing of children is still a matter of old-fashioned accident, the number of children can hardly reflect the mental pattern referred to as a standard.

But that definition of standard of living is unsatisfactory even where children are completely subject to planning. It is not only the comforts and luxuries that are pitted against the prospective wife, then the prospective child, then the prospective second child, etc. It is the lecture series, the bowling club, the lure of another college degree; interests of a thousand kinds. Modification of income, therefore, is not likely to have effect in the measure that Ise's standard-of-living definition would lead one to expect; and the effect is likely, even, to be in the opposite direction. If a man with an income of $5,000 has that income increased to $7,000, his chance of having a child is probably not increased at all. Perhaps Ise would say that man's standard climbed as his income rose, or maybe he would say the man had a $10,000 standard to start with. But give him $10,000 and you are still not likely to get any reproduction results. The reason is that the *cost* of a child is only one consideration among several. Far more influential are the man's interests.

There would be a somewhat greater likelihood of a reproduction result if the income increase is conditioned on having a child or children. In other words, baby bonuses, if large enough, would lead some people to have babies, as a means of getting income.

But on which economic groups are they likely to have most influence? Assume a flat rate of $500 per year per baby; $500 means more to the man with a $2,000 income than to one with a $5,000 income, because it is 25% of his income, whereas it is only 10% of the income of the higher-paid man. A flat-rate baby bonus, then, has its greatest influence at the bottom of the income scale, with a lesser effect on people farther up the income scale.

What will be the relative effects of a baby bonus on groups classified by education? The more highly educated people have the wider array of interests and the more intense interests. Not many of them merely drift. They have goals. Babies, at least in prospect, get in the way of these goals. In contrast, the people with very little education are much less likely to have either many interests or intense interests. A baby is less likely to get in the way of their interests. So a baby bonus is much more likely to get a response from them. Definitely, a baby bonus increases the antisocial differences in birth rates.

Canada passed a "Family Allowances Act" in 1944; Great Britain adopted one in 1945; New Zealand has one; so has Chile. Several other countries, and some of our own states, with somewhat similar legislation have unwittingly directed their sovereign influence toward increasing the proportion of their witless citizens.

The U.S.S.R. makes parenthood an occupation (which might make sense if there were selection of parents, but there isn't — except the same unconscious and adverse selection that occurs in other countries) .

There are no payments for 1st child and 2nd child, but the 3rd child brings a payment at birth and the 4th child is occasion for payments at birth and payments through its 2nd, 3rd, and 4th years. By that time a subsequent child comes along, and raises the rewards as shown in the following table. Frank Lorimer gives this information in *The Population of the Soviet Union,* a League of Nations publication, 1945.

Russians Reproduce for Pay at the Following Prices

	Rubles paid at birth	Rubles paid per year	Honors to mother
4th Child	1,300	960	-------------------
5th Child	1,700	1,440	Medal, Second Class
6th Child	2,000	1,680	Medal, First Class
7th Child	2,500	2,400	Order of Glory of Motherhood, Third Class
8th Child	2,500	2,400	Order of Glory of Motherhood, Second Class
9th Child	3,500	3,000	Order of Glory of Motherhood, First Class
10th Child	3,500	3,000	Order of Heroine (Gold Star)
11th Child	5,000	3,600	
Each Additional Child	5,000	3,600	

The estimated annual wage in Russia was 4,020 rubles for 1940, so a woman having a child every year received, for her 7th and subsequent children, more than her average worker husband received for his work.

However, she can't stop having children, because if she does, the down payments cease at once and the flow of income stops after four years.

Ralph H. Blodgett, in *Comparative Economic Systems,* tells us that incomes in Russia have substantial differences, the highest being about 64 times as high as the lowest. To a family getting 65,000 rubles a year a bonus of 2,500 rubles for having a baby, and a wage of 2,400 rubles for taking care of it and the earlier six, would be less attractive than those payments would be to a family with an ordinary annual income of 3,500 rubles.

Besides, the men in managerial and other government positions have a variety of interests which take the focus off sex. We can expect the usual differences of birth rates in Russia. Data are lacking, but the fact is conspicuous that the government representatives of Russia in international affairs have fewer children than the Russian average.

•

You noticed that some of those reasons for the *decline* in birth rates apply more forcibly as the total population grows. You noticed that the alert, sensitive people are soonest and most affected by the changes. They are the ones who reduce the number of their offspring most. The changes result in part from the more crowded condition that the biggest families bring about. The complexity of interests is very definitely connected with population density. The chain of cause is direct. The big families of the people who graduated from the third grade, by making the population denser, prevent the college graduates from getting married or, if married, from having very many children. If the third graders had no children or few children the college graduates would have more children, because population, being less dense, would present fewer interest magnets, and less uncertainty for offspring.

Ferdinand Lundberg and Marynia Farnham in *Modern Woman: The Lost Sex,* abridged in *Omnibook* for November 1947, remarked that if the Catholic Church did not interdict contraceptive appliances the American birth rate would be very much lower than it is. But I think the "very much" is an overstatement. We have seen that birth-rate differences follow the same pattern among Catholics that it follows for the rest of the population. According to Father Coogan's study, accomplished Catholics reduce their birth rates; the dumber ones, not so much. The top-flight Catholics and other accomplished Americans who do reduce their birth rates do so

because of the conditions that arise in the denser population. The denser population is denser because the
dumber Catholics and dumber others are having so many
children.

So the major influence of the hierarchy's campaign
against birth control is that they trade away their alert
Catholics and get dumb ones.

Lundberg and Farnham went on to say that the remedy
for the psychic disorder of planned childlessness does not
lie in a taboo on contraception but in an attack on the
psychological causes underlying the disordered attitude.

Psychic disorder seems not an appropriate description.
It is a psychic *adaptation* to the environmental disorder
of supercomplexity—the actual physical disorder of too
many people. And the people who are readiest to adapt
are the bright ones.

If you want the bright folks to have children, don't
put out a general plea to go forth and multiply. Since
the order is a misfit in a crowded world, the bright ones,
being first to see that their circumstances are inconsistent
with the plea, are most likely to disregard it. The dumb
ones conform, and thereby make the conditions worse
and the accomplished people still more likely to disregard the plea. It would seem more appropriate to aid the
unaccomplished ones in avoiding reproduction, thereby
making for less complexity of problems, a less hectic flow
of stimuli to act against the accomplished people.

Population congestion from any source is an influence
in the same direction—makes the accomplished people
more inclined to the unmarried state or to childlessness.
Thus *immigration* cuts down the birth rate of our college grads. The flow of Puerto Ricans to New York City
will do that.

I talked about immigration in this connection at some
length in *Human Breeding and Survival*.

The big point is that once a country is pretty much

settled, additions to the population from any one source are not entirely additional to the numbers that would otherwise be there. In part, the additional people prevent replacements by the folks already there—particularly by the most accomplished of them.

Thus to encourage one group is to discourage another. And any general encouragement to the extent that it actually takes effect will act as a particular *dis*couragement of the reproduction of the most accomplished citizens.

In summary, this chapter has shown, or I think it has, (1) that the more accomplished a person is, the less representation he is likely to have in the generations to come. (2) The most influential reason for that is that the person most likely to accomplish anything worth while is sensitive to his environment, and develops interests accordingly, which subtract from the usual focus on sex and reproduction. (3) Even when unaccomplished persons and accomplished persons plan families of the same size, the unaccomplished persons will have the larger families, because the thought and action patterns that lead to failure in life in general carry over to failure in limiting the number of offspring. (4) One aspect of the environment that hops up the alert man's interests is the complexity created by an increasing or a dense population. (5) Births by dimwits, by making the population more crowded, thus reduce the birth rate of alert people.

Probably some of my readers think that alert people have no better heredity than the dimwits have, so it doesn't matter who has the babies. In the next chapter I plan to show (1) that even if there are no differences in heredity, the birth-rate differences are nevertheless important, because they place the majority of babies in relatively unfavorable environments. And (2) actually the alert people do have the more distinctively human heredity.

Chapter 7

Too Many Fathers

Time, November 10, 1947, page 51, reported that Man-o'-War, greatest of all U. S. race horses, was dead, age 30 years. What a horse! In two years of racing he won 20 of his 21 starts. Betting odds on his winning were 100 to 1. His owner, Sam Riddle, "once refused a $1,000,000 offer for his wonder horse." Riddle retired him from racing in the prime of his career because of the confidence of horsemen in horse heredity. Said *Time:* "Only the choicest mares were bred to Man-o'-War—at $5000 a try. The results were top quality, as with everything Man-o'-War did.

"He sired 383 foals. Some of his famous sons and daughters: Mars, Crusader, American Flag, Scapa Flow, Edith Cavell, War Admiral."

Few people doubt the importance of heredity for bone and muscle quality. People argue about *proportion* of influence of heredity and environment in physical affairs, but there is general agreement that heredity does play a big role in making race-horse winners, bovine milk factories, Olympic champions.

The human blood types affected by heredity became known only a few years ago, and the Rh factor, an attribute of the red corpuscles, was discovered by Dr. Alexander S. Wiener and Dr. Karl Landsteiner as recently as 1940. The Rh factor gets its name from the first two letters of "Rhesus monkey" in which it was discovered. There is a good technical discussion of the genetics of the Rh-Hr blood factors by Herluf H. Strandskov in the *Bulletin of the New York Academy of Medicine* for April 1949, and another by Alexander S. Wiener, Eve B. Gordon, and Lillian Handman, in *The American Journal of Human Genetics* for December 1949. The authors of the latter study had tested a total of 923 families with 1,567 children for the eight Rh types and had worked out the applicable heredity rules.

That a man is the father of a specific child cannot be affirmatively proved by blood tests, but in approximately 45 percent of cases in which a man is not a child's father, that fact can be definitely proved by use of the A-B-O test, the M-N test, and the Rh test.

It is well known that color blindness, some other eye defects, weakness in various body parts, susceptibility to certain diseases, are influenced by heredity.

But some people draw the line when they think of brain cells being in any meaningful way dependent on heredity.

They don't deny that the cells themselves are inherited. And they do not doubt that the inherited cells do have a function in behavior. Their thought is that, with respect to those inherited cells, people are near enough alike in their heredity that the influences that make people measurably different from one another come out of environment. Who, in your block, is to be a great inventor? The environmentalists think *each* person has enough surplus of hereditary capacity to become the great inventor if he has the right environment. Is he supposed, additionally, to be able to keep up with world politics and local politics, read all the latest books, and play a winning game of chess, if he has the environment favorable to all those? I don't know how they would answer that. But they, the environmentalists, do hold to the idea that almost everybody has plenty of inborn capacity.

However, average intellect may be too low. Here is an article in *Nation's Business* for November 1947, by Leo P. Crespi, Assistant Professor of Psychology at Princeton, on the subject, "Are We Getting Dumber?"

Crespi recognizes that birth rates of educated people, and otherwise accomplished people, are low, and that birth rates are high as an average among unaccomplished people. He thinks it is "probably true" that the influence of birth-rate differences is toward a declining IQ. But he holds that there are IQ gains that balance the losses, in the fact that education is reaching a larger number of people. His idea is that IQ is partly and essentially dependent on environment, and so is affected by education.

And so it is! But let us bear in mind that the IQ is also partly and essentially dependent on heredity. Otherwise, with training, we should be able to make an Aristotle out of an ape. Since education does not increase the *hereditary capacity* for education but merely makes more use of that capacity, the IQ gain from education does not offset the hereditary loss when we breed a disproportionately large number of people from the bottom of the IQ scale.

Crespi seems to be one hundred percent environmentalist; he ignores heredity.

Suppose one were to observe that erosion of our soil is decreasing its fertility. It would not be adequate to answer that the total productivity is being temporarily kept up by wider or more frequent cultivation. Crespi's thought about the greater cultivation of the nation's diminishing hereditary capacity seems to me to be comparable. Even if there is, as Crespi thinks, a "rise in the IQ of the average American" through the stimulating effects of education, there isn't anything fundamental about it; its limits are near and getting nearer. The hereditary basis for America's IQ's seems to be undergoing a "sheet erosion" which is much more serious than that reported by the immediate result in the crop of IQ's. With the hereditary soil getting thinner each season, its increased cultivation must soon be powerless to keep up the IQ yield.

In the Milbank Memorial Fund *Quarterly* for October 1947, Professor Gardner Murphy states the case for heredity (or really for environment *and* heredity) in this way:

"What we do know is that marked improvement in opportunity does jack up the I. Q. a good many points, and that the earlier the process begins the more salutary the results are likely to be. We also know, however, that there are always limits, and that human protoplasm talks its own language instead of yielding completely to forces which would try to make of it anything they wish."

"There are always limits" to the learning possibilities of any person, and those limits may be substantially different from the limits of the person next door. The limits are comparable to the limits of productivity of an acre of ground; and its limits differ from those of the acre across the valley. Incidentally, one's efforts both in the cultivation of the acres and in the education of the persons are subject to the law of diminishing returns.

But though Crespi thinks there has been a rise of IQ average for the country he doesn't think it has been enough. "Now that the atom is unleashed, one of the prime requisites for survival," he says, "is as much intelligence as the human race can muster."

He is still talking about a superficial sort of intelli-

gence—more intensive cultivation of the same old acres
—but the point is worth considering in connection with
intelligence from both sources: more education and better heredity. Civilization might crumble even if thought
power were not *declining,* merely because the modern
complexity of problems requires *more* problem-solving
ability than has ever before been necessary, and the average human being may not have it. Crespi scores a point
there. Our current social and political problems seem
not now to be handled with any extraordinary insight.
We need to provide "as much intelligence as the human
race can muster," but we need to do it by working on
heredity as well as on education.

Time, for December 5, 1947, told the tale of Robert
Justus Kleberg, Jr., cattle-monarch of the vast King
Ranches in Texas at the Gulf of Mexico. Kleberg bred
a new kind of beef cattle that grow fat without grain.
The genetics of his Santa Gertrudis breed is reported by
A. O. Rhoad in the *Journal of Heredity* for May 1949.
Kleberg also bred fast cow horses, bred better grass. Once,
when the possibilities of breeding were in discussion, and
a friend remarked that nobody can breed better people,
Kleberg didn't agree. "Don't know. Maybe you could.
Nobody's ever tried it."

Bob Kleberg must feel pretty sure—as you must—that
the only obstacles to breeding better men are the folkways of men. It becomes essential to the well-being of
the human species that we revise those folkways to make
use of new knowledge.

Environment and heredity point in the same direction.

What Crespi thought about hereditary transmission of
problem-solving ability was not clear; he seemed not to
have thought about it, seems to have assumed a limitless
innate capacity. All his stress was on the effects of education.

Everybody will agree, I suppose, that inadequate environment of children does have a mentally stunting effect—that children reared by uneducated parents, or in poverty-stricken homes, or by criminals, are handicapped.

Some critics say, let's go all out to educate them. Some say, let's discourage the supply of children from such sources. Some say, let's do both: reduce the supply of them, but educate such as we get.

That discussion may take place entirely on the basis of environment. Without reference to heredity, there is reasonable argument that the offspring of inadequate parents should be few. Even with an assumption that the children of the dull may be brightened up "with sufficient polishing," the process is seen to be socially costly—and wasteful. Better get the replacements from sources where the polishing would take place as a matter of course.

But heredity considerations do add argument in the same direction. Education cannot get very good results except as it has something precious, and apparently rare, to start with.

Though preoccupied with environment, Crespi arrived at a point not very far from where he would have been if heredity had been included in his guidebook. And he had a good observation for us about modern problems requiring *more* intelligence.

Let us look next at an article by Dr. Harold F. Dorn in the Milbank Memorial Fund *Quarterly* for October 1947. Dr. Dorn is in the Division of Public Health Methods of the U. S. Health Service. Also he was recently Secretary of the Population Association of America, the man to whom I mailed my checks for $3 as dues in that organization.

I guess he would be happy enough with heredity if he could just get his tape measure around it. Measuring it is what stymies him. He recognizes that Mr. and Mrs. Numbtop are having more than their share of

younguns, but, he asks, is that lowering the average quality of the kids in the Numbtop School? "Not," he says,
"until the general concept ability is separated into specific measurable components can the scientific evidence
necessary to answer this question be accumulated."

I think that sort of a rule, consistently applied, would
send us back to the taboos of the Stone Age. Suppose the
boys of the 4-H Club are about to have their calves
weighed to see which one has gained most during the
contest. "You can't do that," County Agent Dorn would
say; "not till we find some way of weighing the eyeballs
separate from the rest of the critters. The hair must have
a separate weighing too. Then we'll put the figures together to see what each calf weighs."

The boxers weighed in at 152 and 153? You can't let
them fight, Boxing Commissioner Dorn would say (if I
interpret him correctly); you can't let them fight until
you can weigh the bones separate from the flesh!

Hi, Professor Finnigan. I'd like to talk with you a
minute. How about my entering the next track meet, to
run the hurdle events in Harrison Dillard's place?

You ask, would my presence on the Baldwin-Wallace
team in his place lower the athletic quality of the team?

Eddie, it's like this: "Not until the general concept
. . . [speed] is separated into specific measurable components can the scientific evidence necessary to answer this
question be accumulated." The evidence that you have
seen—stop-watch records, etc.—that's all cancelled. As I
interpret the Dorn rule, until you can measure and compare our rhythms and the tensile strength of our tendons,
you have to consider that I am as fast a runner as Harrison is.

You baseball prophets who try to estimate which team
will win the pennant by following the team performance,
that's all wrong! According to what I take to be the Dorn

formula the teamwork doesn't count. You have to measure the *components!*

I think it is not "unscientific" to compare trees by their fruits, generators by their horsepower, and, in general, conglomerates by their results.

Race-horse breeders thought they were incidentally breeding nerves. Maybe they were. On January 18, 1946, in *Science,* John Macleod and Eric Ponder told them they were also breeding different red blood cells than plow horses have. Macleod and Ponder had been studying Col. C. V. Whitney's horses. They found that race-horse blood has smaller red blood cells and that each cell contains less hemoglobin, but there are more red cells and there is more hemoglobin for a given amount of blood.

This "specific measurable component" was not what Colonel Whitney was breeding for. He was breeding from a result and for a result. The speed had been increased with no knowledge of one of the components.

It is possible that, after further testing for correlation of speed with blood attributes, blood tests may be one basis of selection for breeding. But it must be recognized that successful breeding for speed did not await the discovery of the corpuscle differences. (It did not await even the progeny test, though that has probably hastened results.) It followed the rule expressed by Warren Wright: "Just mix the best with the best and hope for the best."

Actually, Dr. Dorn did come around—though on an environmentalist basis entirely — to conclusions harmonious with those of the 4-H boys and you and me and most of the scientists. He said:

"We do have sufficient evidence to be sure that a large proportion of the recruits of the next generation come from the classes of our population which are the least able to provide maximum cultural and health advantages. So long as differential fertility operates in a way that denies opportunity for maximum development of innate ability it acts counter to the professed ideals of our society and as such is a matter of serious concern."

That's reasonable. Said more directly, in the Numbtop family there has been one father too many.

•

Dr. Dorn doesn't believe that human problem-solving capacity is limitless. In that, as well as in seeing the differences in birth rates as a social blunder, our positions are the same.

In my own concept of the limits of problem-solving capacity, and I think it is a widely held concept, one does not bump into the capacity limits suddenly, but in terms of diminishing returns from mental effort. The many pieces of *land* in a given area, though cultivated by many men, will yield roughly according to the fertility of the separate fields—and reflect their comparative fertility by their yields. Similarly it seems probable that some people have a lot more hereditary mental capacity than other people, and that the capacity is roughly reflected by achievement. Achievement is evidence of capacity.

Let's think a minute about achievement as a workable test of hereditary capacity.

Consider some difficult objective, like running the 220-yard low hurdles in 24 seconds. Everyone who accomplishes that objective must have *everything* that is required to accomplish that objective. The heredity alone isn't enough; the training alone isn't enough. Both are necessary. Not merely 50 percent of the winners, not merely 90 percent of them; 100 percent of those who attain the objective—*every one of them*—must have *both* the necessary heredity and the sufficient training.

Line up a hundred men who have run the 220 low hurdles in 24 seconds or less. There can be no slightest doubt that each of them has, or at least had, what it takes.

Now line up a hundred men picked at random. Have they as good heredity for running the hurdles as the first group? No; maybe some of them, with training, might be able to do it; but train them all to the nth degree, and yet not all of them could ever match that 24-second mark. Average heredity doesn't provide what is necessary.

Pick one of that second hundred, at random. Could he match 24 seconds? Maybe, but since he is in the group who never have done so, he may lack the required heredity. In fact, since fewer than 50 percent of people, no matter how hard they train, can ever match the 24-second time, the *chances* are that this Mr. X doesn't have the necessary hereditary capacity.

Of course the same reasoning applies if the "difficult objective" is the passing of an intelligence test with a score of 130. Those who do it have the necessary heredity and the necessary education. They have *both*. A person who gets a 115 score lacks something. Maybe it is the education; maybe the quality of brain cells; maybe both. Since fewer than half of the people could ever score 130, the chances are *he* lacks the necessary hereditary capacity. This 115 scorer fits in with a group most of whom never could under any circumstances score 130.

However, even he has something that the average person lacks. The chances are that his heredity is better for problem-solving than is the heredity of the man who scores 100.

The school system involves, in part, a weeding-out process. To graduate from high school in the top fifth of one's class requires some capacity to learn. Maybe the lad who got discouraged and quit school in the 5th grade has as much capacity—but the chances are against that, because his conduct is like the conduct of a lot of kids who are dumb.

If you had to choose the fathers for the country's future, would you select the students in the top fifth of the high-school graduating class, or the students who quit school in the fifth grade?

Would the country's future be safer in the hands of the children of men with IQ 130 or those of IQ 90?

You may protest that we shall have no chance to make such a choice; why be bothered?

But I think that unconsciously we have been favoring the IQ 90 people in their reproduction, by the laws and customs that we make. It hasn't been exactly a *choice*, since there has not been a conscious weighing of alternatives, but the results have been as if we had made a choice, an antisocial one.

•

Newsweek, April 28, 1947, page 60, put the spotlight on the ancient argument, is heredity or environment the more important?

In 1924, John B. Watson, in his book *Behaviorism*, led an attack against the then prevalent interpretation of action as an unfolding of heredity. *Newsweek* quotes him as saying, "There is no such thing as an inheritance of capacity, talent, temperament, mental . . . characteristics." Watson and his followers developed some valuable knowledge, but they sealed over some valuable knowledge too. In their antithesis they went too far.

At a meeting of the Society of Experimental Psychology in April of 1947, says *Newsweek*, five of the country's most distinguished psychologists

"swung back to the importance of heredity in determining human behavior. Armed with carefully documented papers, each based on a separately conducted research program, . . . not one called environmental factors of primary significance in shaping the psychological character of the individual. All emphasized the power of inheritance. . . ."

I suppose what should be emphasized is what has been neglected. There has been a neglect of heredity in the past quarter of a century. The behaviorism influence in psychology, and the institutionalist influence in economics and sociology, teamed up in putting exclusive faith in environment. The bulk of the political scientists, and other social scientists, tagged along. The biologists, most of them, were willing to await their time. A few of them, like J. B. S. Haldane, got some cheap publicity by pointing out to their hard-pressed fellows how easy it would be to declare bankruptcy. (See *Atlantic*, March 1947, for example.)

The five scientists, reported by *Newsweek* as restoring heredity to attention, were: Dr. Frank A. Beach, Yale psychologist; Dr. Leonard Carmichael, President of Tufts University; Dr. Karl S. Lashley of Yerkes Laboratories of Primate Biology, and Harvard University; Dr. Clifford T. Morgan of Johns Hopkins University; Dr. Calvin P. Stone, Stanford University psychologist. Their work should lead us from the antithesis of the past 20 years to an unemotional synthesis in which both heredity and environment are seen as active, dynamic factors.

•

Time, April 21, 1947, cited an article in the *Journal of Heredity* by Calvin S. Hall of Western Reserve University, which is further evidence on heredity of psychological traits. The inheritance he tested was in mice. Two strains of mice were bred for many generations, and then tested for "audiogenic seizures"—convulsions from fright at a sudden noise.

Hall put a loud electric bell inside the rim of a wash-tub. Then he put in some of each of the two strains of mice. One strain was black, the other brown; that assured identification.

When Hall rang the bell, nearly all of the brown mice in the tub scurried around, had convulsions, and died. Nearly all of the black ones survived.

But maybe their mothers had trained the brown mice to be scared? Dr. Hall had thought of that possibility, and tested that too. He had transferred fertilized ova from a brown mouse to the womb of a black one. All of the heredity of those ova was from brown mouse ancestors; all of their environment was with black mice.

When the special brown mice were given the bell treatment, two-thirds died. Dr. Hall concluded that the tendency to die of audiogenic seizures is hereditary.

•

Professor R. C. Tryon of the University of California has conducted an experiment that we should consider. His account of it is in the 39th Annual *Yearbook* of the National Society for the Study of Education. It is relayed in Professor Gardner Murphy's article mentioned a few pages back, and also in Norman L. Munn's textbook in *Psychology*.

This time, learning capacity is in focus—in rats; does a rat's ability to learn its way through a maze depend on heredity?

Tryon tested a rat in the maze, then mated it according to the results. In the beginning generation, composed of

142 unselected rats, the number of errors made in 19 trials ranged from 5 for the "brightest" rat to 214 for the "dullest" rat. The rats that made few errors were mated with others that made few errors. Those that made many errors were mated with others that made many errors.

By the eighth generation, that is the 7th generation of descendants of those 142 rats, there were two distinct strains. The bright strain, made up of 85 rats, averaged approximately 20 errors for the 19 trials. The offspring of the dull rats averaged approximately 100 errors for the 19 trials. Almost no descendants of the high IQ ancestry made as many as 50 errors. Almost no descendants of the dull rats made as few as 50 errors.

•

Dr. Arthur Kornhauser conducted a poll of experts, and published it in the *American Magazine* for May 1946. The experts numbered 63, and were listed with the article—some of the most outstanding human behavior scientists of the country.

Heredity was judged to play *a leading role* in intellectual ability by 91 percent of them. Eleven percent thought the differences between individuals are determined *almost entirely* by heredity. Eighty percent thought that the differences are due *in large measure* to heredity, but are considerably affected by normal differences in environment. Only 8 percent judged that our differences in intellectual ability are affected somewhat by heredity but in larger measure by environment. Not a single one of them ruled out heredity entirely, but one thought that no judgment is possible from existing evidence.

Concerning musical talent, 4 out of 5 believed that it depends in large measure on heredity. Heredity was thought to be most important also for dexterity and energy.

The heredity influence on psychological characteristics, particularly on intellectual capacity, is of profound importance because of the differences of birth rates. Fuzzy-minded people have more babies than clear-thinking people. *Each generation of American citizens is the product, for the most part, of the woodenheaded portion of the previous generation.* So each generation has less above the ears—less capacity for education—than the previous generation.

R. B. Cattell estimated that the English average IQ is declining at the rate of 3 points per generation. Fraser Robert's sample declined 1½ points per generation. Sir Cyril Burt estimated an English decline of 5 IQ points in 50 years. T. F. Lentz calculated a decline in the U.S. of 4 to 5 points per generation. Frank Lorimer and Frederick Osborn thought it as little as .9 of a point per generation.

The *Journal of the American Medical Association* of November 2, 1946, reported that several studies have shown an average decline of 2 to 3 points in the U.S. IQ average with each generation.

But they all (except Crespi) believed that the average IQs of England and the United States have been going down.

At the same time, it is interesting to note, the speed of race horses has been going up.

Chapter 8

Prospects for Posterity

We sometimes speak of "civilization" as if there has been only one, and as if it is continuous. In that sense the word means complexity in ways of living. Since complexity is a matter of degree, so is civilization.

But in an important sense there have been several civilizations, most of them lasting four hundred or five hundred years, then gradually sinking into a condition of muddling government and miserable people. Egypt had successive dark ages of disorganization spacing its periods of magnificence. The parade of civilizations in the valleys of the Tigris and Euphrates Rivers—Sumerian, Babylonian, Assyrian, and Chaldean—followed invasions and infiltrations by outlanders. China's civilizations have been rhythmic in their flow and ebb.

Some areas have had a single heyday, like that of Persia, and then what seems to be a cultural slumber.

But whether in any one geographic region a civilization has been a single flash in the long dark of the eons or has been one unit in a series, it has followed a pattern of rise and fall; there has been no permanence.

A civilization is essentially (but never exclusively) an economic system. In every case it involves DIVISION OF OCCUPATIONS. That is what the characteristic is called when one takes a view of the producing activities as a whole. SPECIALIZATION is its designation when it is viewed in the tasks of the single workman, the single factory, or sometimes the single area. The division of occupations permits at least some of the persons who participate in a civilization to have economic surpluses, and those surpluses permit the support of various supplementary activities such as music, art, architecture, formal education, gladiatorial combat, professional baseball.

The activity which unifies a civilization is TRADE— the buying and selling of goods and services. Except for arrangements for the exchange of goods the specialization could not exist. The key to the time and space scope of a civilization is the time and space scope of its system of trade.

Civilizations have not had definite geographical boundaries; rather, at their far margins, trade with persons and organizations nearer the core has been a less regular activity; has been less a dependence of the people, and so a less trustworthy vehicle for ideas.

A well-developed TRANSPORTATION SYSTEM has been a characteristic of each of the civilizations. That, of course, is essential to the trade. The transportation methods have ranged through river floats and boats, seagoing sailing vessels, and slave-propelled galleys to steam and Diesel power; and on land from a variety of saddle and pack animals through carts and wagons, railroads, autos, and motor trucks. And now for the first time in all time we are traveling in the air—and fast.

A system of COMMUNICATION has been necessary, and each of the civilizations that got very far has developed writing. This has been a requirement for accumulating the expanding body of learning, and passing it on to later generations, as well as for transmitting bits of information for day-to-day use. Development of printing and other means of making multiple copies is a distinctive aspect of our civilization, as are also the electrical devices for sending messages with the speed of light.

There should be advantage in stressing items that have been common to several civilizations. Men who have searched for causes of declines have put their work on the things civilizations have had in common, with a hope of finding the weak spots in our own. However, I have not stressed *trade* with an idea that trade is a weak spot; I have used it by way of definition, to show what the unifying trait of a civilization is. Of course the trade will stop when the civilization crumbles, just as the blood of a person will stop flowing when any vital organ ceases to function, but the seat of the disease may be elsewhere.

•

The realization that civilizations have not been very durable is, in our own civilization, a recent concept. Until the end of last century, people had not thought much about it. Boys in their play had known that "all that goes up must come down"; physicists had known that for every action there is an equal and opposite reaction; and in a variety of common experiences men have been aware of rhythm in the universe. Night alternates with day; sleep with waking; a butterfly is in rotation with the grub in a cocoon; sunspots show at eleven-year intervals; an eclipse is repeated every eighteen years and 10 days. Halley's comet comes every 76 years. The tide flows and ebbs and flows again. We come to expect these and similar pulsations; we build our lives accordingly. The seasons are in an orderly succession: after spring comes summer, then autumn, and winter; then spring again. Year after year the same cycle repeats.

Such phenomena were in the consciousness of some of the ancients. As Greece took its place in the yesterdays, and the Roman Republic was about to be transformed into a dictatorship, the Roman poet Lucretius presented his readers with the thought that nations die. Toynbee says the concept was commonplace in ancient philosophies.

But almost everybody in modern times, and especially in America, up to sixty years ago had taken our civilization for granted as something permanent. Since then a few analyzers have taken the long view. Their findings deserve our attention.

First, and with great respect, I must mention Brooks Adams, who in 1896 published *The Law of Civilization and Decay*. Charles A. Beard, in an introduction to a 1943 Knopf edition of the book, speaks of it as one of the outstanding documents of intellectual history.

Before Brooks Adams wrote, there had been in America a vague but widespread assumption that history is a one-way street toward better and better conditions. In its vagueness it seems to have been a comfortable assumption that whatever *is* is somehow better than whatever *was,* but not so good as things in the trend, which are yet to be. It was an assumption of social improvement, of "progress," of major movement in one direction, an approved direction.

Brooks Adams replaced the beautiful illusion of a one-way social evolution with the harsh fact that earlier civilizations had not only risen but had fallen. He thought that a civilization involved an increasing centralization of power, which gradually choked out the individuals on whom it fed. One civilization after another had thus gone down, he thought, and our own civilization was following the perilous path of ancient Rome.

Felix Morley, in *Power of the People,* makes clear the fact that economic power transferred to a government administration is power still further concentrated than when it is in multiple lesser organizations. The stultification of individuals is consequently surer.

We must agree with Beard, in his introduction to *The Law of Civilization and Decay,* that *in its details* history does not repeat, that there is uniqueness of events and personalities. Yet history does show us broad parallels of rise and fall as demonstrable fact.

I think Beard's implication is that if understanding were broad enough we could get away from the parallels —could prevent the crash. That was Theodore Roosevelt's position in his 1897 review of Brooks Adams' analysis too, and Roosevelt's later trust-busting efforts were probably designed to prevent the over-centralization of economic power that Brooks Adams seems to have thought inevitable. Though Roosevelt's war on the trusts was futile, I agree nevertheless with his 1897 generalization and with Beard's implication. Logic is with us in that intelligence has avoided many of the lesser repetitions of human experience, when they were unfavorable. If understanding and will are great, we can control our major moves too—not so completely as many "institutionalists" have thought, but within the laws. Our maintenance of a civilization indefinitely, beyond the usual span, will be, however, like the controlled flight of a glider. It successfully resists one physical law by the use which its operator makes of another, and so keeps aloft. If ever the vigilance ceases, the glider's flight is soon over.

Brooks Adams' thesis that concentration of power is a cause of the decline of civilizations is in harmony with the thesis of Willis J. Ballinger that *democracy* declines as a consequence of concentration of economic power. Ballinger's analysis is contained in a 1946 book, *By Vote*

of the People, published by Charles Scribner's Sons. The
doctrine that presents concentration of economic power as
a cause of the decline of civilizations is not inconsistent
with the conclusions reached herein. And whatever may
be said of the details, Brooks Adams' general demonstration of the two-way possibilities of social changes administered a needed jolt to America's complaisance in the
notion that all things automatically work out for the best
in the end.

•

About two decades after the publication of Brooks
Adams' volume, Oswald Spengler, a German schoolteach-
er, came out with a study which in its English edition is
called *The Decline of the West.* Spengler observed the
succession of the seasons, and likened the stages of a
civilization to the course of a year. In its springtime it is
organized around agriculture; by the time of its autumn
its efforts have turned largely to industrial production.
Like the work of Brooks Adams, it is a "cycle" theory.

But there is a mysticism in the Spengler version of the
story that civilizations grow old and die, and little in his
analysis to explain their rise. He reports that they have
periods comparable to the four seasons. But the comparison is given with greater confidence than the facts war-
rant. There seems to be no dependability about that
parallel. For some civilizations the conquering hordes
have come early; for some there have been revivals.

•

After Spengler's publication, the next important treatment of the general theme seems to have been an article by S. Colum GilFillan, Professor of Social Science in the University of the South at Sewanee, Tennessee. He had an article in the *Political Science Quarterly* for September 1920, called "The Coldward Course of Progress." He presented the thesis that later civilizations have, as a rule, been successively farther north than those of long ago. That same point was made by Vilhjalmur Stefansson in articles, and in his book *The Northward Course of Empire,* published by Harcourt, Brace & Co., in 1922. The theme is carried along in *New Compass of the World,* a 1949 book of which Stefansson is one of the editors and one of the authors.

In the treatment of GilFillan and Stefansson there seems to be a tacit recognition that civilizations have weakened and died—but no elaboration of that; no discussion either of the causes of the rise of the next one; there was attention only to the question of where the next one arose, and the answer: it arose farther north.

One might question if the evidence bears out their generalization. Pitirim A. Sorokin, Harvard sociologist, in *Society, Culture, and Personality,* concludes that GilFillan and Stefansson "unduly generalize a partial case into universal uniformity."

But I think that at least they served a useful purpose in bringing attention again to the fact that great centers of culture do decline: that "progress" is not inevitable.

•

Another observer with the long view is Dr. Carle C. Zimmerman, a colleague of Sorokin at Harvard. In his recent Harper & Brothers book, *Family and Civiliza-*

tion, he has interpreted the declines as a result of the fact that members of a family become so independent of each other and so wide apart in their interests that the family itself disintegrates, and with it the civilization. That dispersion of interests has been correlated with the disintegration of the family in other civilizations as in our own.

Leaving Zimmerman's doctrine for the moment, but continuing to examine the area he studied, one must observe that a large part of the reason for the contraction of family influence is the creation of new institutions which take over the family's functions—and the new structures are themselves attempts at adaptation to previous partial inadequacy of the family. Education is one of the functions which the family has been losing; amusement is another. Economic opportunity for women is still another. Guidance of members of the family is another.

There is government aid in bringing about the amputation of what in earlier stages were functions of the family. The government hastening of the family disorganization conforms to majority conscience, and follows the failure of *some families* to perform a function themselves. Thus a local government sets up or extends a school system, because educating becomes too skill-requiring for *some* dads and mothers to carry it on as a side line. The rest of the families are induced if not forced to terminate most of their educating too. For general education that happened a century ago. A generation ago the change occurred as to instruction in cooking. Right now it is occurring in sex education.

Amusement gradually loses out as a *family* function when *communities* start competition in amusing. After a while commercial enterprises, specializing in amusing, terminate the amusement entirely in some families, reduce it in most. The movies have a few self-imposed restraints against building disintegrating interests, but not many. Currently their most devastating influence is in picturing intoxicants as if they were a casual and appropriate part of everyday life.

As to the radio and television, let's not fall for the usual fallacy that they are influences that tend to revitalize the family. The divorce rates do not support such a conclusion. And the 13 murders per day which are telecast from six Los Angeles stations cannot be expected to strengthen family psychic patterns, even though all the family may be in one room when they experience the stimulation. The net impressioning of the auditor-observer is not from his living room but from the portrayed story. What sticks in mind is not what Brother Bill said as he switched off the screen, but what the villain said as he pulled the trigger.

The specialized units that take over family functions do not hold the integration of society or the correlated psychological condition of their patrons as an objective.

To be sure, most of the tangible functions that used to be family functions *are performed,* though by other institutions, and most people think they are performed more satisfyingly than most *families* could perform them. In effect a man expresses the opinion that economic opportunities and educational opportunities and amusement opportunities are better in institutions other than the family. He expresses that opinion by his *participation* in those other institutions. Most people join in destroying the family institution by depending on it so little. It becomes almost useless compared with its previous status. The disintegration of the family is correlated with a high degree of complexity of the social environment. The complex of newer institutions, with no integrating objective among them, seems to be cause for the chaos into which a civilization evolves. Perhaps we should say it is the unintegrated complex, rather than the decay of the family, that takes the life out of a civilization.

But, at least, we may think of the decline of the family institution as a sort of marker on which is disclosed that dangerous stage of specialization which in the past has been close to a civilization's undoing.

However, Doctor Zimmerman, whatever may be said for your conviction that the salvaging of a civilization lies "in the making of familism and childbearing the primary social duties of the citizen," I don't think you have dug deep enough. Specialization, we learned, is essential to a civilization—but taken in excessive doses it can be in the chain of change to a civilization's demise. The excessive specialization of institutions, which contributes to both the family decay and the decay of civilization, you haven't dealt with. We may not be able to avoid the excessive specialization, but I think we must contrive a *change of incentives* to counteract and offset the unsocial incentives that grow out of specialization. I shall dwell on that in later chapters.

Another point: you write as if you haven't been conscious of any *overpopulation* problem in former civilizations or in our own. If our Plutarchs were to propagandize for more children, as you suggest — no strings attached—they would, to the extent of their success, lead individuals not only to forego their individual adjustments, but also actually to worsen the prospects for the civilization via overpopulation.

Most serious, you fail to take heredity into account in your recommendations. Magnifying familism and child-bearing, as an objective to be applied indiscriminately, would leave the numbtops in an increasing majority.

•

Specialization is most persistent in *economic* life. First it took the man out of the home; gave him a set of interests in which his wife and children could not share. Recently it has developed economic opportunities for women. In various other ways economic specialization makes for complexity of environment—and lack of cohesion.

The specialized new units do not synthesize their objectives. Governments attempt a synthesis, but to do that they have to take over more and more management. The job gets too big.

Brooks Adams, Oswald Spengler, S. Colum GilFillan, Vilhjalmar Stefansson, and Carle C. Zimmerman have given us valuable help. And though wide apart in their approaches they seem not at all inconsistent. In fact, with a little bridging and bracing here and there their analytical structures fit neatly together. And none of them denies the validity of still other probings. I have in mind among the "other probings" the accumulating literature on (1) overpopulation, and on (2) the destruction of geographic resources, and especially on (3) the relation of reckless reproduction to the destruction of geographic resources. Zimmerman's *recommendations* are out of line with the population and resources findings, but I think his *analysis* as such is not. The population and resources literature is illustrated by: H. H. Bennett, *Soil Conservation,* particularly his chapter on "Erosion and Civilization"; E. Parmalee Prentice, *Hunger and History,* and his *Food, War and the Future;* Guy Irving Burch and Elmer Pendell, *Population Roads to Peace or War,* republished by Penguin Books as *Human Breeding and Survival;* Frank A. Pearson and Floyd Harper, *The World's Hunger;* Fairfield Osborn, *Our Plundered Planet;* William Vogt, *The Road to Survival;* and W. C. Loudermilk, *Conquest of the Land Through Seven Thousand Years.*

That last is a 33-page mimeographed publication of

the U.S. Soil Conservation Service: MP-32. Lowdermilk, who is Associate Chief of the Soil Conservation Service, concludes that civilizations die when their supporting agriculture fails. When erosion steals the soil, or silts up the water supply, the social order is in desperate straits. He tells us that in ancient Mesopotamia, when the great public works of cleaning silt out of canals were interrupted from time to time by internal revolutions and by foreign invaders, the people faced their greatest disaster in canals choked with silt. The silt "depopulated villages and cities more effectively than the slaughter of people by an invading army."

Lowdermilk reports results of the accumulation of silt on a Cyprus plain, so persistent that the level of the land was 13 feet above the old level of a church floor there. And he tells of great Roman cities in North Africa, buried, until recent excavations, by dust.

He pictures an opposite effect of erosion too—in a hundred ghost towns in Syria, where land has washed away from the buildings and has left the doorsills 3 to 6 feet above the exposed rock that has been rained clean before them. The accent, of course, is not on the fact that the towns have become uninhabitable—that is merely a graphic measure of the force that ruined the food sources.

Lowdermilk described the silt-laden Yellow River of China, winding 40 to 50 feet higher than the farm land on the floor of the valley, kept up there—when it is kept in control — by bare hands carrying baskets, working on dykes. He followed the course of silt to its sources; the raw hills, that for a thousand years had been repeating their protest against the ravage of the forests that once protected them and all the plains below.

One other summary of the rises and falls of civilizations is in order here—that of Arnold J. Toynbee. In view of the scholarly nature of Toynbee's *Study of History* there is encouragement and gratification in the tremendous amount of popular acclaim which that study is receiving. The one-volume abridgement by D. C. Somervell, published by the Oxford University Press, has already sold out many printings. That is the edition I am using. I quote from that book by permission of the publishers.

Challenge and *response* are key words in Toynbee's formulation. A group receives a challenge from the environment. The challenge may be a problem which arises from geographic conditions or a problem which arises from the action of other groups. The way the group handles the problem is its response. A response is likely to change the environment enough to present another challenge, and over the years the challenges are in a long series. In effect, "Necessity is the mother of invention," and invention makes a new necessity which calls for another invention.

The challenges are not met by all the individuals in a group but by a creative minority. A group in which the creative individuals are too few or insufficiently inventive does not bring about a civilization, but a group which effectively solves its successive problems does initiate the activities and institutions known as a civilization. Toynbee examines 21 civilizations.

Most of the civilizations have faded out or have been absorbed by others. They have broken down because of a failure of creativeness.

I shall have more to say about Toynbee's thesis; much of the factual data he has used is available as evidence supporting my own position. And for aught I know he may come out of the woods at the same place I came out; it is reported that he still has some volumes to add to the

six already in print. At any rate, notice again that the
conclusions reached by all these men of the long view
are not conflicting—at least in their broad outlines.
Their findings fit together to help solve the haunting
problem—why is there impending jeopardy for the things
we cherish?

And now I shall launch into my own analysis, which
logically harmonizes with all of those you have just been
considering.

•

In the fall of 1620 the first of the Pilgrims arrived at
Plymouth. George F. Willison gives a fascinating account
of the adventure in *Saints and Strangers,* a 1946 book
published by Reynal & Hitchcock. Within three years,
234 persons had arrived or died on the way. Of those,
85 were "Saints," 123 were "Strangers," 5 were hired
men, and 21 were servants. Of the 234 persons, 108 were
men, 51 were women, and 75 were children.

The question has occasionally been raised as to whether
or not the Pilgrims were a select group, a superior people.

At least the "Saints" among them were less motivated
by the primitive urges than are average people. They
were Separatists, who in disapproval of the easygoing
ways of the Church had broken away and established
separate congregations even while in England. There
must have been some sorting in that separation. There
was a further sorting in the escape to Amsterdam, another
sorting in the decision to go to Leyden, in 1609; and
still another weeding out for the hazardous prospects in
the New World.

The "Strangers" were mostly impelled by a hope of

worldly advantage, yet for them to forsake the comparative security of the homeland for the hope of a gain so distant and unlikely must have required a forecast of the future that is far beyond the average mental scope.

The culling process was severe and obvious in the rigors of the first New England winter. One voyager had died at sea; 6 died in December of 1620; 8 of the 104 on the *Mayflower* died in January, 1621; 17 (which is practically 17 percent as well as 17 people) died in February, 13 in March. Of the 41 *men* who had signed the *Mayflower* Compact, only 20 were left alive by the end of March—less than four months later. There were 6 more deaths by the time the ship *Fortune* arrived in the fall of 1621, making a death toll of 51 of the original 104.

Besides those deaths of the first year, there were others resultant from famines, in 1622 and 1623.

Conditions were not so harsh by 1630, yet of 2,000 who migrated to the Massachusetts shores in that year, 200 died in the winter of 1630-31.

Not many of the details were known until recently, and in the haze of legend that enveloped the subject, most Americans overlooked the tremendous truth that had shaped their country's course. The truth is that the process of biological evolution, the weeding out of the less hardy and the less adaptable and the less wise, which applied among wild creatures and among primitive peoples, was reapplied to the Founding Fathers of the New World. And in so observing we come upon the key with which Darwin unlocked the wonders of the biological world: namely, the hypothesis that the weeding-out process brought about creatures of increasing effectiveness. For us it may reveal the answers to some of civilization's riddles.

But you still may ask, is there evidence, besides the logic of the evolutionary process itself, to show that the surviving Pilgrims were superior to average Englishmen?

Ellsworth Huntington reported a profound series of studies in his 1945 book, *Mainsprings of Civilization,* published by John Wiley & Sons, Inc. He sorted New England names according to dates of first appearance in America; classified them in four groups: those arriving 1620-1635, those coming 1636-1643, those appearing 1644-1692, and those of 1693-1790. He found what proportion of people in 38 cities of the United States bear those names; and then found how they rank according to the proportion of them that have achieved distinction. He points out that the present bearers of those names are diluted, yet "the differences between people descended from Puritans who arrived in America early in contrast with those who arrived later are surprisingly great." Of the fourth group, arriving 1693-1790, "which did not undergo such difficulties as beset the earlier migrants," not nearly so large a proportion have achieved distinction.

One of Huntington's studies is of entries in *Who's Who*. In each occupational field the people whose ancestors came into this country 1620-1635 are achieving distinction in much higher proportion than are the persons whose ancestors came 1693-1790, averaging about twice as high. A "control" of British names arriving at all dates: Adams, Brown, Edwards, Jones, Smith, Stone, Williams, and others, are achieving distinction in still less proportion, though not remarkably less than the descendants of the 1693-1790 group.

As one of his tests, Huntington investigated the name groups in relation to persons taking out more than one patent per year in 1907, 1908, and 1937-39. He found the same direction of differences, though the extent of difference was substantially less. It appears, then, that the Founding Fathers, at least those of them who survived and became the actual fathers of their colonies, *were a superior people.*

In this connection we should also refer to a scholarly study by Stephen Sargent Visher, entitled *Scientists Starred, 1903-1943, in "American Men of Science."* This book gives a great amount of interesting and useful information about the scientists who have been voted by their fellow scientists to be the outstanding contributors to scientific knowledge. It was published by the Johns Hopkins Press in 1947.

Visher found that of the fifty *women* who were starred between 1903 and 1943 as outstanding scientists, almost all are of Puritan descent. Of the starred men, a larger number are from Puritan ancestry than from any other group.

The beginning of the American civilization was unique in its details, but not in its general pattern. The weeding out of the weaklings, and the consequent improvement of the average biological level of the group, seems to have been a condition precedent to civilizations in general—and the more rigorous the weeding out, the more phenomenal the subsequent achievements. *The rise of civilizations has been based on the process of biological evolution as surely as the rise of man above the other animals has been based on the process of biological evolution.*

I have referred to Massachusetts as an example of the culling-out process, but *Virginians* paid for their later achievements too. Five thousand people had migrated from England to the vicinity of Jamestown in the 18 years from 1606 to 1624, but by 1624 only 1,200 had survived. Three-fourths of the migrants had succumbed to starvation, and Indian attacks, and malaria and other maladies.

The *German* people suffered a special application of the evolutionary process in the THIRTY YEARS' WAR. The Cambridge History entitles its volume IV *The Thirty Years' War.* That was was fought in the years

1618 to 1648, when war was still in considerable measure a man-to-man combat. That war was a slaughter of the innocents that involved millions. We are told on page 418 of the Cambridge History Volume IV that the population of Germany was diminished from over 16 millions to under 6 millions. Wives and children often followed the armies, and suffered a terrific death toll. There was much emigration too, but the persons who clung most tenaciously to their old homes and places of business were those who had ownership claims. Most of the peasants starved or were killed by roving brigands or emigrated.

It took Germany 200 years to recover from the Thirty Years' War, yet it is probable that to that conflagration we owe the concentration of talent that resulted in the music of Bach and Beethoven and Brahms and Mozart, the poetry of Goethe and Schiller, and the scientific achievements of Bunsen, Humboldt, Mendel, and a host of others.

Far back in history we find evidence indicating that the culling of human flocks was basic to that evolutionary process by which human beings acquired sufficient mentality to form a civilization.

We know that any large group of people have wide variations, and that with regard to any one measurement they conform to a normal curve. In a primitive environment, to be at the left end of a normal curve representing almost any helpful quality, is to be in jeopardy of loss of life. The variations among the offspring of the survivors lead to an average endowment of a high order, and at the right end of the normal curve, of leaders capable of accurate appraisals and efficient judgments.

Thus the Semites of Akkad, who, at about 2900 B.C., began nibbling at the Sumerian civilization in the area which became Babylonia, were able to develop such master minds as that of Sargon in the 25th Century B.C., and that of Hammurabi in the 20th Century B.C. The Sumerians, as such, disappeared after Hammurabi's time, absorbed by the conquerors, and the language of Babylonia became Semitic, though supplemented by words conveying Sumerian concepts.

Further south and west, at about 1200 B.C., Palestine was occupied by Canaanites—apparently a people of mostly Hittite stock. The Israelites came east and north from Egypt, a people of substantial intellect, sharpened by the killing hardships of the journey through the wilderness. By a "peaceful penetration" method they took over Palestine.

Something of the biological basis for the rise of civilizations can be learned from China. The great plateaus, deserts, and mountains by which China proper is surrounded have been sources of repeated invasions. Resistance to the invasions accounts for the Great Wall of China. One notable invasion was that of the Tartars, about 588 A.D. Another notable event was the rise of Genghis Khan, during which he conquered China by 1215.

There is drama in the story of Genghis Khan, that nomad who came out of the Gobi desert with his wild riders and conquered most of the earth. He had been a herder of beasts, but he outgeneraled the armies of three empires. He could not write—but he drew up a code of laws for 50 nations. Harold Lamb tells us about it in his book named for the Asiatic warrior. Genghis Khan was representative of a "scourge that comes every so often out of the desert to destroy decadent civilizations."

Genghis Khan was born 1162 A.D.; began his rule in 1206. In the great Oriental desert the people are "born to suffering," says Lamb; with "scant meat and millet in winter." Tribes raided each others' cattle and horses. His father was master of 40,000 tents, but a rigorous turn of events forced Genghis Khan to begin his career at the bottom. Can there be any doubt that the explanation of his abilities is in the ordinary process of biological evolution?

And for every civilization its originators must have developed by the processes of biological evolution to a heredity level which would support a civilization. Says Huntington, "That some of the invading races achieved great things because they possessed innate ability seems certain." Yes, of course; they all must have had what it takes, and in most situations it takes, among other things, innate ability to achieve great things.

●

But the questions intrude themselves—why does a civilization which has risen to the heights collapse? Why, though it may have been able easily to hold a wilder group in check for centuries, has it suddenly been swept aside by that same wild group? The wilder group has been developing its capabilities through the elimination of its less fit, but is that the complete explanation?

S. Colum GilFillan and Vilhjalmur Stefansson gave us no hints. Oswald Spengler helped, though he believed too definitely in history as a regular and axiomatic unfolding to appraise any causation factors. The centralization that Brooks Adams reported could be important, though it seems sometimes not to have proceeded far enough to be causal of collapse. The unintegrated specialization that weakens the family institution is part of the story in some instances; and the devastation of crop land has been widely influential in weakening the material basis for various civilizations.

Most persistent of all the causes of cultural declines, however, is the decline of heredity.

We have only to look at the 1940 census of the United States to see how the decline of heredity comes about. The Americans who accomplish much, whether or not descended from the Founding Fathers, seem not to be the Americans who are doing most to mold America's future. As usual, the brainiest ones have the widest array of interests. Reproduction as an interest is in severest competition in them—and they have fewest children.

The 1940 census discloses on a nationwide scale a condition that has previously been seen by samplings. The unaccomplished people are reproducing rapidly; the people who win championships, or who invent patentable devices, or who make scientific discoveries, or even those who get a good education, are having few children. We have already given attention to the census figures. Among other data I reported that the women who never got beyond the fourth grade have more than four times as many children per thousand as the college graduates have.

Let us pause for a moment to see where those comparative birth rates lead us. At the rate of 776 children per thousand women graduates of the colleges, a thousand of them will have, five generations from now, 282 descendants. At the same time 1,000 of the women with fourth-grade education or less will have, at the rate of 3,561 children per 1,000 women, 572,610 descendants. The college grads constitute 50 percent of the total we take for comparison. Their descendants, five generations hence, will constitute only slightly more than *one-tenth of 1 percent*. The other 99 and almost 9/10 percent, at the rate of 3,561 children per 1,000 women would be descendants of the women with a fourth-grade education or less. Paraphrasing the Ivory Soap slogan, Americans five generations from now will be more than 99 44/100 percent IMpure.

Actually there will be a variation from these figures, but if the influences continue the same, probably not an improvement. Many of the descendants of the 4th-grade women will become well educated. But they thereby become the cream which will be skimmed off. The least accomplished offspring of the least accomplished people will continue to inherit the earth—unless influences change.

Aldous Huxley in "Whose History," an article in the September 1947 issue of the magazine '47, writes as follows:

"Fertility in the democratic countries is in inverse ratio to ability. . . . Whether a qualitatively deteriorating society is capable of democracy remains to be seen."

Channing Pollock, writing in the *American Mercury*, was convinced that democracy could not withstand the adverse birth-rate differences — that civilization itself must vanish. "Among civilized races," he said, "the unfit are a multiplying majority which recurrently overwhelms civilization, until its destruction destroys them."

Ancient Rome seems to have suffered from the same sort of differences of birth rates. The people without abilities were having more children than those with abilities. Historians are in agreement about that, I think. Professor Tenney Frank, in his *Economic History of Rome*, page 153, shows that of forty-five patricians sitting in Caesar's Senate, "only one is represented by posterity in Hadrian's day" (a hundred and seventy-five years later). Of the families of nearly four hundred senators recorded in 65 A.D. fewer than half had any offspring.

Guglielmo Ferrero made frequent references to births in *The Women of the Caesars*, published by G. P. Putnam's Sons. Observed Ferrero: "That glorious Roman aristocracy which had escaped the massacres of the proscriptions and of Philippi, ran grave danger of dying out through a species of slow suicide." Among a variety of social laws which the emperor Augustus proposed and had adopted in 18 B.C. was *"The Lex de maritandis ordinibus,"* which attempted by penalties and promises to constrain the members of the aristocracy to contract marriage and to found families, thus to combat the increasing inclination to celibacy and sterility. The law fixed at three the number of children which every citizen should have "if he wished to discharge his whole duty toward the state." But Augustus himself, who had formulated the law, had only Julia, I understand, and complied with the law by *adopting* two sons of Julia. Adoption was common. The aristocracy was becoming "less numerous, less prolific, less virtuous."

Said Ferrero: "The increase of celibacy was rendering sterile the most celebrated stocks; the most lamentable vices and disorders became tolerated and common in the most illustrious families. . . . All this had grown up after the conquest of Egypt. . . . The ladies especially took up the new oriental customs. . . ."

And thus is the finger pointed to the still older civilization, that of Egypt, where careless living among the established classes is at least partial proof of the usual differences of birth rates there.

That period after the Roman contact with Egypt was late in Egypt's history, after several pulsations, and long after the complex organization of the pyramid building. We can go back to another period of violent change, a disturbed period a little before 2000 B.C. Dr. J. O. Hertzler, in *The Social Thought of the Ancient Civilizations,* a McGraw-Hill book, quotes Ipuwer, who was reporting his country's chaos to the Pharaoh. The description may reflect the usual differences in birth rates, but the learned man's language is not, I think, unmistakably clear about it. Said patriot Ipuwer:

"the virtuous man goeth in mourning because of what hath happened in the land. Strangers are become Egyptians everywhere. Nay but the land is full of troops of brigands. . . . Every man saith 'We know not what hath happened throughout the land.' Nay but women are barren, and there is no conception. Khnum (creator of man) fashioneth men no more because of the condition of the land. . . . Nay, but the high-born are full of lamentations, and the poor are full of joy. Plague is throughout the land. Nay, but the river is blood. Nay, but great and small say: 'I wish I were dead!' Little children say: 'He ought never to have caused me to live'."

And Ipuwer boldly charged his sovereign with part of the responsibility:

"People conform to that which thou hast commanded. . . . It is because thou hast acted so as to bring these things about. . . ."

Part of the original document is destroyed, but at the end is a fragment that may have population meaning. Ipuwer seems to be discussing the imagined ideal of a ruler; but in relation to whom?

"Would that he had discovered their character in the first generation. Then he would have stretched forth his arm against it. He would have smitten the (seed) thereof and their inheritance. . . ."

But it should not be necessary to prove the differential birth rate for each, or even for many of the civilizations. It should be necessary only to show that a relatively low birth rate of accomplished people is to be expected in the usual sorts of incentives that are present in complex living.

Over in Babylonia, under Hammurabi's Code, women

could be judges, witnesses, elders, and scribes. Some of the women were in business on their own account, and some were professional secretaries.

Honors and responsibilities for women, outside the home, in a society which depends on the home for offspring, are almost sure to be associated with the differential birth rate. We can be reasonably sure, then, that in Babylonia the women of more than average abilities, since they would be the ones most easily adaptable to the nonfamily opportunities, were having fewer than average numbers of children.

This conclusion that the usual birth-rate differences applied in Babylonia seems to be supported, though not surely, by an old Babylonian proverb: "The strong live by their own wages; the weak by the wages of their children."

But all in all we can be reasonably sure that the leveling down of the biological quality of Babylonians was one of the chief reasons for the decline of the Babylonian civilization—one of the chief reasons for the contrast between the brilliant Bablyonia of Hammurabi's time and the Iraq of today.

North and East of Babylonia stretched the mountains and valleys of Persia, the Iran of our new maps. Zoroaster was a lawmaker and a priest of the ancient Persians, living about 600 B.C. He didn't believe in birth control. He wanted his people to have babies, and still more babies. There is no reason to believe that Zoroaster had any more wisdom concerning population than Mussolini had in the recent past, but Zoroaster is recorded as having related a "vision" that probably reflects differences in birth rates of the ancient Persians comparable to the differences that threaten the civilizations of the present time. He is quoted by Dr. J. O. Hertzler. Said Zoroaster:

"I beheld a rich man without children, and he was

not exalted in mine eyes; and I beheld a poor man with many children, and he was exalted in mine eyes."

Zoroaster's civilization rose and fell. It came into prominence with the military success of Cyrus, and subsided with the invasion of Alexander the Great.

•

Some of the long-view analyzers seem to me to have supported the heredity analysis whether intentionally or not. Pitirim A. Sorokin, on page 541 of his 1947 monumental volume, *Society, Culture, and Personality*, published by Harper & Brothers, included heredity as one of five basic factors in the rise of new social systems. He apologized to the narrower institutionalists for the inclusion thus: "One is not obliged to subscribe to the claims of extreme hereditarians and racialists to perceive that a fortunate heredity is a prerequisite condition."

Then, listing several creative persons who had made notable changes in our ways of living, he observed that training alone could not account for their achievements —and in some cases the achievements had been made in spite of the training having been very meager. Those men had a special start in heredity. And finally, said Sorokin, the fact that few social groups have been creative suggests that those that were creative had a favorable biological heredity, "especially when it can be shown that the environmental opportunities of many uncreative groups have been better than or as good as those of the few creative groups."

But though Sorokin recognized special heredity quality as essential to the development of cultural supersystems, he didn't think of heredity as dynamic, and he did not discuss the development of the especially favorable heredity. Also, because he failed to take account of the fact that the heredity of a group undergoes changes as its personnel changes, he did not follow through to recognize the *decline* of heredity as a cause of the disintegration of a civilization.

Brooks Adams thought of a civilization as dependent on human *energy,* including mental energy. He thought that a society disintegrates because the energy of its people has been exhausted, and the group "must probably remain inert until supplied with fresh energetic material by the infusion of barbarian blood."

The "energy" idea as such seems untenable. Often a society contains many more people, with a total of vastly more physical energy, when it is on the verge of disintegration than when it is young and brilliant and flexible. But since Adams linked the energy restoration with new "blood," in effect what he said was that the breakdown of a civilization results from some sort of a failure of heredity, and that a revival or a new civilization depends on a capable heredity. Though the social processes which lead to changes of heredity were out of Brooks Adams' picture, nevertheless he seems to have believed that in its heredity a group does change, and that the deterioration of its heredity is connected with the downfall of the group.

In *Arnold Toynbee's* analysis the successful responses to challenges depend on the presence of creative individuals in the group. And is the creativeness due to heredity or to environment? To both.

"It is clear," he says, "that if the geneses of civilizations are not the result of biological factors or of geographic environment, acting separately, they must be the result of some kind of interaction between them."

Toynbee told of the delta near the outlet of the Tigris and Euphrates rivers. The marshmen there, who came under observation of the British soldiers during World War I, had learned to adapt themselves to the environment in a passive way. "But they have never yet girded themselves for the task which the fathers of the Sumeric Civilization accomplished in similar country nearby some five or six thousand years ago, of transforming the marshes into a network of canals and fields."

Apparently the difference was not in the environment in that case but in the heredity. And the challenge of the great tropical trees and fast-growing bushes at the north of the Isthmus of Panama called the Mayan civilization into existence—but the same challenge "found no response on the other side of the Isthmus."

"Society is a 'field of action'," says Toynbee, "but the source of all action is in the individuals composing it." "All acts of social creation are the work either of individual creators or, at most, of creative minorities." "Growing civilizations differ from static primitive societies in virtue of creative individual personalities. They never amount to more than a small minority."

Toynbee finds no explanation of civilizations in "race," as such, but his repeated dependence on creative individuals seems to disclose heredity of those individuals as the special causal factor leading to the upswing of a civilization.

The rest of the society must have some quality too, to maintain a civilization, Toynbee observes—and actually, of course, it can be shown that there is no sharp line between the creative minority and the others. If, on the basis of their adaptive qualities, the whole population were arrayed, they would probably form a bell-shaped curve, with the creative individuals at the right end of the curve.

The "uncreative majority" will prevent a civilization's development "unless the pioneers can contrive some means of carrying this sluggish rear-guard along with them in their eager advance." Imitation is called into play. The many must make an effort to adopt and adapt the products of the inventiveness of the creative few.

As to the manner in which the quality of a group is improved, Toynbee uses figurative language—but it seems to report the elimination of weaklings. Repeatedly he concludes that, except for extremes, if the challenges are tough many groups will fail but the eventual response of the successful group will be the more brilliant. The Cossacks were under crushing pressure from Mongol nomads. They met the pressure; they transformed the nomad cattle ranges into peasants' fields. They had been "tempered in the furnace and fashioned on the anvil of border warfare."

As to the *breakdowns* of civilizations—what happens to the supply of creative individuals? Toynbee doesn't say—except, page 246, there has been a "failure" of it. The failure can't be expressed as a "racial" degeneration, he thinks (page 249). Perhaps in the volumes yet to be written Toynbee will give consideration to the differential birth rate.

•

In overall view it appears that the cause of a new people rising to the heights of adaptation and invention necessary to establish a new civilization is the same cause that brought about early civilizations; the same cause as that that made civilization possible at all. It is the process of biological evolution. Many more individuals are born in a wild primitive environment than can possibly survive through the reproduction period. There is a struggle in which the weaklings die early, in greater proportion than the strong. Those who can think fastest or clearest have a better chance of surviving than the dim-wits have. The clear-headed ones know better when to run and where to run, when to fight and how to fight. They know better how to avoid exposure, and how to combat diseases. They survive, and the lesser folk die young. Thus, generation after generation there is a weeding out of the mentally weak; and generation after generation the group is bred mostly from the best.

So a civilization is a precious thing, paid for in advance through many generations of pain and bloodshed and suffering that kill off weaklings, and leave only those with good bodies and sound minds.

Finally a stage is reached when there are seen to be advantages to individuals in interdependence, in co-operation. Co-operative living, interdependence, is the essence of civilization.

A group may, in its developing wisdom, remain where it has been as it grew in its powers, or it may invade and in part destroy, and later rebuild, an older civilization. Invasion has been the more usual procedure.

But when co-operative living gets much developed, there ceases to be so much weeding out. The strong build a pattern of living that protects themselves but also protects the weak. Then arises the cause of the eventual collapse: THE WEAK MULTIPLY MORE RAPIDLY THAN THE STRONG.

Thus comes a gradual weakening of the essential humanness, the brain power of the group. Eventually the wisdom necessary for complex organization is available in too small a proportion of the people. At the same time, because of greater congestion of people, the problems become more complex. Judgments are more often misfits.

Government gets farther from the people. Issues have to be settled by force. Suffering increases. Long-time objectives play less part in people's lives; they live more for the moment. The civilization may then be overcome by conquering invaders, or it may sink into dark ages.

Civilizations crumble because for capable people the incentives for breeding are removed, replaced by incentives for social accomplishment. The breeding is left mainly to those who are not capable of achievement of any sort.

THOSE TWO FORCES: (1) THE CULLING OUT, WHICH IMPROVES AVERAGE INTELLECT, AND (2) THE DIFFERENCES IN BIRTH RATES, WHICH IMPAIR AVERAGE INTELLECT, ARE THE UNDERLYING FORCES WHICH EXPLAIN THE RISE AND FALL OF CIVILIZATIONS.

Essentially, as I have pointed out, a civilization is cooperative living, interdependent living. But basically it is made possible by a widespread possession of high quality brains.

•

A civilization is, in part, an accumulation of skills, and of know-how, and of buildings, and of tools, and of means of transportation and communication. Notice that in regard to its physical artifacts *it is an ACCUMULATION*.

Civilizations are in an interwoven pattern with intelligence. Since a civilization is an accumulation it must necessarily *lag behind the concentration of brain power on which it depends*. The biological evolution of intellect that makes possible the inventions and adaptations is a condition *precedent* to the artifacts and practices that constitute the accumulation.

Likewise, since the manifestion of a civilization, its visible structures, are an accumulation, they may linger on for decades or even centuries after the average intellect, the inherited brain power, has declined far below the level that would have been necessary to develop it.

Lag of a civilization behind the rise and fall of the brain power on which it depends

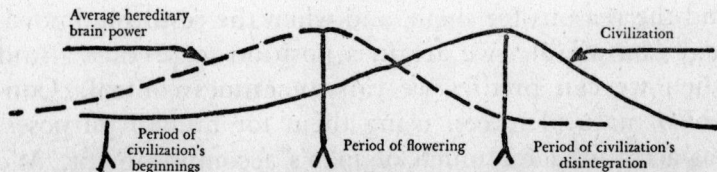

Average hereditary brain power

Civilization

Period of civilization's beginnings

Period of flowering

Period of civilization's disintegration

Environment is harsh at this stage; weaklings probably have more children than problem solvers, but the children of the problem solvers *survive* in greater numbers, so average brain power increases.

After group living becomes sufficiently developed, co-operation keeps mental weaklings alive, and, their birth rate being higher, they survive in greater numbers than the problem solvers, so average brain power declines.

Social organization has held up, has even increased in complexity, in spite of declining problem-solving ability—has held up because of the stability of institutions and the cumulative process. But at this stage average mentality has gotten so low, and problems have become so difficult, that chaos becomes widespread. The devil takes the hindermost; the weaklings cease to survive in such a great majority.

The importance of brains to civilization is generally overlooked because of the lag in the accumulation of the visible structures after the evolution of the brains, and the lag in the timing of the crumbling of the visible structures after the decadence of the brain power, the biological basis of the civilization. The LAG is the chief reason why the birth-rate cause of the crackup of civilizations has not been seen.

The objective of this chapter is to bring into focus the whole process: the building up of average intellect and the resultant accumulation of a civilization; the birth-rate differences and the resultant collapse; and the lags which have blinded people to what was going on.

Throughout the centuries there have been recurrences of like events because of the regularity of the causes of those events. When we study data to find the regularities and the reasons for them, and when the resulting knowledge is available, we are in a position to predict. And when we can predict we can sometimes control. Control of natural forces, using them for human purposes, has accounted for much of man's accomplishment. We may be able to control even the population forces, and thus for our own civilization prevent the decadence that has doomed the others.

Most people believe in biological evolution as the process which enables human beings to do things which would be out of the range of dogs and monkeys—but not many people have thought of biological evolution as the process which enables some human beings to do what other *human beings* cannot do. There has been a superstition that human beings in general have a great reserve of intelligence, so that with a little guidance any individual is capable of filling any role in the civilization in which he lives.   That same superstition is basis for the fallacy that all problems of society will be solved rightly by those who are in positions of leadership.   The belief about the excess of brain power will not hold up. The assumption that anybody can be made capable of filling any position is folly.   The faith that persons in leadership jobs will make the appropriate decisions is dangerous.   Most of us probably live rather close to the limits of our possibilities, with not very much reserve power.   The considerable occurrence of stomach ulcers and nervous breakdowns is some evidence.   And in the civilization which is now undergoing severe strain we collectively seem unable to form the judgments which would make for a smoother operation of the social machinery.   We don't even know for whom to vote to make the judgments for us.

How much intelligence is required in how large a proportion of a population to originate a civilization? What amount can keep a civilization going?   Perhaps no definite measures are possible.   Perhaps it depends on the complexity of the particular civilization.

In that connection it is well to note that as a civilization accumulates it becomes more complex.   The job of running it grows tougher at the very time the brain power is being bred out.

•

If the sequence of events that leads to collapse follows a similar pattern for all or many civilizations, must we conclude that collapse is inevitable?

There has been a regularity of pattern, and there has been a regularity of the forces back of the pattern. But that does not, I think, mean unavoidable doom for our own civilization. Perhaps it is a law. There is a law of gravity, too; but in spite of it men can fly; and in spite of it men can build dams which hold water from rushing to the sea. By wind action and by water rams, as well as by various types of pumps, they even lift water to higher levels. The law by which civilizations have declined operated because people did not understand it. I think the "law" can be counteracted if it is understood by enough people. But I do think that the rhythm of events will lead to disaster except as understanding becomes sufficiently widespread to assure drastic action.

•

In deciding on the action we must keep in mind that the benefits of a civilization are closely connected with its decline. The benefits in focus may be summarized as *co-operation*. The co-operation, in part of its working out, becomes *security*. When security is provided, the weak share it, and *the social organization is weakened through the increase of its weaklings—its burdens*. Actually, security kills itself, through wrecking the organization that provides it.

Earnest A. Hooton, famed Harvard anthropologist, tells us, in *The Twilight of Man,* published in 1939 by G. P. Putnam's Sons:

"Material prosperity encourages the preservation, pampering, and reproduction of the biologically inferior elements which are parasitical upon rich civilizations. Then some cleaner-blooded, and culturally crude stock crashes in and wipes clean the slate. . . . We can either prune off our own rotten branches or submit to a ruthless cutting down and thinning out by more vigorous conquering stocks."

Security, socially paid for, would probably be safe for the organization if it were always accompanied by the proviso that the beneficiaries refrain from increasing the burden by having children.

We must parallel the constructive aspects of biological evolution. In the absence of social organization, biological evolution ordinarily causes the increase of intellect by eliminating the slow-witted, and persons who are otherwise weak. Essentially they are prevented from having offspring. Civilizations to date have terminated that weeding-out process. *To prevent the collapse of a civilization we must somehow restore the weeding out, so far as it relates to offspring—not by killing, but by preventing reproduction of persons who, by being burdens, are civilization's enemies.*

•

It seems evident that lack of co-ordination in the specialized performances of functions that once were functions of the family has a weakening influence on a civilization. Also, economic specialization leads to controls which increase centralization; centralization proceeds until rigidity of organizations including governments smother individual initiative and prevent adaptation in emergency. It is true, too, that when governments increase their functions they seem never capable of a sufficient co-ordination of the activities they regulate or manage; that when governments increase their proportion of judgment making they take much of the spark out of individual living and thus reduce the vibrant and virile quality of a civilization. It seems evident further, that overpopulation complicates the problems and stupefies the individuals, and thus contributes to the disintegration of a social order; and that the destruction of geographic resources, especially the land sources of food, is a powerful cause of the waning of a civilization. Any one of those influences would be important, and under the impact of multiples of them a civilization would have rough going.

All those influences have been operative in various previous civilizations, and in different measures have been causes of their declines. But if those are validly causes of the declines of civilizations, is the differential birth rate to be placed in parallel with them as just another contributing cause? I don't think so. My point is that, if brain power were increasing instead of declining as the problems of a civilization became more complex, the people would be able to synthesize the objectives of their institutions, control their population numbers, conserve their resources—and, if necessary, even reverse the direction of environmental change. In short, if capable, intelligent people had most babies, society would see its problems and solve them.

PART II

Chapter 9

Joe College Has Learned About the Bees and Flowers

I confess there is just a touch of irony in that chapter title; Joe has learned so woefully little about population compared with what he needs. The two textbooks that have had most widespread recent use will show what I mean. Both are entitled *Population Problems*. One is by Thompson; the other by Landis.

Dr. Warren S. Thompson is head of the Scripps Foundation, at Oxford, Ohio, an organization engaged in population research; and he teaches the population course at Miami University, too. His text was published by McGraw-Hill Book Co., Inc., editions in 1930, 1935, and 1942. Quotations are made, by the publisher's permission, from the 1942 edition.

I discuss here not the objective, factual material that comprises most of the 471 pages of Thompson's book, and not the points of evaluation on which we agree, but those concerning which his expressions are most at variance with the conclusions and formulations worked out in POPULATION ON THE LOOSE.

Thompson prescribes a policy of appeasement. On page 277 he says:

"The only way to avoid war is for those powers which hold land they are not using and that they are not likely to use in the near future, if at all, voluntarily to cede some of this to the crowded peoples."

We have seen the value of surpluses of resources, in the early chapters herein. Since all the resources are bases for the well-being of the human groups who own them, and insurance for their own descendants, it is doubtful that any significant acreage of usable land exists which we could expect to be "voluntarily ceded" to the crowded peoples.

And as to any benefits of the Thompson policy, a statement of Dr. Frank Notestein applies. In a Milbank Memorial Fund publication of 1944 entitled *Demographic Studies of Selected Areas of Rapid Growth*, page 150, Dr. Notestein commented that it would be a shame to waste unoccupied spaces by permitting crowded peoples to move in; such a course "could only intensify future problems of adjustment." The outmovement from the crowded areas would do little to relieve the population pressure there, because the high birth rate would fill the places just as full in a short time.

As to avoiding war, there is no evidence that Thompson's appeasement policy would keep the peace even in the short run. Always Mrs. Brink's type of gratitude is the group's gratitude: "a lively expectation of further favors." We have had some experience on this point.

Back in colonial times we wanted land for our expanding population. We put pressure on the Indians to get the land. At first graciously and then reluctantly they tried to appease us; they yielded territory. But we were never satisfied. They "gave us an inch and we took a mile." Our numbers grew, and soon some of our people crossed a treaty line and took more than we had been given. After a while the camel had the whole tent.

When our ancestors couldn't get additional territory without war, they fought. They did not think of the previous concessions as betokening good will; instead, they thought "The only good Indian is a dead Indian."

Does Thompson have any special reason for thinking that the crowded people of the present are somehow more noble, more reasonable, more appeasable, than the American colonists were? Obviously not.

•

Thompson's position concerning heredity, as illustrated on his page 350, is about like that of Crespi, which was discussed in the chapter called "Too Many Fathers." Mostly the heredity is O.K., thinks Thompson; just educate. If we can do something to improve heredity incidentally, he says, let's do it; but let's concentrate on education. He is with Dorn in thinking that the differential birth rate is of importance only "because it affects the opportunities of the children in different social classes" and "impedes the transmission of the social achievements of the race."

Of course those results of the differences of birth rates are important; but I protest at the superstition that almost everybody has an hereditary sufficiency of what it takes, and the assumption that the differential birth rate does not reflect heredity. As a consequence of facts and reasoning presented in previous chapters herein, I am convinced that he is wrong on both those premises.

•

In his chapter 22, on "The Problem of Quality," Thompson plays with the concept of "natural selection." He says in effect that survival shows fitness to survive. He misinterprets completely the contrast between a wild environment and that of present-day America.

People of relatively high intelligence must have had relatively wide interests in whatever age they lived. They may, therefore, have had fewer children than people farther down the intelligence scale—in whatever age they lived. But when we talk of *survival* we make implied reference to *death rates* as well as to birth rates. There is good reason to believe that in an age before much social organization existed, the highly intelligent persons and their children would survive an emergency in much greater proportion and even in greater absolute numbers than those of lesser brain power. At the present time, in contrast, when an emergency occurs, the social organization saves the weaklings and their children. In the present artificial situation, then, survival does not show fitness to survive; it shows only that the group as a whole is providing protection to an increasing proportion of people who could not survive in some other social situation.

The general effect of Thompson's argument, on this point as on others, is to brush aside the importance of heredity, and to soothe a student's uneasiness about the differential birth rate. He does, on page 363, discuss whether the earlier process of evolution was more favorable to superior stock, but not soundly; he ignores the inescapable evidence of the results. After all, men did arise from their simian wilderness. They did build pyramids, and temples, and wheels and compasses, and constitutions. Thompson's rationalization against the general tenets of Darwin seems to be a superficial attempt to argue away some unpleasant facts.

In his section on "Who Are the Superior?" he attempts to rule out *success* as a criterion of superiority, in spite of the fact that adaptation is a generally recognized test of intelligence. And he preaches that if successful folks are so selfish that they don't want children, we don't want their kind anyway.

That sour-grapes attitude ignores the social psychology of ambitions. One tries to do what society says is important. Society, by letting practically anybody have children, has said plainly that reproduction is *not* important. Only a man worthy of respect can become an accountant, or an engineer, or a dentist, or a corporation president, or an inventor, or a composer of popular lyrics. Those require something honorable, says society; they require that one run a gauntlet of some sort. And society renders homage. But to become a father! If a man isn't good for anything else, he is still good enough for paternity, says society. And thus society steers the ambitions of capable individuals away from reproduction. Their success in what they do attempt shows that their kind is valuable; shows that their offspring, if they have any, are likely to be socially helpful in attaining whatever goals society formulates.

Thompson says, 367-370, that if we eliminate poverty, so that all children have good opportunities, they will get more education and have better quality. Of course he is referring to quality in a superficial sense; the better education couldn't improve their heredity. But Thompson, like Tugwell, has hitched his cart with the horse's head over the dashboard. That's a friendly arrangement, but you can't get anywhere with it. You can't eliminate poverty as a first step. Especially in these times of pressure on resources you have to take care of the population problem first.

Thompson would postpone, forever, using the lessons

of success, on the ground that some of the people who fail
have plenty of inherited capacity but have lacked opportunity. Of course that is true of some, but the scattered
instances of excellent heritage at the base of our pyramid
of success should not condemn us forever to breed from
the bottom. I think the chapter reporting too many
numbtops (Chapter 7) showed that the *proportion* of excellent heritage is greater farther up the pyramid, and, if
that is so, it becomes exclusively reasonable to breed predominantly from those people at the higher levels of success. That means that society must establish qualifications
for reproduction—and it means that those who cannot
meet the qualifications must not reproduce. When we
set up requirements for having a child, promptly a child
will become a symbol of honor, a badge of merit. If the
standard is higher for having two children, then having
two children evidences more social approval. We can't
get away from that psychology. The differences in birth
rates that have terminated one civilization after another,
and are now undermining our own civilization, are the
result of society's making reproduction dishonorable by
permitting it to be definitely associated with people who
are without honor.

Thompson's approach amounts to a biological let-alone
policy; it would do nothing to avoid our skidding to dark
ages.

•

What I want is to assure that people approve having a
baby, as they approve a promotion in the factory—something evidencing merit, something requiring special
qualifications, something worth striving for but which
not everybody can attain. You've got to keep the prize

beyond the reach of a lot of them in order to get anybody to look at it as a prize.

Thompson recognizes that the keeping-up-with-the-Joneses incentive applies in reproduction, but he seems to think it applies only to the people who try to keep up; he doesn't recognize that the Joneses themselves fit into the same pattern. On page 442 he says we can work toward the creation of a social atmosphere favorable to the rearing of larger families by getting successful people to have them. Though the reason for his ambition to get the less fortunate classes to keep up their birth rate is not clear, he says the others will want to follow the leaders. But when he gets ready to work on the Joneses themselves, the successful people, he forgets all about the psychology of keeping up with the Joneses.

Educate the Joneses to want more children, he says, but he doesn't say anything about changing the present incentives. By having no children they are not now making a rational adjustment, he says, page 442, and he puts an inappropriate burden on "education." "If our formal education fails to help those who have most of it to make a rational adjustment," he says, ". . . then it forfeits claim to our faith in it. . . ."

Those educated folks do make a rational adjustment to environment by the very process of limiting their reproduction—so education in general does not forfeit its claim to our faith. If a large proportion of the citizenry did not restrain their reproductive tendencies, America would be an overcrowded chaos of poverty-stricken ignoramuses. By limiting their families the educated people do, as individuals, the best they can. I grant that their adjustment as individuals is only a temporary adjustment for society, and it will not prevent the collapse of civilization. For that, a change of incentives is necessary, a change which requires recognition of the psychology of the Joneses.

Make a man show his worth in some way before he is allowed to reproduce—and then the educated people will have an offset to the present incentives to keep their families so small. The sociologists and politicians have been going at this job as Thompson has, without giving any attention to the springs that make people tick. Don't blame the worthwhile folks for not having children; they'll have plenty of them if we prevent our worthless members from reproducing. When we do that, children born more than 9 months thereafter will become walking diplomas, evidences of social approval. In Hollywood every child will be equivalent to an Oscar. I don't know that childless Thorstein Veblen ever mentioned the differential birth rate, but as a disclosure of human motivation, his book, *The Theory of the Leisure Class*, is right on the bull's-eye, explaining why Republican Leader Joe Martin has no children, while the citizens with no education average about half a dozen. Thompson seems not to have studied Veblen.

●

In his chapters on what to do about the fix we are in, Thompson reports the programs of France, Belgium, Italy, Sweden, Russia, Germany, and Japan; and with them as examples advocates indiscriminate government payments for reproduction. France pays premiums for births, has health centers for mothers and children, helps defray cost of education of children in large families, pays wages to working mothers before and after birth of a child, pays for the baby's food if the mother cannot nurse it, pays family allowances.

The programs of other countries are in the same direction.

When Thompson discusses policy for the U. S., he expresses doubt that the economic burden of children is the chief deterrent; he makes some allowance for the climate of opinion. Fine! But his specific suggestions ignore that social atmosphere and fall into the general pattern of France—that has failed from Roman times on down: family allowance, cheap medical and hospital care for the family, payment of special expenses, provision for good housing.

Whether or not such measures have justification in other considerations they are definitely contrary, in their influence, to the correction of birth-rate differences. In relation to the differential birth rate, Thompson's suggestions, and the policies of the various foreign countries, apply the same old upside-down psychology. The lower a family is in the economic scale or the educational scale, or any other scale of accomplishment, the more stimulation to reproduction there is in the Thompson provisions—and the more incentive there is for the accomplished members of society to get out of the stigmatized association that goes with reproduction.

But Thompson believes that there is no heredity significance in the differential birth rate, so he has no idea of what seems to me to be the tragic harm in his suggestions. I think, however, that even on the basis of his own assumptions he may well consider what seems to have happened in ancient Rome and what seems to be happening in France. When reproduction comes to be sufficiently crystallized as a scullion's job, not only the accomplished people get out of it but even people farther and farther down the scale get out of it too.

Population Problems, "A Cultural Interpretation," by Paul H. Landis of the State College of Washington, is a widely used text. It was published in 1943 by the American Book Company. One should read Landis' *Population Problems* with an awareness of the movement of which it was a part. On page 186 of the volume which is now in your hands I pointed out that a generation ago the behavioristic psychologists, and the institutionalists in economics and sociology, thought of the social stream itself as practically the only significant influence on human experience. The Landis philosophy seems to be dated as a part of that insulated "institutionalism." Landis, in the sweep of the current, saw no fixed elements which guided the stream. He admitted no laws and felt no effects of any. "Human social behavior is no longer understood primarily in terms of geographic, biologic, instinctive, or other naturalistic laws, but rather in terms of sociocultural forces," he contended. His use of the word "primarily" was only as a hedge; notice the further assertion: "Population phenomena have meaning only in terms of culture patterns."

I think I have shown in the foregoing chapters that population phenomena do have meaning not only in terms of culture patterns but in terms of heredity, geographic and geologic settings, and economic facts. Geographers have allowed their logical relationship to POPULATION courses as such, in the colleges, to remain dormant, but I noticed this statement in a footnote by editors Weigert, Stefansson, and Harrison in *New Compass of the World:* "The study of demographic developments, while by no means limited to the domain of geography, must be regarded as an important part of Human Geography."

Of course, even though there are biological and economic and geographic facts and laws which limit and channel our action, and give us pain when we make biological, economic, or geographic blunders, yet anything we do by way of adaptation has social aspects. That our frame of reference must be partly social does not mean that we can act apart from the restrictions of the physical environment. The social organization is never in a vacuum, or even free of pressure; it must conform with the economic and other laws, or our action is not adaptation. "Men harmonize with the rules of the universe, or else men suffer."

Landis' position is very much like that of an English teacher friend of mine. My friend insisted that practically all communication, in these times, takes place by means of words. Without a knowledge of words one's efforts in guiding social change would be futile. Therefore the really important subject, as he saw it, is English.

The truth is that English in America is helpful and sociology is helpful—and, for understanding population, geography and economics and biology are also helpful. One is insufficiently equipped for a thorough grasp if he lacks any one of them.

If we make allowances for the exclusive institutionalism — the "cultural interpretation" — which influences the Landis vision, we can find much that is useful in his text. But it is important to realize that in many classes which use the text, its prejudice is not corrected. A student, in the dark, feels one leg of the elephant, and is convinced that the beast is "shaped like a tree."

Illustrative of the pitfalls of the one-leg approach are Landis' expressions about Malthus. On page 38 there is the superficial criticism of Malthus that became fashionable about 30 years ago. Landis expressed faith "that man can easily change the limits of food supply by his ingenuity at invention." He was gambling that inventions not yet made when his book was published in 1943 would nevertheless be available in time to prevent suffering. The extent of current hunger is evidence as to how wild was that gamble.

Landis goes on: "Malthus' premise that food supply is limited in nature cannot be denied. On the other hand, it is just as certain that man has never found its limits."

Actually, Malthus was not reasoning in terms of absolute limits; he was reasoning in terms of diminshing returns, and certainly man finds those everywhere. So long as the people of Puerto Rico increase, said Malthus in effect, they will have less of resources per capita with which to work, and their per capita productivity will diminish. Malthus was right, and his teaching was important in that through increased understanding it opened up new opportunities for adaptation to environment (though mostly the opportunities have been ignored).

"Much of population theory of the past century has looked upon economic forces as something inevitable," says Landis, "rather than as a complex of man's own making."

True; and in significant part, correctly. That law of diminishing returns, for example. It is as inevitable as a law of physics—and in fact, as I think I showed in the chapter called "It's a Small World," it depends on physical truths. It is not "a complex of man's own making." Man can make some uses of resources which are wiser than other uses, but he can no more escape the law of diminishing returns than he can escape the law of gravity.

"Reproductive behavior is for the most part a matter of custom," says Landis; "custom which harnesses, regulates, defines, and even institutionalizes its patterns." That, he says on page 40, is the premise on which his book is based.

The phrase "for the most part" may be an acknowledgment of the existence of the biological and inherited sex urge; nevertheless it draws a camouflage over that, and the statement amounts to an assertion that the elephant *is* shaped like a tree.

Landis continues for several pages to bark up the same old leg: "Our assumption is that human population phenomena are social phenomena and that the processes which determine trends in population numbers are for the most part social and cultural rather than biological, geographical, or naturalistic."

•

When Landis thinks his fights with the rival gangs of the nearby alleys are over, he does settle down, in the area of his specialty, to some good work. His search for *causes of the differences of birth rates* is unusually penetrating, and fortunately it occupies about a fourth of his book. I think it would be worth your time to read some of his points:

On page 83 he shows that trying to keep up with the Joneses involves, for some, such an intensity of struggle as to reduce the desire to have children. (I wonder if he would concede that that desire is an inherited, biological desire.)

Page 83 again: Some people, newly listed on a social register, find the adjustment quite a strain, which may shift their interests away from having children.

On page 84 the point is made that whereas the rural parent is inclined to take his reproduction for granted—a matter over which he has no control—the urban parent thinks of himself as responsible for such economic burden as would be added by having a child.

Page 85: There has developed a sizable group who think it antisocial to have babies without seeing clearly how they are to be supported.

On page 88 he attributes birth-rate differences to differences in *degrees of sensitivity* to culture influences, and to differences in abilities to use contraceptives effectively.

Page 89: "In the long run, birth-rate trends may determine the destinies of a nation."

One wonders at such insight, after the narrowness of the Landis orientation. But over on page 146 he makes clear that he had no heredity implications—only sociological ones:

"Those economic, educational, and high-income groups that have low birth rates do not produce enough children to replace themselves. The significance of this fact is assumed herein to be of consequence primarily to social development of the next generation rather than to their biological quality."

In my language, that generalization would read: The fact that most babies are born of unaccomplished parents must have an unfavorable influence on the social development of the next generation whether or not biological quality is at stake. I would add: And biological quality *is* at stake.

What is the unfavorable environmental influence? Landis tells us on page 148:

"The masses of the next generation are reared by those who, by reason of lack of education and of economic resources, are unable to provide their children with an adequate diet, a completed education, and other advantages necessary to assure the full development of the physical, social, and mental potentialities of the next generation."

Though Landis does not guide a student to an interest in the heredity aspects of population, he does leave the door unlocked; page 104:

"There is also the theory that the farm-to-city migration is in itself selective, draining off the best blood of the rural community to the city, leaving behind the poorer stocks to continue the relatively high birth rate characteristic of rural areas. If this should be the case, the farm-to-city migration has far-reaching eugenic implications."

And in the last sentence of that chapter on differential fertility and class survival, Landis shakes hands with the boys of the Darwin gang:

Page 159: "There is, however, reason for believing that more able biological types are not holding their own."

Then we are agreed, it seems, that breeding from the bottom jeopardizes civilization both by giving the youngsters an unfavorable environment and by giving them an inferior heredity.

•

On Landis' page 179 is a prophecy which is in essence a prescription for a sweeping social reform program: family wage systems, maternity allowances, marriage dowries, free hospitalization for maternity cases, extensive public housing, removal of discrimination against married women working, special privileges to them during childbirth, free school lunches, free food to families with children.

In our consideration of that prescription the question is not on the general arguments for or against those proposals. Just one question is in focus: WILL THEY HELP CORRECT THE ANTISOCIAL BIRTH-RATE DIFFERENCES? The answer is No! The Landis prescription is completely unsuited to that purpose.

Family wage systems cannot lead educated people to reproduce in greater number than they lead ignorant people to reproduce. The leverage is the same as that for a baby bonus—and similarly, to the extent that it works at all it makes the birth-rate differences *worse.* A given amount of money is a greater inducement to a person who has little on his mind than to one who has active interests. A definite number of dollars occupies a larger proportion of thought, and has a greater stimulating influence on uneducated and particularly on uneducable people than on their more alive neighbors. Landis himself reported a related point on his page 170 which indicates in another way the futility—even perniciousness—of the family wage:

"Subsidies designed to encourage the better classes to reproduce themselves are sometimes suggested, but such are generally looked upon with disfavor, since, if given to all groups in a population, they would be less likely to pay adequately the cost of offspring among the better classes than among the classes which are already producing large numbers."

Right, Dr. Landis; and the same reasoning is applicable to maternity allowances. A hundred dollars, or five hundred, look bigger to the poor woman than to one in the middle income group; look bigger to the dimwit than to a person with an intense interest in the book of the month or the quilt contest at the county fair. Maternity allowances would make the present differences in birth rates more pronounced, not less.

The immediate direction of influence is of the same pattern for each item of the rest of the Landis list.

Yet I don't mean to say that he is entirely without basis for his belief. He has seen that an increase of income in a group has in some instances been accompanied by a widening of interests and a change of values which have led to a lowering of birth rates. He thinks that the free services he proposes would act as an increase of income in similarly reducing the birth rates of those classes that would get the most in the process. Could the whole program, then, be different in its results from the sum of its parts; or could the long-time effect of any part be different from its short-time effect?

But consider the places where definitely the plan cannot work—a crowded land like India, for example.

Notice that the first effect of the program would be to reduce deaths, as I have pointed out in previous chapters. Instead of a population increase of 50,000,000 Indians, as there was in the decade before World War II, there would be a decade increase of 150,000,000 Indians—an increase equal to the total population of the U. S.—as the additional population of India in ten years.

Who, in our assumption, is financing such a program? Obviously not the people of India. To support an additional 50,000,000, in a very promising decade, kept practically all of them—350,000,000—down to a bare subsistence; they will probably never again in any decade be able to keep so many additional ones as 50,000,000 alive.

Could the U. S. finance the plan? No. If all our surpluses went to India we nevertheless could not raise the level of living of Indians to the requirements of the Landis plan. And the rate at which Indians would increase, as a consequence of a higher survival rate, would make it sure that the stage could never be reached at which the birth rate would fall significantly.

But what about some state of the United States—say

Mississippi? If the financing of the Landis plan were to be attempted by the people of Mississippi, there simply would not be enough purchasing power available. The level of living high enough to widen the interests and thereby reduce the birth rates of the unaccomplished people would be impossible.

Would the Landis bonuses be effective in California? California already has a low birth rate, the effect of the steady stream of migrants into the state. It is possible that the birth rate would be reduced further by a prolonged application of the Landis plan, but not likely that the birth rate *differences* would be overcome. If the plan did succeed in reducing the birth rate of people far down the social pyramid, it likely would reduce still further the birth rate of those nearer the top. In most historic instances, though the slanted blade of the golden ax has cut the birth rates of all levels of society, it has cut those in the top levels most. Under the Landis plan California could easily become a second France—and France is a nation grown numb through the differential birth rate; and though the overall birth rate is so low that the total population declines, the antisocial *differences* in birth rates continue.

If the Landis prescription were applied to the U. S. as a whole, could it correct the differences in birth rates? No; again the incentives for the Joneses would not be changed unless for the worse. Through a rigorous socialization of income, those farther down the pyramid might conceivably be led to reduce their birth rates, but the Jones would reduce theirs too. And again we would face the strong prospect of an overall birth rate so low that the population would steadily decline. I am not protesting that the Landis share-the-wealth plan might lead to that; there would probably be net benefit in a 30 percent decline in numbers in the United States; I *am* protesting that his plan would *not* correct the antisocial

JOE HAS LEARNED ABOUT BEES AND FLOWERS 245

birth-rate *differences*. Definitely the Landis proposals would fail anywhere and everywhere.

But in spite of the shortcomings of the exclusively "cultural" interpretation on which Landis has relied, and in spite of the misguidance of his prescriptions, I think that the text can be put to good use by the syllabus method. With assignments in the Landis volume, the teacher can take advantage of the good analysis Landis has made of the causes of birth-rate differences.

•

At this point I want to call attention to the *Report of the Royal Commission on Population,* the British study published in June 1949.

Of course it was not composed for textbook purposes, and yet, like the Landis text, parts of it could be used for college classes in connection with a syllabus. I have already digested for you, in the chapter "Joe Martin is a Bachelor," the Royal Commission's findings of the causes of birth-rate decline.

Another notable section deals with the increasing proportion of old people. If old people could get jobs, a lesser proportion of them would be burdens. They could get jobs if their wage rates per hour could be lower than usual union rates and if they could work half as many hours. The health developments that enable people to live longer would also enable them to work longer, except for social obstacles to their employment and social inducements to their idleness. Greater institutional flexibility would reduce the social burden of old age.

In the matter of population quality, the Commission presents material which demonstrates antisocial birth-rate differences. On the importance of the differences they say, "There is a remarkable approach to agreement among . . . [the 'authorities'] on the two essential points, (1) that a considerable element in intelligence is inherited and (2) that the more intelligent have smaller families on the average than others."

And they say, "It is clearly undesirable for the welfare and cultural standards of the nation that our social arrangements should be such as to induce those in the higher income groups and the better educated and more intelligent within each income group to keep their families not only below replacement level but below the level of others."

Then—what a letdown!

The Royal Commission does a right royal flipflop: uses a hundred pages in presenting recommendations for social arrangements which would do precisely what they say would be "clearly undesirable," recommendations which would induce the more intelligent to keep their families below replacement and below the level of others. They propose financial allowances and services to mothers, in proportion to numbers of children. After spending four-fifths of a million dollars in making a nest, they come out with that antique china egg from the second-hand store!

Your Highness, it's a good egg of its kind, but it can't hatch!

The Commission uses the same old upside-down incentives presented by Thompson and Landis. Their program flies in the face of their own warning. As I think I have shown in discussing the Thompson and Landis proposals, it effect must be to make worse the antisocial birth-rate differences.

But if you can blow away the royal chaff and straw, you'll find some good wheat in the Commission's granary.

●

Dr. T. Lynn Smith is author of *Population Analysis,* a textbook published in 1948 by the McGraw-Hill Book Company.

Dr. Smith was head of the Department of Sociology and Anthropology at Vanderbilt University; is now at the University of Florida. He has turned out a creditable piece of sociology, reporting facts and his conclusions in clear paragraphs and with more graphs and maps than usual.

In his preface and first chapter there are various debatable concepts. Smith falls in with the popular idea that the United States is not overpopulated and not likely to be, refers to philosophic phases of population study as "mental gymnastics," speaks overoptimistically of distribution of population with relation to resources as subject to "fairly accurate and facile measurement," thinks the recent baby campaigns of dictators somehow demonstrate an importance of numbers in winning wars (though he does yield some credit to surpluses of productive capacity) .

While we are examining the little indigestible lumps the baker has put in the batter, we should notice that for a man who is writing "science" Smith does use a lot of nonscience words, even after he gets past the pitfalls of the first chapter. For example he speaks of instances of depopulation as "serious" and "severe." Those are attitude words, not objective. Another example: some people have a fear that Asiatics will eventually submerge the white stocks. Smith refers to that fear as a phobia. "Fear" is descriptive; "phobia" has come to be a word of scorn for what is thought by the user of the word to be an unreasonable fear. Smith speaks of a population increase as a "gain." "Increase" is a nonfeeling, descriptive, scientific word, whereas "gain" is a popular word, a word of approval; it isn't scientific.

But Smith does recognize that the stream of human experience flows between banks: that level of living of a population is influenced by its size in relation to resources—in general, the more the people, the lower is their level of living; that the size of population "is not the sole factor determining military capacity. Natural resources, technological skills, and social organization are likewise factors. . . ."

A useful table is given in the first chapter showing density of population by countries, and another showing density of population in the states of the United States.

Smith really gets into his stride in the second chapter. Especially clarifying is the discussion of the census classification of "rural non-farm," which is actually very largely suburbanite. A graph shows the movement toward the cities throughout the country's history, and two of the author's uniquely illuminating maps show that, contrary to the usual idea, the population of our sparsely populated states is not especially rural but that "the bulk of their inhabitants live together in incorporated centers."

The chapter on educational status makes valuable data available from the 1940 census in clear comparisons. Women in 1940 were a little better educated than men; city residents have more education than farm folk; Negro farmers have 4.1 years of schooling to compare with 8 years for white farmers. The South ranks high in the education of its urban white population, Mississippi topping the nation with a median of 11.7 years of schooling.

But the *differences* in schooling are great in the South, the rural whites there being substantially down the scale, and male Negro farmers being at the bottom.

The chapter on *differential birth rates* presents birthrate differences by city and open spaces, by racial groups in the United States, by regions, and by occupations. There is nothing to show birth-rate differences of persons with different educational achievement or any other type of achievement as such, though of course the births for occupational groups do show incidentally the general fact that achievement in preparation for making a living is correlated with low birth rates.

The *declining* birth rates are given a separate chapter. There are graphs showing crude birth rates for several countries and the long-time trend for the United States. The fact is pointed out that birth-rate decline originated in cities and spreads from cities.

I have sketched only scattered samples. Dr. Smith has set out to teach scientific measurement, analysis, and reporting of human relations, in the sociological subdivision of population, and I think that, for the most part, he has done a good job of it, and made it interesting too.

There is, however, a vast body of material about the subject of population that Smith has passed by in the night, and without which population students are ill equipped.

That plunks down before us an unsolved problem of educational administration. For the young people who have resulting problems of course selection, I have to discuss it.

According to returns on a batch of questionnaire post-cards, and the entries in college catalogues, courses with the word "Population" in their titles are taught in more than 200 U. S. colleges. About 95% of them are taught in sociology departments. I think all of the rest are in economics departments.

But whether the courses are in sociology departments or in economics departments the students in most of them are getting materials narrowed to not more than a third of the realistic scope of the subject matter, and often with propaganda to prevent the development of an interest in the other two-thirds.

What I think would be a wholesome organization in a college is a POPULATION DEPARTMENT, on a level with the history department or the department of mathematics. Only two standard-length courses would be taught in the population department, at least at first. One would be a general survey course which would be required of all students in the college. Students could "minor" in population, and many would do so whose major fields would be agricultural economics, anthropology, biology, economics, geography, geology, history, political science, prelaw, premedicine, sociology, statistics, zoölogy. The credits for population as a minor emphasis would be earned in assorted courses in several of those other departments, under guidance of the head of the population department. Students might major in population—on the same basis. For a student to receive credits toward his major, for work done in departments other than his major department, would be a unique setup, but population is a unique field of study.

Correlated with at least some of those courses in other departments there should be supplementary one-hour-a-week courses to keep the student aware of the bearing which the courses in other departments have on population. Thus a group of majors and minors in population might be steered into a course in economic geography which would meet three times a week. A correlated one-hour course in the population department would induce those same students to do the applicable supplementary reading and writing and discussing to keep that economic geography course meaningful in its population implications. All four hours of credit would be usable for the students' credit requirements in population. That is illustrative. A full array of other courses would be similarly utilized.

The second standard-length course actually taught in the population department would be an integrating course for seniors majoring or minoring in the department.

The population department must not be administered by an insulated institutionalist. Such a one usually has a contempt for principles of geography, and a crazy notion of universal sufficiency of heredity. Such a person would do a lot of harm administering a population department—and that means that probably 80% of the professors who have been teaching population *courses* are too lopsided to administer a population *department*. It would be wise to get as an administrator a scholar whose field has been geography or genetics.

No college has such a population department now, yet population conditions are the basis of the world's worst miseries *now,* and they threaten to get worse yet; and fast. Many young people are seeking educational aids with which they may understand and grapple with humanity's woes *now*.

And so I shall direct the next two or three pages to Joe College and Betty Co-ed, and shall assume that they are freshmen, not yet certain what courses they will take.

To be concrete, let's list, from a university catalogue, some courses that have population importance. I refrain from naming the university because I am not in a position to judge the quality of the courses there, and I was disappointed in a recent book participated in by two of the teachers of the courses I name.

•

The X University has BIOLOGY OF MAN as a "core course"—4 hours a week for 2 semesters.

In the geography department I find ANTHROPO-GEOGRAPHY, CLIMATE AND MAN, CONSERVATION OF NATURAL RESOURCES.

Betty, don't be dazed by that word "anthropo-geography"; all it means is "human geography." It reports where the peoples of the world are, how close together they live, how they make a living, and what their levels of living are.

If you have time for a little more rounding out in this direction, the X University geography department has a course called ECONOMIC GEOGRAPHY and another entitled WORLD RESOURCES AND INDUSTRIES.

A good volume on ECONOMIC geography is *Principles of Economic Geography* by Ellsworth Huntington, published in 1940 by John Wiley & Sons. It is not light reading, but a reader who has come this far in *Population on the Loose* would have no difficulty with it. Huntington has sometimes arrived at a "principle" of doubtful general application, but his book does contain much useful information concerning population.

Another noteworthy text is *Fundamentals of Economic Geography* by Nels A. Bengtson and William Van Royen, 3rd edition, published in 1950 by Prentice-Hall.

Under a broader title, I recommend *Human Geography, An Ecological Study of Society*, by C. Langdon

White of Stanford University and George T. Renner of Teachers College, Columbia University, published in 1948 by Appleton-Century-Crofts, Inc.

You will want a lot of statistics. The *mathematics department* will teach you ELEMENTS OF STATISTICS and THEORY OF STATISTICS.

Also in the *sociology department* you will find SOCIAL STATISTICS.

In the *psychology department* there is a statistics course, too; and there are three in the *College of Education*.

These five courses are taught in the *sociology department:* HUMAN ECOLOGY, POPULATION PROBLEMS, POPULATION AND EUGENICS, WORLD POPULATION PROBLEMS, INDIVIDUAL STUDY IN POPULATION AND HUMAN ECOLOGY.

In the *psychology department,* besides the statistics course already mentioned, better take SOCIAL PSYCHOLOGY. It should give you a little better understanding of birth-rate differences.

In the *zoölogy* department you will want PRINCIPLES OF HEREDITY, and ORGANIC EVOLUTION.

The summer session at X University has some offerings with attractive titles too: GENETICS AND HEREDITY, CONSERVATION OF RESOURCES, ECONOMIC GEOGRAPHY, STATISTICS.

But, Betty and Joe, the chances are that you are not at the X University, and will not be able to get that precise array of courses. The listing shows you, however, the types of courses to look for, and the departments where you are likely to find them.

Now I want to send a note to the parents of young people not yet in college—parents who have come to realize the tremendous importance of population as an influence in human lives.

Dear Parents:

Some college will run your Sally and Sam through many examinations after they get there. Before they go, you may appropriately apply tests yourself, both to your young hopefuls and to the colleges. If your son and daughter show interest in the branches of study that lead to population comprehension, you may wish to expose them to learning in the field in which this book is written. Maybe you can't send them to a college with the very best opportunities for population education, but there must be various *degrees* of excellence among colleges within their and your choice. As you look over the catalogues, for our purposes you can test the colleges by four fields of study:

1. Statistics.
2. The relations of men with earth resources.
3. Heredity of population.
4. Social aspects of population.

1. Except for teaching, most of the professional work in Population is in STATISTICS. That must be very definitely known by one who plans a population career. However, if Sally is to pursue the study for a grasp of the forces that shape the course of nations and neighborhoods, but not for a living, then a single semester of statistics will probably suffice, and the colleges can be tested mostly for offerings in 2, 3, and 4. Better check for at least one course in statistics anyway. A college without a single course in statistics hasn't got what it takes to make any sort of a social scientist.

2. In your inquiry about RELATIONS OF MEN WITH EARTH RESOURCES, look in the geography and geology and economics departments for the courses in HUMAN GEOGRAPHY, ECONOMIC GEOGRAPHY, CLIMATE, CONSERVATION. Sally and Sam should know DIMINISHING RETURNS too, but I guess they'll have to depend on this book for that topic— in the chapter, "It's a Small World." No courses concentrate on it. And I don't know of any courses that point out that *specialized production and the money process* throw a haze over the resources, preventing a ready comprehension that they are being overworked. In general, an alertness to the relations of men with earth resources will help your son and daughter to keep aware of the delicate and important problem of whether and where earth resources are used with an intensity and in a manner that will give them 10 years' duration, or a perpetuity, or something between.

3. HEREDITY OF POPULATION is studied in biology and zoölogy departments, in their courses in GENETICS, and EUGENICS, and HUMAN EVOLUTION, and HEREDITY; perhaps in still other courses.

4. SOCIAL ASPECTS OF POPULATION are in prominence in sociology departments in their courses with the word "population" in their labels.

Getting an education in population is an uphill struggle. The colleges themselves are organized against it. The requirement that one must earn credits for a "major" in an existing department leaves little time for acquiring the necessary population courses—scattered as they are in several departments. A realization of the handicaps, however, should give one a better start than most previous population students have had.

You and Sally and Sam will have to co-ordinate the courses, and the rich lore that is in them, as best you can.

Chapter 10

Joe's Dad Has Joined
the Do-Better Club

In the *Cleveland Plain Dealer* for Sunday, November 23, 1947, was an article by Margaret S. Reed entitled "Girl Scouts Fight Against Land Ruin."

"Who is teaching whom is an as yet unanswered question out in East Cleveland, where members of Girl Scout Troop 166 have given their fathers the task of teaching them conservation."

The fathers were boning up on reforestation, stream pollution, and flood control.

"The troop is said to be the first in the country to devote all its energies to the land and its resources."

I wonder if other scout troops are pioneering in that direction now.

There are other organizations working on phases of population. This chapter is not intended to be an exhaustive directory. But it is intended to bring to consciousness the fact that many people are thinking in various sections of the field of population, and it does specify a few of their organizations.

256

The organizations are arranged under four topics:

STATISTICS of population
RESOURCES in relation to population
HEREDITY of population
VARIOUS ASPECTS of population

First I shall list the names of the organizations; then tell a little about them. There are parts of the chapter, as you will see, that are as dry as a phonebook, but perhaps in the same way useful.

Organizations Giving Attention to Statistics of Population

American Statistical Association
Bureau of the Census, in the Department of Commerce
Metropolitan Life Insurance Company
Scripps Foundation
United Nations Statistical Commission

Organizations with Attention to Resources in Relation to Population

American Forestry Association
American Geographical Society
Conservation Club in a school
Friends of the Land
National Council of Geography Teachers
Natural Resources Council of America
Soil Conservation Service of the U. S. Department of Agriculture
United Nations Food and Agriculture Organization
United Nations Population Commission
United States Forest Service

Organizations with Attention to Human Heredity

American Association on Mental Deficiency
American Eugenics Society
American Genetic Association
American Society of Human Genetics
C. M. Goethe

Human Betterment Association of America
Human Betterment Federation
Roscoe B. Jackson Memorial Laboratory
State Boards and Commissions
University laboratories for human heredity
    Dight Institute (U. of Minn.)
    Heredity Clinic (U. of Mich.)
    Human Genetics Laboratory (U. of Utah)

Organizations Dealing with Multiple Aspects of Population

Malthusian League
Margaret Sanger Research Bureau
Milbank Memorial Fund
Planned Parenthood Federation
Population Association of America
Population Reference Bureau
Voluntary Parenthood League

Now to put the addresses with those names, and in some instances to include a little more information.

•

The AMERICAN STATISTICAL ASSOCIATION is composed of scholars associated for promotion of fact-finding and development of statistical methods. They deal, in considerable measure, with population data. The Association has headquarters at 1603 K Street, N. W., Washington 5, D. C. It publishes three periodicals:

The *Biometrics Bulletin;* 6 issues per year; subscription price $2.

Journal of the American Statistical Association; quarterly, $6.00 per year.

Bulletin of the American Statistical Association; quarterly, $1.00 per year.

The BUREAU OF THE CENSUS is in the U. S. Department of Commerce, Washington 25, D. C. It is the most thorough and dependable census organization in the world. Its population findings are available at very low prices.

The METROPOLITAN LIFE INSURANCE COMPANY publishes a monthly *Statistical Bulletin,* at 1 Madison Avenue, New York 10. Its studies relate to birth rates, death rates from various causes, life expectancy, and other aspects of population, mostly limited to the U. S.

The SCRIPPS FOUNDATION, Oxford, Ohio, is a population research organization under the directorship of Dr. Warren S. Thompson, who also teaches a course in population at Miami University. I discussed his textbook a few pages back. Some of his work is reported in Chapter 15.

The UNITED NATIONS STATISTICAL COMMISSION, from its STATISTICAL OFFICE, publishes a *Monthly Bulletin of Statistics* in parallel English and French columns and tables. Population figures of countries are shown in comparison, including birth rates and death rates. The subscription price is $5.00 per year; single copy 50c. It may be subscribed for at the International Documents Service, Columbia University Press, 2960 Broadway, New York 27, N. Y.

•

We come now to our second grouping: "Organizations with Attention to Resources in Relation to Population."

First on this list is the AMERICAN FORESTRY AS-
SOCIATION. You have probably noticed that some of
the organizations named have a direct membership; others are agencies of government. The American Forestry
Association is one you can join directly. It was organized
in 1875, as an instrument for conserving our forests "and
related resources of soil, water and wildlife," and through
its membership of several thousands of men and women
it works to build up public understanding of and participation in its objectives. Members receive each month the
American Forests, a magazine of many pictures and well-
selected articles. The subscribing membership fee is $5
per year; contributing memberships higher. The address
is 919 Seventeenth Street, N. W., Washington 6, D. C.

The AMERICAN GEOGRAPHICAL SOCIETY is
also an organization with attention to resources in relation to population. The organization doesn't concentrate
on the conservation objective; it is a scientific society, facilitating the study and report of geographical facts. Yet
the logic of its members' findings points impressively to
the relations of resources to human experience. The
American Geographical Society has offices on Broadway
at 156th Street, New York 32. There are 4,500 members.
Annual fellowship dues are $10 per year, optionally
more, but a subscription to its quarterly, the *Geographical Review,* may be had for $6. Among its other publica-
tions the Society has a new four-page monthly leaflet entitled *Focus,* with a subscription rate of $1 a year.

In Janesville, Wisconsin, is a CONSERVATION
CLUB in the public schools. Pat Dawson, Director of
Recreation, tells us about it in *Recreation* for November
1947. Each session opens with a pledge
"to save and faithfully to defend from waste the natural
resources of my country, its soils and minerals, its forests,
waters and wildlife."

Congratulations, Janesville!

Carrying on another foresighted movement—on a nation-wide scale—are THE FRIENDS OF THE LAND, "A Non-Profit, Non-Partisan Society for the Conservation of Soil, Rain and Man." In a folder stating its objectives is this statement:

"We of the FRIENDS OF THE LAND are bringing to the public the findings of Federal, state and private research agencies and encouraging our members, and all citizens as well, to take an active and aggressive part in maintaining and restoring all those natural resources, particularly soil and water, which are the real wealth of the nation and the ultimate base of all prosperity and health."

Members of the society pay dues ranging from $5 to $100 per year, a special $3 rate applying to specified philanthropic groups. Subscription office: 1368 North High Street, Columbus 1, Ohio.

Members receive (1) *The Land Letter,* published every 12 weeks as a field report on conservation; (2) various pamphlets and informational services, and (3) *The Land,* a quarterly magazine edited by Russell Lord, airy enough in its style to be alluring, earthy enough in its substance to be fruitful.

The NATIONAL COUNCIL OF GEOGRAPHY TEACHERS, like the American Geographical Society, deals with the relationships of men to earth. Loyal Durand, Jr., of the Department of Geography at the University of Tennesee, is its 1950 President; and M. Melvina Svec, of State Teachers College in Oswego, N. Y., is Secretary. The Council publishes the *Journal of Geography* monthly except for June, July, and August; subscription price $3 per year.

Next on our alphabetical list of organizations dealing with the relationship of men to resources is the NATURAL RESOURCES COUNCIL OF AMERICA. Its secretary is C. R. Gutermuth, Wire Building, Washington 5, D. C. Said Mr. Gutermuth, in response to my letter:

"The organizations which make up membership in the Council are not directly concerned with POPULATION, but, of course, the increasing human population on this continent has a direct bearing on their activities. So long as the population continues to increase, there will be a greater need for the type of work to which all of the member organizations are dedicated."

Members are scientific societies in the natural science field, and conservation organizations as follows:

American Forestry Association
919 17th Street, N. W.
Washington 6, D. C.

American Geographical Society
Broadway at 156th Street
New York 32, N. Y.

American Museum of Natural History
Central Park West at 79th St.
New York 24, N. Y.

American Nature Association
1214 Sixteenth Street, N. W.
Washington 6, D. C.

American Nature Study Society
P.O. Box 1078
Chapel Hill, North Carolina

American Ornithologists' Union
J. M. Linsdale, Chairman
Jamesburg Route
Monterey, California

American Society of Limnologists
and Oceanographers
P. O. Box C
Put-in-Bay, Ohio

American Society of Mammalogists
Donald F. Hoffmeister, Secretary
University of Illinois
Urbana, Illinois

American Society of Range
Management
W. J. Anderson, Delegate
205 Littayer Center, Harvard Univ.
Cambridge 38, Massachusetts

American Society of Zoologists
Thurlow Nelson, Delegate
Rutgers University
New Brunswick, N. J.

American Wildlife Foundation
709 Wire Building
Washington 5, D. C.

Better Fishing, Inc.
509 South Wabash Avenue
Chicago 5, Illinois

Conservation Foundation
30 East 40th Street
New York 16, N. Y.

Ecological Society of America
Paul B. Sears, Delegate
77 Prospect Street
New Haven, Conn.

Friends of the Land
1368 North High Street
Columbus 1, Ohio

Game Conservation Society
1819 Broadway
New York 23, N. Y.

Grassland Research Foundation
Dr. J. M. Aikman
Iowa State College
Ames, Iowa

Izaak Walton League of America
31 North State Street
Chicago 2, Illinois

National Association of Soil
Conservation Districts
Waters S. Davis, Jr., President
League City, Texas

National Audubon Society
John H. Baker, President
1000 Fifth Avenue
New York 28, N. Y.

National Fisheries Institute
Charles E. Jackson, Gen. Mgr.
724 Ninth Street, N. W.
Washington 1, D. C.

National Parks Association
1214 Sixteenth Street, N. W.
Washington 6, D. C.

National Wildlife Federation
3308 Fourteenth St., N. W.
Washington 10, D. C.

National Conservancy
1214 Sixteenth Street, N. W.
Washington 6, D. C.

New York Zoological Society
30 East 40th Street
New York 16, N. Y.

Pacific Northwest Bird and Mammal
Society
Mrs. Margaret A. Ivey, Secretary
University of Washington
Seattle, Washington

Sierra Club
1050 Mills Tower
San Francisco 4, California

Society of American Foresters
Mills Building
Washington 6, D. C.

Soil Conservation Society of America
Room 411, Center Building
Upper Darby, Pennsylvania

Sport Fishing Institute
R. W. Eschmeyer, Vice-President
Bond Building
Washington 5, D. C.

Wild Flower Preservation Society
3740 Oliver Street
Washington 15, D. C.

Wilderness Society
1840 Mintwood Place
Washington 9, D. C.

Wildlife Management Institute
709 Wire Building
Washington 5, D. C.

Wildlife Society
Ian McTaggart Cowan, President
University of British Columbia
Vancouver, British Columbia

The SOIL CONSERVATION SERVICE, a subdivision of the U. S. Department of Agriculture, is a tremendously important organization of which as citizens all of us are members. It was brought into existence by a Congressional Act of April 27, 1935, and has been organizing conservation districts since 1938.

As of January 1, 1949, a total of 2,094 conservation districts had been organized, 25 of them in the territories, 2,069 of them on the mainland. The 2,069 districts on the mainland contain 4,387,000 farms. A few of the 2,069 are called wind erosion districts, grass conservation districts, etc., but 2,021 of them are "soil conservation districts," made up of 4,339,906 farms containing 1,123,067,-759 acres.

Those four and a third million farms constitute three-fourths of all the farms in the country. Eight of our states are completely organized in conservation districts: Alabama, South Carolina, Delaware, Rhode Island, New Hampshire, Vermont, Massachusetts, and New Jersey.

The readiness with which the farmers have recognized the importance of conservation is very encouraging, and the extent to which they have organized into conservation districts is nothing short of phenomenal. Yet, as one conservation speaker cautioned us in a Cleveland meeting, the organization into districts is only the beginning. Conservation plans have to be worked out for the separate farms. That requires a lot of surveying and plan-making by specially trained men. The requests for such work have run several years ahead of the possibilities of the Soil Conservation Service staff. As I understand, of well over a billion acres in the conservation districts, there are now about 160,000,000 acres under active conservation plans. In other words, only about 14% of the area in the conservation districts has received the necessary technical study. Of that 14% for which plans have been prepared, work has been applied on only a little more than half—a little short of 83 million acres. Additional acres are given attention as fast as technical staff can be developed, considering the limited funds available.

Illustrative practices applied in soil conservation districts are

stubble-mulch farming	strip cropping
contour farming	terracing
cover cropping	making ponds
seeding pasture and range	improving water application
woodland improvement	establishing windbreaks

Group enterprises in drainage, irrigation, and erosion control have been planned, with the assistance of the Soil Conservation Service, in more than 3,500 districts.

According to a report of the Chief of the Soil Conservation Service, the Service has given much consideration to cover crops, to green-manure crops, particularly the legumes—and to conservation rotations. It has tested grasses and plants for conservation purposes, and is encouraging their use in appropriate parts of the country.

There are approximately 14,000 private contractors helping farmers in soil conservation districts to complete the application of their conservation plans. Of nine main types of machines used in the conservation work, bulldozers owned by contractors numbered at a recent date 8,465; bulldozers owned by districts numbered 172; bulldozers owned by the Service, on loan to districts, numbered 313. Crawler tractors owned in about the same ratios totaled 7,956, and power shovels 703.

Flood-control activities have been initiated on 300 watersheds. The activities include revegetation, the making of farm and ranch ponds, detention reservoirs, gully control dams, the working out of roadside erosion control, and terracing.

The Service has conducted water-use surveys, and has prepared guidance reports for conservation districts. A study of ground water in Texas led to a recommendation against its excessive use. Sediment surveys of lakes and reservoirs were made in 15 states.

The benefits of the soil conservation work for the preservation of food sources are great beyond computation, and yet I think that in terms of relative need, a small percentage of the activities of the Service may well be reevaluated. I have in mind the land-development operations—through which it is bringing into use newly created farm units. I have doubts too about some of its irrigation work and most of its marsh-drainage projects. My tendency to protest against these activities is based on

the reasoning in the chapter entitled "Expansion Fever."
I believe in insurance, and so in surpluses. In general,
swamps and marshes lose none of their capacity for productivity with the passing of time. Why rush them into
use now? Left as they are, they are a reserve against possible greater need for food sources in the future. In rare
instances health considerations may make draining necessary; most of the swamps and marshes, I think, should remain such.

That reasoning seems to me applicable to some irrigation projects, and to the little remaining wild land that
can be turned into farms. Certainly, I think, the money
spent in those directions is less well spent than money
which is used to prevent erosion—since erosion involves
the actual shrinking of a land resource.

But the activities against which I protest are only a
small part of the work of the Service. Getting back to its
actual conservation work, the Soil Conservation Service
supplies millions of trees and shrubs to the soil conservation districts, some of them purchased from state nurseries; most of them grown in its own nurseries.

Some experimenting with foreign erosion control
plants has been conducted; about thirty of them have
been accepted into the agriculture of the United States.

The research program of the SCS is fundamental. For
example, leaving wheat stubble on the land was found to
yield less crop the next year than burning it, but leaving
the stubble on the land year after year resulted in very
substantial increases. Experiment showed, too, that surface utilization of the stubble is superior to disking it or
plowing it under; and that retaining winter cover crops
on the surface as mulch increases the yields of corn crops
that follow. On a 3.8 percent slope in Texas, clean cultivation of cotton and corn caused erosion at a rate of 1
inch in ten years, whereas cotton in rotation with sweet
clover lost soil at the rate of 1 inch in 226 years; and un-

der a permanent sod of Bermuda grass the erosion was at
the rate of only 1 inch in 6,000 years.

Study revealed that, in a Missouri area of claypan soil,
production on soil-conserving pasture amounted to 169
to 288 pounds of meat per acre—the equivalent of 27 to
46 bushels of corn—whereas the yield of soil-destroying
corn averaged only 34 bushels per acre.

In Wyoming the pitting and grooving of pasture land
was found to be effective in retaining rain water, thereby
increasing the volume of grass. In other regions the run-
off of rain from pastures was reduced by contour fur-
rowing.

The Service puts out a monthly publication, available
at a dollar a year from the U. S. Government Printing
Office. It has also published bulletins on terracing, methods of tillage to prevent soil blowing, Kudsu for erosion
control, strip cropping, and about a hundred other topics.
Some of the bulletins are free, some have a price; and
the list is available from the Education Section of the
Soil Conservation Service.

The SCS is pioneering. And—rare among Government
employees—its workers have the quiet eagerness of men
who know that they are getting great results. In just a
few years more they may be able to halt our appalling
soil destruction and put the nation's food sources on a
permanent basis.

Chief of the SCS is H. H. Bennett. With him was W.
C. Lowdermilk as "Associate Chief" until Lowdermilk's
recent retirement. The two of them had been with the
organization since its beginning, and with its forerunners
for many years before that. Both Bennett and Lowdermilk have seen their work in its long-time perspective.
I mentioned them in the chapter "Prospects for Posterity."

It would not stand to reason that all the thousands of
hypotheses and inventions that have gone into soil con-

servation had stemmed from just two men. Yet I like the fact that Lowdermilk in his 33-page booklet *Conquest of the Land Through Seven Thousand Years* gives definite credit to farmer J. Mack Gowder, of Hall County, Georgia, for originating the revolutionary soil-saving practice of stubble-mulch farming; that is, leaving old crop litter on the surface instead of burning it or plowing it under.

It seems to me that Bennett and Lowdermilk are among the most fortunate of men—in the fact that, seeing a great need for a far-reaching change, they have been able to reform a nation's thinking to implement that change. Under their eyes and in their charge their dreams are coming true, and a vast land that was bleeding to death is having its wounds closed while there is yet time. Rare is the reformer who lives to see the fruit of his reform and knows the fruit is good.

And we, as heirs of Bennett and Lowdermilk, are fortunate too, in the hope for a future that would be impossible without the work that they are guiding.

The FOOD AND AGRICULTURE ORGANIZATION (FAO) is composed of representatives of the governments constituting the United Nations. It holds a world conference annually to review food conditions, and maintains a council of representatives of eighteen governments for action between the annual conferences. A technical staff, headed by a director-general, constitutes a permanent core for the institution.

The FAO assembles facts and publishes statistical data.

But we must not expect the FAO to accomplish its announced objective of "balancing food and people," and we must not expect it to live up to the purpose expressed in its constitution of "raising levels of nutrition and standards of living of the peoples. . . ." Since the organization proceeds on an assumption that the ratio of people to food can be purposefully modified only on the *food* side of the ratio, the FAO has, in effect, already declared bankruptcy.

And even in the stopgap objective of increasing food supplies it rests its program in large part on the usual fallacy that "modern production techniques" in terms of seed drills, combines, and milking machines can enormously increase food totals. The error of FAO thinking on that point is set forth in the chapter "It's a Small World."

There is validity in its minor objectives of overcoming animal diseases, increasing crop yields through increasing the use of improved seeds and breeds, extending erosion control and reforestation.

If we write off FAO's pretense of balancing food and people, we can evaluate favorably its more moderate achievements and prospects.

The FAO is not the only agency of the United Nations which gives attention to numbers of people. UNESCO is another. Those initials mean UNITED NATIONS EDUCATIONAL, SCIENTIFIC AND CULTURAL ORGANIZATION. And one U. N. body, the POPULATION COMMISSION, concentrates in this field. It investigates problems arising out of quantity of population in relation to resources, problems arising out of growing and declining populations, and problems arising out of migrations. Its work thus far, however, has been of small significance.

Also in conservation work is the UNITED STATES FOREST SERVICE. I have already called your attention to some aspects of the service of the Forest Service. Longer than any other Government body it has been guarding the public interest as that interest relates to resources. With conservation consciousness on the increase, we can hope for more co-operation with Forest

Service efforts—both in legislation, and in personal carefulness.

•

Now I report organizations which give attention to human heredity.

The AMERICAN ASSOCIATION ON MENTAL DEFICIENCY has its office at Mansfield, Connecticut. The purpose of the Association is to study causes and prevention of mental deficiency. There are an annual meeting of the Association as a whole and sectional meetings in eight regions. A quarterly, *The American Journal of Mental Deficiency*, priced at $4 a year, is edited by Dr. Edward J. Humphreys, State Office Building, Columbus, Ohio.

The AMERICAN EUGENICS SOCIETY, Room 1404, 1790 Broadway, New York 19, has membership dues of $3 per year to $100 per year. The Society is primarily informational. Four times a year it publishes *Eugenical News*.

The AMERICAN GENETIC ASSOCIATION has an office at 1507 M St., N.W., Washington 5, D. C. It seems to have as its primary function the publication of a monthly journal entitled the *Journal of Heredity*. Dues, which include subscription to the *Journal*, are $4 per year for residents of the U. S., though subscription price without membership is $5 per year.

The AMERICAN SOCIETY OF HUMAN GENETICS, after preliminary meetings in 1947, was formally organized in 1948, with Dr. J. H. Muller of Indiana University as President, and Dr. H. H. Strandskov as Secretary. The Secretary's address is: Department of Zoology, University of Chicago, Chicago 37. (His courses there include "Human Genetics" and a seminar, "The Genetics of Human Populations.")

Already there is a considerable membership from the fields of anatomy, anthropology, biochemistry, child development, cytology, economics, genetics, immunology, medicine, pathology, physiology, psychology, psychiatry, and sociology.

The second annual meeting was held at Hotel Governor Clinton, in New York City, on December 28, 29, 1949. The scholarly *American Journal of Human Genetics* was launched in 1949. Editor is C. W. Cotterman of the University of Michigan. Membership dues, including subscription to the *Journal,* are $8.00 per year.

This next entry reports an individual philanthropist rather than an organization. He is C. M. GOETHE, 720 Capital National Bank Building, Sacramento, California.

Mr. Goethe is the author of at least two eugenics books. Occasionally and rather frequently he publishes *Eugenics Pamphlets.* Those are distributed mainly to college libraries and classes. Each pamphlet presents a great number of separate facts showing the importance of human heredity. The materials are written up in a leisurely yet concise style.

The HUMAN BETTERMENT ASSOCIATION OF AMERICA, INC., 2 East 103rd Street, New York 29, N. Y., is engaged in research and the education of the public in the field of selective sterilization. It is supported by voluntary contributions.

This society was organized in April 1943 as "Birthright, Inc.," changing to its present name in June of 1950.

Mrs. Marian S. Olden, its founder, was its dynamo until about the middle of 1948.

The Human Betterment Association of America is national in its membership. Its president is Dr. H. Curtis Wood, Jr., well-known Philadelphia obstetrician. Miss Irene H. Armes is Executive Director. Medical Director is Dr. Fred O. Butler. While he was Superintendent and Medical Director of the Sonoma State Home, in Eldridge, California, before his recent appointment to his present position, Dr. Butler had performed or supervised approximately 5,000 sterilization operations.

Thirty-six publications relating to eugenics, genetics, and sterilization are available from the organization's headquarters, and are announced in a catalog which is furnished on request. Publication No. 5 is a folder showing which states of the United States have sterilization laws, and reporting the number of persons sterilized under the laws of each state. A 1950 inclusion in the catalog is "Human Sterilization — Techniques of Permanent Conception Control," a 40-page illustrated study by Robert L. Dickinson, M.D., and Clarence J. Gamble, M.D., intended primarily for surgeons, social workers, and teachers, and yet interesting and understandable to the general reader. Its bibliography contains 355 entries. Another recent addition to the list of publications available from the society is a reprint of an article by Moya Woodside entitled "Sexual and Psychological Adjustment after Sterilization." Mrs. Woodside interviewed 48 married women who had been sterilized. She found that these women were happier; that they were freed from recurrent anxiety about pregnancy; that sexual and marital relationships were felt to be much improved; and that the physical relief from constant childbearing was important. She concluded that sterilization had conferred great practical and psychological advantage to the group as a whole, and in a number of cases could have been even more constructive if undertaken earlier.

Other publications distributed by the Association report that estimates of mentally deficient persons in the United States vary from 1,400,000 to 2,000,000, and that only about 8% of these are in institutions; that maintaining public psychiatric hospitals, institutions for the feeble-minded, and various other services for defectives costs over a billion dollars a year; that a large proportion of the feeble-minded reproduce at much more than average rates; that there is a considerable degree of correlation between juvenile delinquency and mental inadequacy; that during part of World War II the cause of 1 out of 4 rejections by our Selective Service was mental disease or mental deficiency.

The publications of the Human Betterment Association comment that no court will knowingly allow a child to be *adopted* by feeble-minded or insane persons, yet no restriction is put on the number of children which feeble-minded or insane persons may have by birth except in those states which by law provide for sterilization.

They show that more than half of our states and Puerto Rico now have sterilization laws and that about 50,000 persons have been sterilized under those laws. (Incidentally that *total* for the U. S., as Nils von Hofsten shows in the *Journal of Heredity* for September 1949, is about the same as the *yearly* number would be if we had the sterilization *rate* that Sweden has.)

The Human Betterment Association publications show that for either man or woman closing a pair of tubes one-eighth of an inch thick yields full security from pregnancy and that sterilization involves no other alteration than such closure. No organ is removed. In most cases there is no change in sex response; in a few persons it is lessened; in more it is intensified.

In California one institution for mental defectives released a number of selected sterilees. Except for the sterilization they would have had to remain in the institution—at an estimated cost of $650,000 annually.

The Human Betterment Association of America advocates:

1. Selective sterilization as the most immediate and effective method of checking the increase of those least qualified to exercise the privilege of parenthood.
2. A continuous state census of all mental defectives similar to the census in South Dakota where every feeble-minded person is made a ward of the state. This program of social control has for its purpose the proper care of every mentally defective person and the prevention of, either by segregation or sterilization, his or her procreation.
3. Vocational and other training to enable sterilized defectives to support themselves and to live in the community so that they may acquire a sense of self-respect as useful members of society.
4. Supervision or parole, as in California, for two or more years, of sterilized individuals to assist them in adjusting to their work and to the community.

The research program of the Association includes a legal and sociological study of sterilization in Europe and the United States. Dr. Philipp Weintraub of Hunter College has completed the first section of the program with a comprehensive investigation in Norway and Sweden. Plans are now under way for publication of his findings.

Medical education on sterilization is under the direction of Dr. Butler and the Medical and Scientific Committee, headed by Dr. Dickinson and located in the New York Academy of Medicine. This phase of the Association's work covers instruction for the medical profession, preparation and presentation of scientific papers, field visits to state institutions, exhibits at national conventions and regional conferences of organizations in allied fields, and consultation with groups requesting assistance in the formulation of sterilization laws.

In June 1950 the Human Betterment Association of America started a periodic *Newsletter,* compact and neatly printed. It is mailed to members without charge.

THE HUMAN BETTERMENT FEDERATION, founded in October 1949, has headquarters at 512 Ninth St., Des Moines, Iowa. The Federation is the coordinating organization for Human Betterment Leagues in five states, with addresses at

2521 Fifteenth Avenue South, Birmingham, Alabama;
P. O. Box 174, Augusta, Georgia;
512 Ninth St., Des Moines, Iowa;
P. O. Box 184, Lincoln, Nebraska;
P. O. Box 3036, Winston-Salem, N. C.

All these leagues have been formed since 1946. Their chief objective is to decrease the transmission of hereditary handicaps, by encouraging the voluntary sterilization of persons with such handicaps. To accomplish this they distribute pamphlets and reprints of scientific articles pointing out the hereditary nature of certain diseases.

The ROSCOE B. JACKSON MEMORIAL LABORATORY, Bar Harbor, Maine, is a biological research institution which studies the influence of heredity and environment in experimental animals. Its year-round staff of 75, including 12 outstanding scientists, are studying cancer, abnormal growth, and animal behavior. Presumably their studies will be revealing of human behavior too. The Laboratory is headed by Dr. C. C. Little, formerly president of the universities of Maine and Michigan.

North Carolina's EUGENICS BOARD, by January

1, 1949, had administered a total of 2,152 sterilizations. That organization is on the front line of the battle for civilization.

North Carolina is not the most active state in weeding out its defectives, however. Its 1949 rate was 6.4 sterilizations per 100,000 people, whereas Virginia's rate was 6.9. The rates for that year for some of the other states were:

Iowa	6.2
Delaware	6.1
Georgia	5.2
North Dakota	3.8
California	3.6
New Hampshire	2.6
Utah	2.1

These rates are only a start. They offset only a fraction of the current additions to the crop of people with weak heredity. Feebleminded persons constitute not less than 1% of the population; so, for example, in North Carolina, with about 112,000 births per year there are at least 1,120 feebleminded births, yet sterilizations in 1949 numbered 249, and even of the 249 about a fourth were a safeguard against insanity rather than feeblemindedness.

Comparable with North Carolina's Eugenics Board is North Dakota's STATE COMMISSION FOR THE CONTROL OF THE FEEBLE-MINDED. Probably there are similar organizations in the rest of the 24 states whose laws are, in some measure, enforced. Those commissions and boards are parts of the state governments.

The DIGHT INSTITUTE FOR THE PROMOTION OF HUMAN GENETICS was organized as a part of the University of Minnesota (Minneapolis 14, Minnesota) as a consequence of an endowment by Charles Fremont Dight, M.D. Under the Institute's former director,

Dr. Clarence P. Oliver, it has sponsored lectures, initiated a file of records, maintained a consultation service, published occasional studies, somewhat technical. Under the new director, Dr. Sheldon C. Reed, the genetic counseling is continuing, and the educational functions of the organization have been expanded. For its research activity it has received from the Carnegie Institution the largest collection of human pedigrees in America—that which was built up in the Eugenics Record Office at Cold Spring Harbor, N. Y.

The University of Michigan, at Ann Arbor, maintains a LABORATORY OF VERTEBRATE BIOLOGY, and in it an HEREDITY CLINIC which is open to the public, and the services of which are without charge. The Clinic is in close co-operation with the University Hospital and the School of Dentistry, and works with any other units on the campus which are concerned with human heredity; also with other state institutions and with private physicians, social workers, and others.

Dr. Lee R. Dice is Director of the Laboratory and the Clinic. Says Dr. Dice:

"We maintain a record office for families covering traits that are or may be hereditary. Most of our records are of Michigan families, but we do not stop at the state line. However, we are unable to offer advice on heredity unless the members of the family concerned are able to come to Ann Arbor for examination. We are convinced that hearsay evidence is not satisfactory as a basis for advice in such a difficult field."

Dr. Dice continues:

"It is evident as a result of our experience at our Heredity Clinic that most families are very much interested and concerned with their heredity, especially if it is known that there is some serious defect in the family which is suspected to be inherited. We are convinced that a tremendous amount of progress in the elimination of bad heredity from the population could be achieved if the families and their physicians could be given proper advice. . . . Every large center of population should in my opinion maintain an heredity clinic and record office, supported at public expense. . . ."

The program of the Laboratory includes studies of the role of heredity in the development of human traits: studies of diseases and abnormalities; of antigens, especially those produced in the blood groups; of dental characters; of speech pathology, anthropologic characteristics, and mental traits. There are also included studies of frequencies of blood-group genes in human population. Several studies have been published in scientific journals by members of the Laboratory staff.

In the Heredity Clinic the groups of related persons on record total over 1,200.

In the University of Utah, Salt Lake City 1, is a School of Medicine, and therein is a LABORATORY OF HUMAN GENETICS, with Dr. Fayette B. Stephens in charge. The purpose of the Laboratory is to study a wide variety of disorders which have hereditary bases. Dr. M. M. Wintrobe of the Laboratory's staff wrote me:

"We seek to accumulate as much information as possible about the inheritance of these disorders by tracing family histories, examining as many persons as possible and checking their family histories by the use of blood groups. In the Laboratory of Human Genetics the heredity data are preserved permanently where they are available to doctors and members of the families concerned."

OTHER LEADERS, besides persons connected with the above-named organizations, are Dr. Lawrence Snyder, Dean of the Graduate School at the University of Oklahoma, Dr. D. C. Rife at Ohio State University, Dr. Nash

Herndon at the Bowman Gray School of Medicine, Winston-Salem, North Carolina, Dr. Herbert M. Stecher, City Hospital, Cleveland.

•

The MALTHUSIAN LEAGUE is English, with headquarters at 107 Crescent Road, London, N. 22—but a lot of Americans are members. It was founded in 1877. Its object is "to promote understanding of the economic and evolutionary doctrines of Malthus and Darwin and of the necessity for restricting reproduction, especially of the least healthy and capable individuals. . . ." It publishes *The Malthusian,* an 8-page monthly magazine, 7½ by 10 inches, jam-packed with news and comment. Membership is $2 a year and includes the magazine; a separate subscription costs $1 a year.

The MARGARET SANGER RESEARCH BUREAU, 17 West 16th Street, New York 11, received its present name in 1942. It was founded in 1923, by Margaret Sanger, and for nearly 20 years was known as the Birth Control Clinical Research Bureau. The Bureau has given contraceptive information to over 130,000 women; interviews each year between 20,000 and 30,000, of whom 5,000 to 6,000 are new patients. Director of the Bureau is Margaret Sanger. Its Medical Director is Abraham Stone, M.D. There are also an Associate Director, an Assistant Director, an Executive Secretary, 25 staff physicians, 10 full-time nurses, and 5 secretarial and clerical assistants.

The Bureau trains senior and graduate medical students in contraceptive techniques, and holds seminars for staff physicians from contraceptive clinics. Harvard,

Yale, Long Island College, and Bellevue Medical Schools send their senior classes for lectures, demonstrations of techniques, showing of films, observation, and training.

Research includes, for examples, tests on the effectiveness and suitability of various contraceptive techniques, degree of fertility during menopause, use of plastic cervical caps, analysis of delayed menstrual periods.

An infertility service, and marriage counseling, are other activities of the Margaret Sanger Research Bureau.

Another fact-finding group works under the name MILBANK MEMORIAL FUND, 40 Wall Street, New York 5. The organization publishes a quarterly bulletin at $1 a year. That has been an important source of information about the differential birth rate.

The PLANNED PARENTHOOD FEDERATION OF AMERICA, INC., endeavors to bring to the attention of the public the need for making parenthood a matter of deliberation rather than of accident, and it maintains clinics to make its objective socially possible.

The Planned Parenthood Federation has a periodical: the *News Exchange,* which is a monthly newsletter, at $1 a year. I have referred to *News Exchange* frequently in the foregoing chapters. The Federation also sends out folders and pamphlets, some at a small price, and some free. More than 2,000,000 copies of its literature have been circulated within the last five years.

According to information from the Planned Parenthood Federation, contraceptive services and fertility services are available in the U. S. mainland in

> 231 Public Health Department units
> 60 hospitals
> 214 extramural clinics
> 45 referral stations.

In six states, birth-control services are a regular part of

the state public health maternity care programs, namely Alabama, Florida, Mississippi, North Carolina, South Carolina, and Virginia. Texas has taken a first step.

The extramural clinics are most active. The main reason for the comparative inactivity of the public health offices and the hospitals is that, in parts of the country where the Catholic clergy has a leverage, they force the public health offices and the hospitals to conform to the policies of the Pope.

There are 55 fertility services located in 19 states and the District of Columbia, to help persons who desire children but who have seemed to be infertile.

Not all of the service centers record the religion of the patients. Of those who do, the approximate proportions of patients are:

Protestant	54%
Catholic	27%
Jewish	18%
Other	1%

Church membership of the general population runs about

30%	Protestant
18%	Catholic
3½%	Jewish
48%	nonmember

The figures showing religion of the clinic patients, since they specify no nonmembers, appear to report preferences—not necessarily membership. The figures do not disclose, of course, what proportions of the various religious groups have previously been practicing birth control, or what proportions get their information from private physicians, or what proportions remain helpless.

The Planned Parenthood Federation of America, Inc., has as its Honorary Chairman Margaret Sanger, a stalwart Joan of Arc who pioneered the movement out of the dark ages at the beginning of the century into its present high state of respectability and influence. The Federation is an associate member of the *National Health Council* and the *National Conference on Social Work.* Its child-spacing program has been officially recognized by the *U. S. Public Health Service,* which will provide funds in this connection at the request of state health officers in the same way other health requests are met.

Sponsorship of planned parenthood includes church groups, medical talent, health officials, and a great variety of social welfare organizations. A resolution calling upon churchmen to work for planned parenthood services in every community has been signed by 3,600 clergymen from all the states. The principles of planned parenthood have been endorsed by

American Unitarian Association
Central Conference of American Rabbis
Committee on Marriage and the Home of the Federal
    Council of the Churches of Christ in America
General Council of Congregational and Christian
    Churches
Lambeth Conference of Anglican Bishops
Regional and state conferences of the Methodist
    Church
House of Bishops and House of Deputies of the Protes-
    tant Episcopal Church
Rabbinical Assembly of America
Universalist General Convention.

The American Medical Association in 1937 adopted unanimously a report of its Committee to Study Contraceptives, which report recommended the teaching of contraception in medical schools. In an extensive survey of physicians, Dr. Alan F. Guttmacher found that 96% of the physicians of the country approved contraception under at least some conditions. Medical organizations which have endosed birth control are:

Section on Obstetrics, Gynecology, and Abdominal Surgery of the American Medical Association

American Gynecological Association

American Neurological Association

American Medical Women's National Association

National Committee on Maternal Health

Arizona State Public Health Association

Florida State Public Health Association

State Medical Societies of at least 15 states.

Says the U. S. Public Health Service to its personnel executives:

"The counselor should refer married women workers with special problems to the medical service or a private physician for advice on the proper spacing of children as a means of protecting the health of the mother and her children."

Hundreds of social organizations have passed resolutions supporting planned parenthood. They include

American Association of University Women

American Civil Liberties Union

American Eugenics Society

Business and Professional Women's Clubs, State and local

Child Welfare Committee of America

General Federation of Women's Clubs

National Council of Jewish Women

National Women's Trade Union League

Parent-Teacher Associations, State and local

State Conferences of Social Work

Y. W. C. A., National Board

Women's International League for Peace and Freedom

I was planning to include here the addresses of the 530 birth-control clinics in the country, but they would take too much space. For a dime you can get the *Directory of the Planned Parenthood Clinic Services* from the *Planned Parenthood Federation of America, Inc.,* 501 Madison Avenue, New York 22, N. Y. You might ask at the same time for their *List of Publications.* That is free, and tells of about a hundred printed items available from the organization.

The purposes of the POPULATION ASSOCIATION OF AMERICA, INC., as set forth in its certificate of incorporation, are "To promote the improvement, advancement and progress of the human race by means of research with respect to problems connected with human population, in both its quantitative and qualitative aspects, and the dissemination and publication of the results of such research. . . ."

"The Association cooperates with the Office of Population Research, Princeton University, in the publication of *Population Index,* a quarterly annotated bibliography of books and articles in the general field of population, together with statistical tables presenting the most recent data concerning birth, death and marriage rates, life tables, population estimates, etc., and brief comments on items of current interest. Members of the Association receive *Population Index.*"

The editors are Frank W. Notestein, Irene Barnes Taeuber, and Louise K. Kiser. *Population Index* probably comes nearer to tying together the scattered threads of population knowledge than any other source of information.

Membership in the Association is open to individuals who are interested in advancing its purposes. Dues are three dollars per year. Application for membership should be addressed to the Secretary, Dr. Henry S. Shryock, Room 2029, Bureau of the Census, Suitland, Md. Applications are passed upon by the executive committee.

The Association has an annual meeting in May. The membership gets an opportunity in advance to vote on topics for discussion at an annual meeting.

The POPULATION REFERENCE BUREAU is located at 1507 M Street, N.W., Washington 5, D. C. It was founded in 1929 by Guy Irving Burch, as a non-profit, scientific, educational organization for the purposes of gathering, co-ordinating, and distributing population data. Its distinguished council is composed of Frank H. Hankins, Willford I. King, Clarence C. Little, Edward A. Ross, Karl Sax, Joseph J. Spengler, Stephen S. Visher, and A. B. Wolfe. Guy Irving Burch is Director of the Bureau. Its Treasurer is Robert C. Cook—whose book on population, I understand, is scheduled for publication in the fall of 1950. The Secretary is William Vogt, author of the best seller *Road to Survival.*

Mr. Burch was coauthor with me of *Population Roads to Peace or War,* which was published by the Population Reference Bureau in 1945, and republished by Penguin Books, Inc., in its Pelican series in 1947 as *Human Breeding and Survival.* Penguin Books, Inc., is now *The New American Library of World Literature,* 245 Fifth Avenue, New York 16, N. Y. *Human Breeding and Survival,* by Burch and Pendell, is in the pocket-size series and is priced at 35c. Here are a few quotations from people who have read it:

The *United Nations Councillor* said about it:

"Without population limitation, there will never be freedom from want and security from war. The authors present comprehensive evidence, disprove many demographic fallacies, and suggest how population information should be extended through the UN agencies."

A Sacramento businessman: "More than ever am I impressed with the fact that herein lies the way to lessening the frequency of war."

H. L. Mencken: "It is an excellent book."

A California social worker: "Rereading the book, one realizes more than ever that here is the one revolution that matters."

The wife of a college professor: "I think this is one of the most important books written in many years and one whose subject has been near to my heart and mind ever since doing welfare work and seeing the futility of much of it. . . . It seems to me that 90 percent of the problems discussed today could find their solution in your book."

A professor of life science: "The book . . . is in my opinion one of the most significant that has ever been published."

Miami, Florida, *Herald,* January 25, 1948: ". . . the single most important new book now published in this country. . . ."

Those and the hundreds of other favorable appraisals of that book are deeply gratifying.

The Population Reference Bureau publishes the *Population Bulletin,* of which Mr. Burch is editor. Each issue presents one or more special topics. These topics illustrate:

America's Manpower in the Postwar World
Needed—Higher Birth Rate Among Scientists
The Tremendous Waste of Births in India
Puerto Rico, a Miniature India
Differences in Birth Rates
Level of Living of Earth's People
Puerto Rico—A World Population Laboratory
World Food Crisis—"Temporary" or "Chronic"?
Birth Rates and Education
America Takes Stock of Its Resources
Differences in Growth of Earth's People
Is American Intelligence Declining?
Can America Support a Multiplying Europe?

America's Displaced Persons
Speculations in Population Growth

Primarily, the bulletins of the Population Reference Bureau are intended to supply population information to newspapers, and the substance of every issue is widely redistributed in that manner. But many readers want more regular and complete reports than the newspapers give, and so they subscribe directly. The subscription price is $1 per year.

Another active organization working for reasoned reproduction rather than the old fashioned accidents is the VOLUNTARY PARENTHOOD LEAGUE, INC., 1211 Madison Ave., New York 28. It has 3,500 enrolled endorsers. Mrs. George Engelhard is Treasurer.

•

There they are—more than two dozen organizations that have population significance. Several of them would welcome your membership or your subscription to their publications. It is your cause they are sponsoring.

Chapter 11

Parenthood Should Be Planned

"You are Cordially Invited to Attend the Eighth Annual Meeting of the Virginia League for Planned Parenthood, Inc. . . . Second Baptist Church and The Jefferson Hotel, Richmond, Virginia."

I guess I'm a member of that organization; anyway I paid some dues to it. Let's notice what is on the program. First a joint session with the Richmond Ministerial Union, at the Second Baptist Church, the Reverend Frederick J. Warnecke to preside, and Dr. Leland Foster Wood, Secretary of the Federal Council of the Churches of Christ in America, scheduled for an address on "Marriage and the Home." Then there is to be a business session, at the hotel, and a board meeting dinner, with the Reverend Carter H. Harrison presiding. He is Vice President of the Virginia League for Planned Parenthood. An evening session is arranged, for a round-table discussion, with Dr. Hudnall Ware, Jr., presiding. Topic for that discussion: "Responsible Parenthood in Relation to Delinquency."

It looks well worth-while!

I'm glad those planned parenthood groups changed their names from "birth control" societies; the present names are better to show the balance of objectives. Members of the League for Planned Parenthood believe that families ought to have a reasonable number of children; that's one objective. But they believe that a family ought not to breed like animals, with no thought of the consequences; that's the other objective. Of course, for a family to plan its parenthood program effectively, it has to know and practice birth control.

What is birth control?

Normally, we are told by biologists, a man produces at least two hundred million microscopic pollywog-like spermatozoa per week. That's enough for one lone man to repopulate the whole world with the spermatozoa output of less than three months, if each sperm cell could engage in the man-sperm-man cycle. But even under conditions favorable to that cycle, almost all of them swim out their brief lives uneventfully. Even under favorable conditions only about 12 spermatozoa, in a man's lifetime output of half a trillion of them, ever become anything but long-tailed tadpoles. The half trillion figure may be found on page 118 of Amram Scheinfeld's *Women and Men,* a Harcourt, Brace & Company book of 1944.

It puts quite a strain on reason, don't you think, to attribute a religious glorification to those tiny biological creatures? Surely they are wonderful; the whole reproduction process is wonderful. But about 499 billion 999 million 999 thousand 988 of a man's output of the brainless little wigglers live and die without mating. Should we be concerned that nine more of them must join that great majority in order that human beings may live in comfort?

The glands which produce the spermatozoa also produce a hormone—a chemical. Family life involves more than reproduction. The hormone which I have referred to has, as one of its *psychological* results, sex desire. Thus there is a chemical basis—a biochemical basis—for sex desire.

There are limits to the number of people that can live on earth, and much nearer limits to the number that can live in a manner we think appropriate to human beings. It is only with a practice of some sort of birth control that people can afford education, or medical conveniences, or in fact anything at all above a bare subsistence. With a complete absence of birth control even that bare subsistence is available to some people only because many others do not get a subsistence, and so die early.

If, without birth control a man should have 12 children, then even without birth control all but 12 of his estimated half a trillion sperm cells would live their short and uneventful lives without being part of the man-sperm-man cycle. It is not typical—it isn't normal—for one of those little sperm cells to be in a man-sperm-man cycle. But if we would make the living conditions favorable for human beings, we must frustrate about nine more of those sperm cells, so that the ratio of cells that actually complete the cycle will compare with those that do not complete the cycle as 3 compares with 499,999,-999,997.

George W. Corner, in *The Hormones in Human Reproduction,* a 1943 book put out by Princeton University Press, makes graphic the size of a sperm cell. It is really tiny! Though it is only one cell, it is shaped like a head with a tail. Two thousand five hundred of the heads laid like bricks in a pavement would be required to cover the period at the end of this sentence.

The usual birth-control procedure includes putting a thin layer of rubber in a position which prevents the spermatozoa from swimming to a region in which they might cause trouble. Sometimes, instead, some chemical is placed where those little tadpoles come in contact with it, and are immobilized—200 million of them at a time. Of course, all but one out of a month's output of at least 800,000,000 would have been immobilized anyway in a short time, because, once they have a good place to swim they rather rapidly swim away all their energy. One of the most widely recommended methods of birth control involves the use of both a chemical and the rubber wall.

It so happens that an ovum is in an area where it can be reached by a sperm cell for only a few hours; then this pin-point egg disintegrates. After that, until the next month's ovulation, no matter how many spermatozoa may be swimming in that area, there can be no pregnancy. That is the so-called "safe" period. But it isn't very safe. There are too many uncertainties.

So none of the state-operated birth-control clinics in North Carolina recommends the "safe" period method, otherwise called the rhythm method of birth control; it fails too often. I don't think any birth-control clinics, either publicly or privately financed, in other states, recommend it either, though most are ready to convey information about it on request.

In the problem of birth control we are confronted with an alternative. Are we to agree to the inclusion in the man-sperm-man cycle of eighteen more billionths of 1 percent of those little single-celled aquatic animals—with a correlated reduction of the life span for human beings to 27 miserable years—or, in contrast, are we to promote a life span of 65 years for human beings, letting the additional eighteen billionths of 1 percent of the spermatozoa go unmated?

Members of the Virginia League for Planned Parenthood believe that where the welfare of humanity requires the celibacy of nine more tadpoles in each half trillion of them, they'd better be kept away from the ova.

Chapter 12

Priestly Rationalization

"Doctors Hear Priests Score Birth Control"

That headline was in the *Cleveland Press*, Thursday, October 16, 1947, on page 4. In the article which followed it, Walter Lerch reported that Rev. Fr. Francis W. Carney, in an address before the Catholic Physicians' Guild of Cleveland, classed contraceptives as immoral. The Rt. Rev. James McDonough followed, saying, according to the news account, that the Catholic Church opposed contraceptives but is not against a reasonable form of birth control such as the natural rhythm method.

About the time of that meeting of physicians, a friend of mine sent me a little pamphlet by the Reverend Daniel A. Lord, S.J., entitled "What Birth Control is Doing to the United States," 10th printing, August 1946, with "Statistics and other factual data revised and brought up to date for seventh edition by Dr. Clement S. Michanovich." It was printed by The Queen's Work, Inc., 3115 South Grand Boulevard, St. Louis 19, Missouri. Judging from the number of printings, it is probably reaching many thousands of people.

The "S.J." following Rev. Mr. Lord's name means that he is a member of the Society of Jesus, a Jesuit organization within the Roman Catholic Church. I understand that the details of reasoning in such a brochure do not necessarily represent the thoughts of other Catholics, but that they are likely to carry a lot of weight. The Rev. Mr. Lord is editor of the Catholic magazine *The Queen's Work*.

Let's see what the reasoning is in that pamphlet.

In "What Birth Control is Doing to the United States," its author attributes the success of the birth-control movement to "the selfish element in every human being" (p. 3). The basic ideas seem to be (1) that in sex relations there is a yielding to selfish desire; (2) that except for birth control the yielding to selfish sex desire would result in unwelcome children; (3) that if one does not know birth-control technique, he will be prevented from yielding to the selfish desire, prevented by the prospect of acquiring unwelcome children.

Is sex desire selfish? What difference does it make? It is like hunger, in that whether selfish or not, everybody has it. As to fulfilling the desire, that is comparable with eating, and in practice, whether selfish or not, most married people do it.

Author Lord seems to imply that if people know birth-control techniques, they do not exercise restraint from sex relations. He seems to say that people who do not use contraceptives *must* exercise restraints or else there will be too many babies, and so they *do* exercise the restraint.

But in actual life the *must* is not followed by the *do*. From the standpoint of the general welfare, and often of their own welfare, (1) persons without birth-control information *do not* exercise restraint on enough occasions, and (2) not enough of them exercise restraint. In other words, among persons who are ignorant of birth-control methods, there are, in any one year, too many fathers.

Particularly that is true among persons whose offspring are most likely to be social liabilities.

The practical result of the sex satisfaction of married people is that some of them do harm to society, and some of them do no harm. Are the people who practice birth control the ones who do harm—in their sex activity—or are the ones who do not practice birth control the trouble-makers? The evidence in this book is abundant on that problem. Some people do harm by practicing birth control too much—having fewer children than they should. More people do harm by having more children than they should—in other words by not practicing birth control enough. If a couple have extra special qualities, problem-solving abilities, for instance, *and* can furnish a good environment for children, they could ordinarily do more good by contributing to the heredity of the future than by putting all their efforts on improving the environment of the present. If a couple have *ordinary* qualities, and can furnish only ordinary environment, they ought to have fewer children than the present average, because the present average makes for too much growth of the total population. If a couple have *less* than ordinary qualities *or* less than ordinary environment, they do harm by having any children at all. Of such parents there are too many. And the question is applicable: if one, however well-intentioned, stands in the way of their getting birth-control knowledge, does one's action amount to a participation in the harm they do?

The question of whether or not birth control permits a larger fulfilment of selfish purpose is irrelevant to the public welfare; the glaring fact is that *without birth control there is enough gratification of sex desire to bring about wars and malnutrition and a variety of other harms.*

•

Plato and Aristotle are mentioned by Author Lord as having been worried by the prospect of overpopulation, but now after 2,300 years, he says, overpopulation has not yet developed. If they were right, says Lord, we should expect overpopulation to be actually threatening by this time. But Texas and South America and most of South Africa and Canada and our western states are, as he thinks, evidence to the contrary. And he makes the wild assertion that Texas alone could feed the entire United States.

It appears that the wise men of ancient Greece probably had basis for their concern about overpopulation. During most of those 2,300 years Greece has been an area of misery, because of overpopulation—and it is such right now. On September 11, 1947, the Greek economist, Demetrious Calitsounakis, stated before the International Statistical Conference that the Greek economic situation is a problem of *too many people per arable acre*.

And Europe as a whole, for most of those 2,300 years, has been recurrently ravaged by famines and wars.

Europe had a golden age, after the discovery of America, an age of relative abundance, especially in the 19th Century. Some writers attribute its prosperity to the fact that many people left Europe for the New World, and that products of the rich new continents went back. Some think the agricultural improvements, and the Industrial Revolution, account for the better living conditions. All of those developments must have been causative. But the population has continued to grow, and now overpopulation not only shows "some signs of being imminent"; it is all but overwhelming!

The Industrial Revolution might go on much further, but it involves an increasing complexity of organization that stifles freedoms, on the one hand, and on the other hand requires more brains than are available. And the New World isn't new any longer. Aid to Europe, under arrangements obtaining in 1950, being without recognition of overpopulation as the heart of the problem, is likely to have disastrous results.

The statement that Texas alone could feed all of the United States seems to ignore completely the scarcity of water and the law of diminishing returns. Even if it could be true, the level of living it would require is that of the Russian prisoner camps.

Author Lord implies (pp. 7 and 8) that God has been taking care to see that there has not been any real overpopulation. But let this be kept clear: that since wars, disease, famine, and malnutrition are the major *processes* by which overpopulation has been reduced, Lord's implication, in effect, is that God is the perpetrator of those most oppressive evils in all human experience—and that, in America, He is instigator of the gentle art of contraception.

But why, Rev. Mr. Lord, attribute them to God? It is *men* who engage in the sex activity that makes the overpopulation, *men* who struggle on death-strewn battlefields for scarce resources, *men* who contaminate the air and the water supply with their disease germs; *men*, too, who have the opportunity to make those scourges less likely by using contraceptives. We might reasonably say that the responsibility for overpopulation is on the people themselves, and "ignorance of the laws" of population does not relieve the people from the suffering involved in the violation of the laws. They, in their uncontrolled response to sex impulse, make a degree of overpopulation and thus bring the conditions that lead to war and disease and famine and malnutrition. The people themselves, when they exercise foresight, tend to avert overpopulation by practicing birth control.

Putting the analysis in objective language, the population pressure itself, as it reaches a stage of some intensity, leads people to go to war to protect their livelihood;

population density itself makes for the spread of disease. Where people are so numerous in relation to resources that they have nothing to turn to when something goes wrong, they starve. As an alternative to the evils of slum conditions and starvation people must practice birth control.

What constitutes overpopulation? Overpopulation is a condition in which long-run average productivity is lower than it would be with fewer people. If we think in terms of avoiding war, disease, famine, and malnutrition, the 2.3 billion present inhabitants of the earth constitute a substantial overpopulation. Allowing for a usual amount of clumsy organization, bad judgment, weather upsets, etc., the conditions for happiness would probably be better with a stationary population of about 1,600,000,000. Of course some areas, like China, India, Japan, and Italy, and our own Puerto Rico, are *tremendously* overpopulated.

•

Urban people always tend to die out, whether or not birth control is practiced, says Lord. Others are brought in from the rural areas "to save the cities." Cities need no birth control for their destruction; that is just one means of annihilating them, added to other means. So says Author Lord.

It is true that both the positive and the preventive population checks, of which Malthus wrote, have their greatest impact in the cities. Wars are most destructive there, disease spreads more readily there than in rural areas, starvation takes its greatest toll in the places most removed from food production. And, as to the preventive

check, people marry later, or not at all. It is the considerable degree of overpopulation in the cities that brings
about those results. Birth control in the cities is an added
means of wiping them out, only in the sense that it is *an
alternative* means of keeping their numbers in check—to
the extent that it is used. The "recruiting" of city
dwellers from the rural districts makes birth control more
imperative by congesting the housing conditions, making
rents higher, and transportation and trucking costs more
severe.

In connection with city conditions the alternatives can
be vividly seen: either there will be sprawling slums in
which people live in squalor and die young and in misery,
or there will be a widespread practice of birth control.

•

How birth controllers can assert that there are world
shortages of food in the face of surpluses of food, Author
Lord (p. 10), and perhaps some of his readers, do not
readily see. "Cuba is snowed under by its sugar," for
example—and if we had more people in the United States
to eat the sugar, thinks Lord, the Cubans would be more
prosperous.

The economic relationships are truly complex; I'll do
what I can to clarify them. To start with, why don't the
Cubans (or our own Puerto Ricans—they are in a still
worse plight) sell their sugar to the Chinese? There are
lots of people in China, and they haven't been eating
much sugar, probably not a tenth as much per capita as
the people of the United States eat. The reason is that
the Chinese are so numerous, in relation to their active
resources, that they are working under conditions of diminishing returns, so their productivity is low. Their

productivity being low, they can't afford much sugar. If
the people of the United States were more numerous,
diminishing returns in agriculture, and diminishing resources of timber and minerals, would reduce their productivity too. If we increased our numbers in some relatively small measure, we might increase our total demand
for sugar, and thus increase the price of it for the Cubans
and the Puerto Ricans, but we would at the same time
reduce our own level of living somewhat. And foreign
people who depend on our lands for foodstuffs would be
forced to eat less. If we increased our numbers to match
the Chinese, the chances are that there would be an
actual reduction in our total demand for sugar, and both
the sugar islanders and we should suffer. If Author Lord
is desirous of keeping up the demand for Cuban sugar
he will have to advocate birth control in the U.S. at a
stage of population moderation which will permit the
level of living to include sugar.

It is frequent that specializers produce more than the
market can take at prices above costs. In the sugar islands,
and particularly in Puerto Rico, the part of the costs that
goes to laborers as wages gives them only a bare subsistence. Then why do they stay in sugar production? Because, considering the amount of land available to them,
they would run a risk of getting still less in any other line
of production.

The way out of their misery is not to increase the population elsewhere, but to reduce their own birth rate, so
that their per capita production can be greater or their
total specialized production less in relation to demands
for it.

England is discussed by Writer Lord (pp. 14-16) as a land threatened with depopulation, showing a "deficit" in reproduction. If fertility remains unchanged the population will soon reach its height and will then soon decline at the rate of 24 percent in every generation.

The reproduction rate did change. It increased, so that by 1947 the birth rate was just about enough for replacement of the numbers in the reproductive age groups. But that is probably temporary: a postwar bulge. In the longer sweep it is probable that the trend reported by Lord and the men he cites will continue for awhile, possibly until the approximately fifty millions now in England and Wales have declined to the 17,685,000 predicted for the year 2000. Lord thinks of that as "alarming," but, as a quantity matter, what's alarming about it?

Englishmen have been getting their living only in part from the mines and the downs of the homeland. Investments scattered all over the wide world gave Englishmen a right to goods. The empire is breaking up, and four-fifths of the investments were drained away in the titanic struggle so recently ended. And anyway, the overseas lands in which Englishmen sold finished goods and from which they acquired raw materials have been developing their own manufacturing establishments. The outcome has been clear for decades now. Average income in England would have to decline, or else England's population would have to recede.

Malthus analyzed today's situation a hundred and thirty years ago, when England's population was only about 10,000,000. In a passage already cited in Chapter 2 he discussed a contemporary's idea that Europe ought to let America grow its grain while Europeans devoted themselves solely to manufacturing and commerce. But even

"if by such means Europe could raise a population greater

than its lands could possibly support, the consequences ought justly to be dreaded."

The populations would grow in the new lands, Malthus pointed out, and they would eventually develop their own manufacturing.

"But when upon this principle America began to withdraw its corn from Europe and the agricultural exertions of Europe were inadequate to make up the deficiency, it would certainly be felt that the temporary advantages of a greater degree of wealth and population . . . had been very dearly purchased by a long period of retrograde movements and misery."

For England World War I was the beginning of the long period of retrograde movements and misery. England and Wales together are only as big as Michigan, but they have seven times as much population. England has less than an acre of land per person, less than enough to produce enough food to keep 50,000,000 Englishmen alive.

Martin Ebon quotes Group Captain Wilcock of Derby, speaking in the English House of Commons:

"I suggest that it is the duty of the government to decide whether this country can carry a population of fifty million. It is interesting to remember that at the time of our greatest prosperity our population was about thirty million."

And even for those thirty million, the English were depending heavily on foodstuffs from outside of England and were depleting the coal supply on which England's export trade depended.

England will have to reduce its numbers very substantially, or else put up with a level of living much lower than that to which Englishmen have been accustomed. Probably they will take a little of each—and the birth-control process will greatly reduce the misery of the transition.

To contrast with birth-control-minded England, writer Lord says (page 17) , "let's take two Catholic countries," and he presents Ireland and Italy.

Ireland, practically barren of mineral resources, must live almost entirely on its annual production from soil and muscle. Yet, with a little less than six acres per capita, the Irish earn a level of living that compares well with that of the most nearly prosperous of the European countries. Ireland has attained its relatively high degree of well-being by two auxiliaries to its industriousness. First, it has, for many years, exported a stream of migrants approximating about a fourth of its number of births. (But not many doors now remain open to migrants.) Second, its citizens have used the Catholic clergy's own form of population control; that is to say, an unusually large proportion of Irishmen refrain from marriage. Some of those refrain only for a few years, however.

To renounce sex relations for fifteen or twenty years beyond puberty must require a lot of determination, and so that course must be limited to individuals stronger than average. However conducive to single-minded leadership may be the practice of celibacy by either clergy or laity, one may well raise a question of its result on the quality of average heredity. It fits in with the antisocial differences in birth rates at least as dangerously as the more conventional birth-control methods do.

The present well-being of Ireland as contrasted with the distressed condition of England can hardly result from the differences in their present birth-control methods, but seems primarily to depend on the fact that England, fattening as she was on the products of other lands, practiced her birth control "too little and too late," whereas Ireland, goaded by the famine of the 1840's, was earlier to apply her Malthusian wisdom. Ireland must refrain from reproduction still more rigidly, however. Not for long can she find a place for the fourth of her people that have customarily been sent abroad to be fed. Either her birth rate or her level of living must inevitably decline. It is anybody's guess as to whether marriage age will go up still higher, or the rhythm will become a more popular gamble, or contraceptives will have a wider distribution, or waistlines will become smaller and cheeks more haggard.

●

Lord's brochure on page 17 reports a birth rate for "Catholic Italy" of 23.7 per 1,000 and a death rate of 13.8. Its population increases more than 300,000 per year. "And Italy moves ahead."

One could wish that the Italian story had been told more fully. If few Italians are practicing birth control we might expect a higher birth rate than 23.7—more like China's 40, or the 55 of early America.

But 23.7 is much too high for Italy's "state of life," and her past birth rates have been much higher. Forty-six million people are sardined on 76 million acres. Seventy million acres are in agriculture, which averages about an acre and a half per capita—much of it not very productive.

The Italian level of living is not much above that of the Orientals now, and must necessarily go lower than it is.

"Italy moves ahead," says Rev. Mr. Lord. Toward

what? For Englishmen there is hope; for Italians there is hardly a chance. The main difference in the prospects depends on their contrasted attitudes on birth control.

•

Japan, we are informed (p. 17), had an average, for the period 1935-1939, of 29.7 births per 1,000 population, and 17.4 deaths. Russia's rates were 44.1 births and 20.2 deaths. These misery generators are cited with a "go thou and do likewise" implication.

And now that birth control finally is getting a hearing in Japan, the Catholic press and Catholic clergy in Japan are fighting the movement even there. So clear it is that Japan's invasion of China and her role in World War II resulted largely from her overpopulation, we can hardly avoid the conclusion that the hierarchy favors war as a method of keeping population and resources in balance. The clerical opposition to Japanese birth control is reported in *The Catholic Universe Bulletin*, published in Cleveland, in the issue of June 3, 1949, page 12.

Of course I should not be surprised; the Catholic clergy has always wanted more and more souls to be available for saving. A condition of poverty and misery of people on earth is unimportant, as I understand their other-worldliness, if it conflicts with their objective of processing more and more souls. So it is better, by Catholic clergy standards, to have innumerable babies born, even if they can live only in famine conditions and most of them for only half a dozen years, than for fewer to be born and live in happiness. India, with its 27-year life span, conforms more closely to the Catholic clergy standards than the U.S. does with its 65-year life span, because India's reproduction patterns make more souls available for saving.

If and where scantiness of resources in ratio with population leads to war rather than to starvation, nevertheless the large population is desirable from the Catholic clergy standpoint, because it is in the direction of gratifying the priestly hunger for more souls.

I have made a distinction between the Catholic clergy and the Catholic laity, because I think that not very many of the laity go along with the clergy in their heartless orientation. Catholic laymen are not supposed to do any independent thinking on such matters, but apparently a brain is something that acts, whether invited to or not. The fact that Catholic women attend birth-control clinics in about the same proportion as the proportion that they constitute of the population is evidence of their practical adaptation. A *Fortune* poll I shall report a few pages farther along is additional evidence.—Watch for it.

Don't misunderstand my excursion in this section. Author Lord does not in so many words advocate either war or famine. Nevertheless he does attempt to crowd more and more people into the bus, and he persistently rationalizes about plenty of room at the rear, though it is perfectly plain that every seat is taken and people are unavoidably jostling one another in the aisle. To attempt any earth-based justification for more population in Japan is nothing short of ridiculous!

Birth rates for the U.S. are reported as 55 per thousand of the population in 1800; 17 per thousand in 1940. Suppose there had been no practice of birth control in the United States; suppose the action of Americans had been 100 percent in accord with economics-writer Lord's prescription. Would the results be what he would like? Would they be what you should like?

If the United States as a whole had, for the last hundred years, followed the course he prescribes, as to birth control—and had followed his prescription for restraint only as well as it has—the population in this country would probably have increased at the rate of 35 percent per decade, as it did in the early 1800's, and so would probably be 450 millions. The death rate would be high; the level of living would be low. If, right now, the United States were to adopt that no-birth-control attitude, at that same rate of increase, in a mere 40 years the United States, instead of its present 151 million inhabitants, would have about 475 million. That is not a projection from the aforementioned 450,000,000; it is what would happen in your own lifetime, starting now, with 151,000,-000 inhabitants of the country, if we were all to follow Rev. Mr. Lord's anti-birth-control prescription. Colleges, and automobiles and airplanes, and bathrooms, and telephones, and radios, and other "semiluxuries" would be scarce.

In still another 40 years, if all the U.S. continued to follow the no-birth-control attitude, those semiluxuries would have disappeared, and since the computed billion and a half of people would be utterly impossible, the death rate would have risen to the level of the birth rate, and the average age of death would probably be, as in India, about 27 years.

Obviously, writer Lord's advice against birth control could not be given general application without dooming us and our descendants to a hell on earth. The basis of that hell: too many people! And leading toward that hell, the Rev. Daniel A. Lord, S.J.!

•

The next point which the little pamphlet takes up is age distribution. If the birth rate falls off, the *proportion of old people* will be larger. Their own number will be no larger, but there will not be so many young people on whom to draw for their old-age benefits.

Of course; but we have to face that condition sometime —unless we keep packing the people in till they reach an Asiatic level of living.

And one thing in favor of Grandpa, as a dependent, is that you don't have to send him to college.

But actually, with a low birth rate there would be less likelihood that Grandpa would be a dependent. There would be fewer young persons against whom an oldster would have to compete. In such a competitive condition more old fellows could take care of themselves.

Not only that, but with a lessened pressure on scarce resources, the production processes would extend not so far down the scale of diminishing returns; average productivity would tend to be greater.

•

Lord admits a soaring abortion rate. Dr. Christopher Tietze, at the 1949 meetings of the Population Association of America, reported on 363 cases of abortion done in 1948 by two abortion specialists in a large Eastern city. Of the 363 women for whom the abortions were performed, 102 were single, 180 were married, and 81 were previously married. About half of the 81 previously married women were widows, and half of them were divorced. A large proportion of the married women had had two children before the abortions. Sixty-five women were repeaters; 14 reported two previous abortions, and 8 reported three or more. The cases seem to indicate that many of the women used abortion as a means of limiting the size of their families.

Vera Connolly, in *Colliers'* for January 22, 1944, voiced the widespread conclusion that the solution of the abortion problem "for married women, is country-wide contraceptive education."

•

On page 28 of Rev. Mr. Lord's interpretation of "What Birth Control Is Doing to the United States," he recognizes the differential birth rate and attributes it to the advocates of birth control.

The support for that position is an array of examples of the usual differences of birth rates—unaccomplished fathers having the most youngsters per capita.

Consider: in 1850, if the subsequent hundred-year span of birth control could have been foreseen and compared with an alternative century of large families, which would have been chosen? If Annie Besant and Charles Bradlaugh, and the Drysdales, and John Stuart Mill, and Margaret Sanger could have clearly seen that their recommendation would have made more serious an already existing differential birth rate, would they nevertheless have been "birth controllers"? Assume that in making that judgment they would have been basing it entirely on the welfare of the citizenry of today. How would they have decided? Do you, halfway through the 20th Century, deplore what they did a century ago, and since then? Remember that the alternative would have been a present population more than $2\frac{1}{2}$ times what we now have— a population submerged in poverty and characterized by the ignorance that accompanies poverty.

But a present-day birth controller in the United States can know that his or her success against poverty and suffering is not in any measure offset by a loss in hereditary capacity. To the extent of his or her success there is gain, both against poverty and against low IQ average.

Let me try to explain that.

In 1,000 families on relief, 210 children were born, says Lord, citing a Metropolitan Life Insurance Company study of 1935. And to families with incomes over $2,000, 107 children were born.

A very large proportion of families with incomes over the 1935 purchasing power of $2,000 already know birth-control methods. That is part of what Lord's figures mean. The work of the birth controller is to try to get the information to the families of lower income.

In general, the better qualified a family is to have children the fewer does it have, as Lord agrees. Now let's take the other side of the situation which Lord's booklet reports:

The *less well*-equipped the parents were to bring children into the world and give them their opportunities for success, the *more* likely were they to have children.

These less well-equipped parents and prospective parents are the ones that the birth controllers are trying to reach. It is clear, then, that the work of the birth controllers, to the extent of its success, will make for better opportunities for America's children by reducing the proportion of children in homes where the opportunities are scantiest.

Lord reports some deplorably low birth rates of college graduates, and of people in *Who's Who*. And he says that the immigrant and underprivileged families are keeping up America's "appearance of a stable population."

How can he talk of an "appearance of a *stable* population" when the country's *increase* in a ten-year period is enough to populate an area twice the size of New England?

But he doesn't mean a *stable* population; he means an

expanding population—the immigrants and the underprivileged are keeping our population expanding. Lord
means that the ignorant people are having most of the offspring. And that, I agree, is a deplorable fact; deplorable
in that the ignorant ones are having too many offspring,
and also in that the accomplished people are having too
few. But remember the evidence in our chapter "Joe
Martin is a Bachelor": the birth rates of educated folks
are as low as they are partly because of the conditions
caused by the too many births in the uneducated families.
So actually the birth controllers, to the extent that they
are successful in reducing birth rates of the uneducated
people, tend to *prevent* the fall in the birth rates of the
educated.

Birth control has been dysgenic; *is* dysgenic—because
it is practiced mostly by the alert people, whose shortage
of offspring is part of the explanation for the present low
level of average intellect. But with birth control in use
by alert people, any *extension* of its practice does constitute a eugenic advance, because it reduces the excess of
births of the nonalert in comparison with births of the
alert.

The persons who are now making the alert members
of society a smaller proportion of the total are not the
birth controllers but those who resist the birth control
movement: Rev. Mr. Lord, for example, since he tends
to prevent those nonalert people from reducing their
birth rates.

•

In the sociologist's outlook, conforming to a ritual is
not necessarily moral. What is moral depends in part on
expected results. Morality is conformity with practices

which are generally thought to have long-range social
benefits in excess of harms.

Is birth control moral?

Yes; it is generally thought to have long-range social
benefits in excess of harms. *Fortune,* August 1943, page
24, bears that out. The survey question was:

"Do you believe that knowledge about birth control
should or should not be made available to all married
women?"

The responses from women classified as indicated were
as follows:

	All Women	College Women	Grammar School only	Catholic Women
Should be available	84.9%	92.6%	70.2%	69.0%
Should not _____	10.0	4.9	18.2	24.4
Don't know _____	5.1	2.5	11.6	6.6

Of course the public is often wrong; some things are
moral which are actually correlated with a preponderance
of harm. But the public is right about birth control, particularly if it is extended so that it will have a chance to
reduce the antisocial differences in birth rates.

There are occasional other instances in which the
papal position against birth control and sterilization, if
not "damned by faint praise," is at least made suspect by
inconsistent support. In *The Sign,* "National Catholic
Magazine" for October 1947, is an article by C. J. Enzler,
in which improved use of soil is presented as a complete
and sufficient measure for solving the problem of population pressure.

Mainly Enzler's remarks relate to the U.S., and his position depends heavily on a quotation from former Secretary of Agriculture Clinton P. Anderson. Anderson had said that we have about three and a third acres of good crop land per person, whereas 2½ acres is a necessary minimum; and Anderson had said that if our population levels off short of one hundred and seventy millions, there will still be about 2¾ acres of crop land per person in the United States.

Enzler's argument that we need not give any attention to the birth rate to preserve that favorable land-man ratio depends solely on Anderson's assumption that the population will level out by itself while it is still in a favorable ratio with the crop land.

That assumption by Anderson, adopted by Enzler, is an essential part of Enzler's argument. Now note well that Anderson's assumption as to when the U.S. population will cease to grow is really a rewording for *the rate at which the practice of birth control has been increasing.* So Enzler's argument that we do not need birth control really depends on the assumption that we are going to have an increased use of birth control!

Almost in so many words Enzler has said that we need not advocate birth control because birth control will be practiced anyway.

In recognizing that the welfare of the country depends on an early leveling off of its population, Enzler has, in effect, declared ethical bankruptcy for the Pope's position. And since Enzler depends on that leveling off of population, and thus depends on the increased use of birth control, his protestation against birth control really amounts to this: "I've got to write against birth control, but I hope not many people follow my advice; if they do, we'll be in one awful fix!"

Chapter 13

There Can Be Acres for All

In Chapter 4, "Nightmare on the Isle of Dreams," I reported the hunger-punctuated level of living which, under U. S. guardianship, has been the chronic plight of most Puerto Ricans. We Americans hold ourselves forth as leaders of the world, but we must excuse those who smile at our smugness or accuse us of hypocrisy, since we have failed so miserably with the only economic problem we have had which compares in difficulty with those that confront most of the world.

In part the inadequacy of the U.S., as mother hen to Puerto Ricans, lies with Congress, yet the Administration has usually attempted to give the cues to Congress, so both have responsibility. Want in the Island, and news about it, must be embarrassing to an Administration that is trying to represent the U.S. as a messiah to other suffering regions. Of course there is a way out of the want and so a way out of the embarrassment.

It was shown in Chapter 4 that over 600 inhabitants per square mile constitute an adversity that no amount of fuss-budget concern with superficialities can counter-act. Of Puerto Rico's 2,176,000 acres, about 1,000,000 acres are suitable for tillage. With the population at 2,200,000, there is less than half an acre per capita. Since the land area of the Island is definitely limited, and the man-land ratio is in constant focus, none of the subter-fuges of rationalization which are usual elsewhere will serve in Puerto Rico. People *have* to admit the popula-tion cause of the poverty if they lay claim to reason at all.

Then why hasn't the Puerto Rican poverty been ap-proached in terms of its cause? Now at long last is a change in prospect, or is the Administration planning to continue sweeping the dirt under the rug? We shall have an answer, I think, in 1951.

To open up the subject of policy for Puerto Rico I use an article by Dr. Christopher Tietze, an M.D. who has made valuable studies concerning reproduction and contraception. He has been a research associate of the National Committee on Maternal Health. He is one of those who has dug out materials which, by showing Puerto Rican poverty to be controllable, has put Puerto Rico in the limelight. Recently he has become an em-ployee of the U.S. State Department. That is why I think Truman's hand will be revealed in 1951. The questions in their immediate significance sum up in this: Did the Government hire Tietze in order to use his knowledge, or did it hire him to gag him?

"Human Fertility in Puerto Rico," Tietze's article which I use as a springboard for discussion of policy for the Island, appeared in the *American Journal of Soci-ology* for July 1947, published by the University of Chi-cago Press.

In reporting the ups and downs of Puerto Rican birth control, Dr. Tietze has made much use of a paper by

Mrs. Carmen de Alvarado, a leader in the Island birth-control movement.

Dr. Tietze tells us that the first birth-control organization in Puerto Rico was started in 1925 in the city of Ponce, under the leadership of Dr. José A. Lanauze Rolon. Its purpose was education and propaganda. "Vigorous opposition on the part of the Catholic church was immediately encountered, and the organization soon ceased to function."

In 1932 two birth-control clinics were started, one in San Juan, the other in Mayaguez, but both were short-lived.

In 1935 Miss Gladys Gaylord, executive secretary of the Cleveland Maternal Health Association, visited Puerto Rico and convinced the officials of the Puerto Rico Emergency Relief Administration (PRERA) that they should include in their activities a program for contraception. A pilot clinic was set up at the School of Tropical Medicine in San Juan, under Dr. José S. Belaval. Soon after that beginning, 53 clinics were established in various parts of the Island. But in December of 1935 the PRERA was discontinued. It was followed a month later by the Puerto Rico Reconstruction Administration (PRRA).

The PRRA set aside $225,000 for maternal health. Depending on money from that fund the birth-control clinics were organized again.

"At this juncture, stiff opposition developed in Catholic circles which had political repercussions in the United States, and shortly before the national elections the maternal health services of the PRRA were abruptly stopped."

A private organization, supported by philanthropy, the Association for Maternal and Infant Health, soon stepped into the breach and maintained birth-control clinics until in 1940 the Insular Health Department established a birth-control program which resulted from Law 136, passed in 1937.

With regard to that law, we should have in mind the governmental structure under which Puerto Rico's laws are made. The general legislation of the Congress of the U. S. applies, but as to that legislation its scope is limited by the U. S. Constitution. However, Congress has power to legislate for Puerto Rico as if Congress were its state legislature. In that role the Congress can legislate over a broader scope. By Puerto Rico's Organic Act (which takes the place of a state constitution) legislative power has been conferred by the U.S. Congress on the locally elected legislature.

Law 136, passed in 1937 by the Puerto Rican legislature, authorized the officers in charge of the institutions supported by the Island government or a city government to request the Island's Board of Eugenics for sterilization for persons within certain classes, and it empowered the Board of Eugenics to decree their sterilization. It empowered the Commissioner of Health to establish contraceptive clinics. Says Dr. Tietze:

"The law enumerated the reasons for which instruction in contraceptive methods could be given, including not only a long list of medical indications but also 'economic poverty and bad social conditions.' Opponents of birth control held that the new law was in conflict with federal legislation. Because this accusation interfered with the opening of clinics by the Health Department, the Asociacion Pro Salud Maternal e Infantil asked for a test case in the courts, and the president, Mrs. Torres, insisted that she be indicted. Judge Robert A. Cooper on January 19, 1939, upheld Law 136 with the exception of that section which recognized the economic and social indication."

Thus Law 136 is partly validated and partly void—partly void because a law previously passed by the U.S. Congress stands in the way.

The United States, bungling benefactor, has never done anything for the Puerto Ricans which gave the slightest chance of long-range improvement of their economic condition. Fifty years ago we barged into the Caribbean in a state of indignation that the Spaniards were misusing the subjects of their decaying empire. After half a century of muddled self-righteousness, and in spite of a cost to the U.S. taxpayers of more than a billion dollars, there is plenty of reason for the conclusion that U.S. control has not in the slightest measure raised the level of living or the level of happiness of Puerto Ricans.

The drift which we have encouraged in poverty and hopelessness might be attributed to callousness on our part. It isn't exactly that. Callousness is hardness, and indifference. Those do not characterize the average U.S. citizen or the average member of Congress either. But the average citizen and, I think, one hundred percent of our Congressmen have avoided the use of clear-cut logic in the problem. Even those who engaged in Congressional investigations cloaked over the issue with a fog of emergency suggestions, doing nothing fundamental, actually leaving conditions worse than they found them.

And why have they been so painstakingly myopic?

Congressmen assume that, in matters on which the Catholic hierarchy has expressed itself, their Catholic constituency applies no independent reasoning; Congressmen know that though Catholics are a small percent of their constituency they sometimes act as a closely knit pressure group; and so Congressmen have thought it good politics to see no population problems anywhere.

And when finally the Puerto Ricans themselves rose to the heights of statesmanship and passed legislation better designed to solve their economic problems than anything else ever tried anywhere else in the world, they found themselves stymied by an act of the United States Congress.

The situation is not without irony. The legislature of Puerto Rico, nearly 100 percent Catholic, and representing an electorate almost entirely Catholic, finally passed an all-important population control bill. Their overlords, the U.S. Congress, are fearful of losing the votes of the 18 percent of their constituents who are Catholic, and so they, the U.S. Congress, sat in dazed helplessness while Puerto Rico's chance for prosperity slipped away as a consequence of a previous act of their own.

Are Congressmen playing wise politics in seeing no population problems? The polls reported in our Chapter 12 indicate that a large majority of mainland Catholics favor population control, and clinic records show that they come to the clinics for birth-control information in about the same proportion of the clinic patients as they constitute of the general population. But the issue at election time is not how they think or feel about such matters. Rather, the question is, Do you favor Candidate John Doe, or Candidate Richard Roe? If a Catholic layman's organization, under guidance of a priest, has disapproved Candidate John Doe, many Catholic voters vote against him without inquiring about the grounds for the disapproval. And, so far, few non-Catholic voters have given any weight to a candidate's position on population issues.

So, if a Congressman's vote margin is thinner than his portion of the Catholic segment of his district, perhaps he plays "good politics" in ignoring population problems. However, it may be well to remind him that the Catholic vote over the U.S. as a whole is only 18% of the total vote; and that, actually, some Catholic voters do think for themselves. Possibly some of the national legislators could afford a little statesmanship.

The Puerto Rican law of 1937, as it was formulated, would have permitted a frank and open attack on poverty. If it could have been that, it could have reduced the danger of the differential birth rate. But as an attack on poverty the legislation was invalidated because of a Congressional Act. However, on July 3, 1950, the President of the U. S. signed a bill giving to Puerto Rico the right to formulate its own constitution. Presumably, then, if the Island's legislature can again muster the courage it will be able to implement the struggle to a higher level of living, unhampered.

The 1937 law was upheld in its health phases, and the Puerto Rican Department of Health by the end of 1946 had established 163 public birth-control clinics. However, each instance of sterilization or of giving out contraceptive information must be in the interests of health or must be made to appear so. A forthright attack on poverty is illegal in Puerto Rico, by Act of Congress.

"That the population problem lies at the root of many of the island's difficulties has been recognized for a long time," says Dr. Tietze. "Community leaders in Puerto Rico are intensely aware of it."

And so, "for a long time" Puerto Rico has been ready for a thoroughgoing reformation, if Congressional enabling acts had been favorable and if somebody with the appropriate training — and the intestinal fortitude — could have been made administrator.

"It is known that contraceptive materials . . . have been imported and sold. . . . Their use has, however, spread only slowly beyond the ranks of the more prosperous and better educated. Organized efforts to promote birth control among the masses are a comparatively new development in Puerto Rico."

The differences in extent of use of contraceptives in different economic, social, and educational groups is a real problem. That is an important reason for the decline in the proportion of high-caliber heredity in a population—the tremendously serious "differential birthrate." And so what? Must we "let nature takes it course" and in this case be resigned to Puerto Rican starvation? Certainly not.

As a guard against the antisocial differential in the birth rate, it is not enough, in Puerto Rico, that only married persons be given the birth-control information, because marriage is less a prerequisite to reproduction there than on the mainland. The proportion of illegitimate parentage is very high. The out-of-wedlock sex relations are and have been considerable; the knowledge of contraceptives would prevent part of their antisocial consequences.

But even if 100 percent of adult Puerto Ricans were to become informed on birth-control methods, there would still be antisocial differences in birth rates. The less foresighted and more careless persons would still have more children than the foresighted and the careful would have. That means that, just as on the mainland, stupidity would tend to increase.

Marguerite N. King, in *Human Biology* for February 1948, had a study entitled "Cultural Aspects of Birth Control in Puerto Rico." Her observations of conditions in Lajas show reasons for the limited use of contraceptives.

"The principal obstacles," she said, "arise from the physical conditions in which the majority live, from cultural and psychological factors, and from the direct opposition of the Catholic Church. It is most probable that the same reasons apply as well to Puerto Rico as a whole."

She was specific about the material reasons: "Few fami-

lies have bath rooms," and there is even a scarcity of
water. "Parents and children share the same room; frequently one or more children sleep in the same bed with
the parents," so there is little opportunity for applying
contraceptives. Distance from clinics and drugstores is a
handicap too, for the rural population.

She also reported psychological reasons for the limited
use of contraceptives. I think they sum up as ignorance,
superstition, embarrassment, horror of being examined
by a male physician, and various weird notions of the
Jane Ace and My Friend Erma level.

•

Sterilization already has a comparatively good start on
the Island—partly because the facilities for rubber and
chemical contraception are often not available. Says Dr.
Tietze:

"According to the testimony of competent observers, the
possibility of avoiding further parenthood by an operation is more widely known among the Puerto Rican people than are more orthodox methods of contraception.
Furthermore, more women seem to be willing to submit
to the operation than are ready or able to practice birth
control with any degree of regularity. The operation is
usually performed twenty-four to forty-eight hours after
delivery and does not prolong the period of hospitalization. Statistics on the subject are scanty. In a group of
seven hospitals—five public and two private, located in
different parts of Puerto Rico—about 1,200 sterilizations
were performed annually during the last three years. The
total number for the whole island may be considerably
larger."

Investigator King found that "sterilization of women is the best-known method of contraception in Lajas," and that "all evidence indicates that it is equally popular throughout Puerto Rico." Evidently, many poor women look forward to sterilization as a means of escape from large families.

In a sample of 49 women, 10 spoke freely of sterilization. Five of the 10 asserted to questioner King that "they would undergo the operation if they found contraception necessary and if they could afford it." "In many cases," said Miss King, "individuals conceive the problem of having or not having additional children simply in terms of whether or not they can afford sterilization."

But those observations apply only to sterilization of *women*. Dr. Tietze found that:

"Very few men have been sterilized so far because of an unfounded but widely spread fear of an unsexing effect of the operation."

The superstition is unfortunate, but since it is completely false, I think it would yield to a persistent campaign of truth. Because of the simplicity of the sterilization operation on the males, they are the ones who, in most cases, should be sterilized.

For a man, the severity of the operation is no greater than having a tooth pulled, and no more dangerous. The effect is to prevent those microscopic sperm cells from leaving the body. They come into being as before, and the male hormone comes into being as before, so there is no change in sex desire or in the psychological effects of sex relations. The sperm cells, as they disintegrate, are taken up by the blood as impurities and thrown off like other waste tissue. Even in total, they normally constitute only a small proportion of the fluid in which they

swim. That fluid is not noticeably diminished in quantity by sterilization, but the microscope would show it to
be no longer a pollywog pond.

●

Whenever sterilization is discussed, a likely question is,
"How far would you go with it?"

In the *Woman's Home Companion* for April 1949,
Edith M. Stern had an article entitled "Should *Anybody*
Be Sterilized?" The implication was in the negative.
That article must have been written on the assumption
that there is food enough for the children of everybody
who is biologically capable of having children, so there is
no need to sort the liabilities from the assets. But since
there is not enough food for "all the world" and all the
children they would normally have, either we must limit
the numbers or else a lot of people are doomed to starve.
The alternative is there; we do not escape responsibility
by a laissez faire policy. And if we are going to limit reproduction we'd better do a little sorting.

Under the laws there are officials whose duty it is to
decide that an individual does or does not fit under the
classifications for sterilization. When Mrs. Stern refers to
those officials she says they "play God." But *by the social
pressures* through which we limit the offspring of ob-
stetricians to about half the general average number of
children of the women they aid, we have unconsciously
been "playing God" since our civilization began. And if
the social pressures against reproduction by accomplished
people are not a sufficient restriction of numbers—and
our attempted laissez faire policy results in mass starvation—in bringing about that result too we "play God."
In one way or another the results, good or bad, are of our

causing. Sterilization is a means by which results can be made more acceptable than the results of a supposed hands-off policy.

Is sterilization a democratic method of meeting the situation? If it is adopted as a policy by the people or by the representatives they select, I think it is. Essentially, democracy is government by the people.

I have pointed out that birth rates are in reverse of capabilities and accomplishments; that, in the harsh environment preceding a civilization, improvement of human quality takes place in spite of the birth rates because the most capable people, though probably having a relatively low birth rate, nevertheless have a high *survival* rate. But, as a civilization develops, the survival rate of capable people, in comparison with the survival rate of incapable people, is low. In the correction of the quantity troubles of a population, it makes sense to correct the quality troubles too—and in the same legislation. To see the simple quality-quantity connection, consider this pattern: *begin at the bottom; sterilize far enough up the quality scale to make the quantity no greater than is appropriate for the long-run drag on the food resources.*

In arranging the quality scale, are we to judge the *heredity* which one would transmit to prospective offspring, or the *environment* one would give them?

Of course all human behavior is dependent on heredity, and all of it is dependent on environment. Suppose the conduct of Mr. X is inadequate to meet his problems in a way helpful to mankind. To what extent such conduct depends on deviations from norms of heredity, and to what extent it depends on deviations from environmental norms, is not easily determinable. Usually there would be no point in coming to a conclusion about that anyway. Whether the influence of an habitual drunkard, or a repeating criminal, or an uncomprehending dullard, is via his chromosomes or by way of the example he sets, we know that children in his household have less than the usual chance of being good citizens.

If you fully realize that any children whom Social Liability X may have, tend to put pressure on other people to refrain from having children; and if you realize that, even so, the children of Mr. X make starvation more likely for somebody, I think you will vote sterilization for Mr. X.

The argument is sometimes advanced that in cases where society, rather than heredity, is the cause of a person's inadequacy, then the individual should not be the place for the corrective measures. Again, the part that the social environment plays, as compared with heredity, in causing the individual's inadequacy, is hard to measure, but even if the cause were entirely attributable to society, if sterilization is the workable way in which society's weakness can be corrected, then surely sterilization is appropriate.

•

Suppose Mr. X and others who are definitely liabilities in a crowded population are all sterilized. That action is suitable but not sufficient. There will be a great mass of people who will be about average. It is true that in a congested population even average people are liabilities, in the sense that they hamper others more than they help. Each would get along better if there were fewer of the rest. And we must realize that if all those average people reproduce without restraint the overpopulation will continue.

I assume now that we are in agreement that the population of 2,200,000 in Puerto Rico should be and is to be reduced, by curtailment of birth rates, to 1,000,000, and then kept at that figure.

That objective would be attained if the Puerto Ricans were to pass a law which would provide, with exceptions, the sterilization of every Puerto Rican male now living who has one or more living children or who hereafter becomes father of one living child. It might be provided that in any case where the father is unknown the mother is to be sterilized.

I recognize the validity of the reasoning that the "only child" is usually in a less helpful environment than multiple offspring are if they have the same economic advantages, but in Puerto Rico's extreme distress the "one child" status is a small price to pay for the accompanying benefits. With that status prevailing, parents would possibly co-operate in the care of their children, and if so, the children would have the advantage of playmates as well as improved economic advantages.

Since, presumably, those individuals who would be definitely unsuitable parents are to be excluded from parentage entirely, the citizens could allocate by vote the quota of those to persons of outstanding achievement at the time of the legislation, and to persons who developed special promise before the due date for their sterilization. Thus, offspring, particularly multiple children born after the passing of the law, would become badges of special honor. In that fact there would be a revision of incentives, which would act as a corrective for the present adverse differences of birth rates.

As the citizenry declined in numbers to a figure near the 1,000,000 established as a goal, slight modifications could be made in the population control law, with a view to maintaining the appropriate ratio of land to population, and to improving the quality of both.

Chapter 14

Aw! Gordon! Let 'Em Get Married!

Time, September 15, 1947, page 16:

"In rural North Carolina, 2068 brides and grooms
waited and waited while the state supreme court weighed
the legal status of the justice of the peace who had married them."

Time! Don't *do* that! Why keep *us* waiting? What was
his status? Didn't he have a right to marry them? Are
they married, or not?

But far more important to North Carolina, and the
country as a whole, than the legal qualifications of that
justice of the peace to perform the marriage *ceremony*
are the qualifications of the officers who issue marriage
licenses. Once a license is granted, somebody is sure to tie
the knot. There is little responsibility on the marrying
official. Marrying parsons and justices of the peace are
expected to hitch Lena the Hyena and Mortimer Snerd,
if they present a license and say "I do." No consideration of hereditary results or environmental handicaps is

expected to stand in the way after one pays his fifty cents for the license.

The *licensing officer* does have some legally imposed duties. In states in which a blood test is required as a protection against syphilis, the licensing officer has to see the physician's certificate before issuing the license. In North Carolina (where live those 2,068 married folks of whose status *Time* left us in doubt) , the licensing officer also has a duty to require that a candidate for marriage be free of T.B. In Maine and Pennsylvania and Indiana the licensing officer is supposed to be sure, as a prerequisite to issuing a license, that the candidate is not a pauper.

In a few states the issuer of a license is duty bound to see that a candidate for matrimony is not a drug addict. In other states he cannot (within the law) give a license to a drunkard.

Some of the states have complicated requirements for marriage—but whether or not complicated they ought to be *severe,* and they ought to be administered with wisdom. The legal qualifications of licensing officers, and the conditions under which they work, can be important as safeguards for the quality of future generations.

The licensing officers should be few enough so that the collection of information concerning candidates, the issuing of licenses, and the keeping of records, can be their entire work, in order that they can know their duties and their responsibilities. Failure to use due care in the investigation of the qualifications of applicants for marriage should be grounds for a licensing officer's discharge.

There is a considerable amount of literature on the prerequisites to marriage, and their bearing on social conditions. John Stuart Mill included a section on the subject in the chapter on "Wages," in his *Principles of Political Economy*. Marriage of persons on relief "appears to be everywhere prohibited." In Norway, a man who married had to convince the person who conducted the ceremony that he had a fair prospect of supporting a family. In Wurtemburg a man could marry only if he could prove that he and his prospective wife together would be able to establish themselves; in Mecklenburg, they had to have a dwelling. At Lübeck a man had to prove that he was regularly employed; at Frankfurt the government prescribed no age for marrying, but "the permission to marry is only granted on proving a livelihood." In several of the cantons of Switzerland there were heavy fines for persons who married without previously proving to the magistrate of their district that they were able to support a family. The minister at Munich is quoted as saying "the great cause why the number of the poor is kept so low in this country arises from the prevention by law of marriages in cases in which it cannot be proved that the parties have reasonable means of subsistence."

In line with those laws that J. S. Mill reported, is a bill introduced in 1949 in the Pennsylvania Legislature by Representatives Albert E. Madigan of Bradford, and Edward W. Tompkins of Cameron County. Their proposed law would prevent issuance of a marriage license to a man on the state public assistance rolls.

The institution of marriage has been, in part, a social regulation of reproduction, and as such it has large possibilities connected with the problems of population.

Our laws have been giving attention to age—getting the youngsters to wait until they are old enough to take on adult responsibilities. In the past I have approved such provisions, on the ground that they reduce the period of exposure to unplanned pregnancies. Take the case of Carl Harvey Blake, Jr., of Michigan. He and his wife were pictured in the Ohio State *Lantern* for April 6, 1949. Carl, age 13, is already a father.

However, the minimum age requirement for marriage is not so important to society if the candidates have a knowledge of birth control.

Of course, birth-control knowledge should be a requirement for a license for *any* marriage in which the woman is under 50.

Four states refuse marriage licenses to habitual criminals—and why not? If criminals are such because of environmental influences, a law against their marriage saves society from more criminals by making criminals a less likely part of the environment of children. If criminals are such because of heredity, a law against their marriage saves society from more criminals by discouraging their reproduction.

With the same approach as the legislators of those four states, the Reverend Gordon Smee of Australia made a statement which prompted the title of this chapter. Please pardon the informality of the wording, Rev. Mr. Smee.

The learned clergyman was convinced that the "steady increase in the number of people of moronic intelligence can be checked only by forbidding the marriage of person who, although subnormal, cannot be certified as insane."

I think, however, that it would be all right for criminals to marry, and for drunkards and dope addicts, and paupers, and morons, and ignoramuses, and insane persons, to marry, if they will have no children: in other words, if they get sterilized as a prerequisite to getting a marriage license. *The enforced nonmarriage seems to be an unnecessarily harsh way of preventing reproduction—and not a very reliable way.*

I agree thoroughly with the conclusion of those legislators and of Reverend Mr. Smee that such people ought not to reproduce. Those are the ones who would be eliminated, for the most part, in the absence of civilization. Elimination of such misfits constituted the upward climb of evolution in the long eons before a civilization. To preserve a civilization, too, we must sort out those people who are social burdens. The rough measures of the wilderness are not necessary, but a rule against their having offspring is indispensable.

But what should be most considered is that *denying* reproduction to persons who make no contribution to the welfare of mankind would *stimulate* reproduction by those who would still have the right to reproduce. The reason is that having children would come to be evidence of the qualities which are made prerequisite to having children. The children would be evidence of approved parent qualities which are not directly seen.

The sort of people that are to make up the citizenry of tomorrow is so important socially that *we must make matrimony the occasion for a thorough sorting on a basis of reproduction qualifications;* we must require higher qualifications for the right to have two children than for having one; and higher qualifications for the right to have three children than for having two. Remember, in considering this, that the stiffer the requirements are, the greater is the incentive to reproduction by the persons who can meet the requirements.

There ought to be a law . . . ! What I want is that a state — *any* state — apply the psychology of keeping up with the Jones to the problem of reproduction. The Joneses are those who are patterned after, and if they are the only ones who can have a large number of children, they'll have them, and other people will want as large a flock as they can qualify for. Your own state might be the one to pioneer the change. I have confidence that the results will be so convincingly beneficial that other states will follow, perhaps improving on the details.

The sort of law I think necessary would be something like this:

In view of the influence of marriage laws on crime, slums, taxes, prosperity, quality of neighbors and of citizens, and on the continuation of civilization itself, it is hereby enacted

1. That no marriage have validity except as it follows a license.

2. That licensing officers be few enough so that the collection of information concerning candidates, the granting of licenses and the keeping of records, can be their entire work, in order that they can know their duties and their responsibilities.

3. That the licensing officers be on salaries and not on a fee basis. If on a fee basis the licensing officer might be tempted to grant a license when to do so would be contrary to the public interest. He would also be tempted to neglect the collection of information and the keeping of records.

4. That no woman under the age of 50 years, or man of any age unless he marry a woman over the age of 50 years, be given a license to marry, unless he or she give ample evidence, either by a physician's certificate, or in an examination conducted by the licensing officer or a member of his or her staff, that the

person is well informed in contraceptive technique. That this limitation be not applied if the candidate for marriage is sterilized.

5. That no woman under the age of 50 years, or man of any age unless he marry a woman over the age of 50 years, be given a license to marry, except as she or he, or her or his prospective spouse, is employed at a net return per month which is at least as high in purchasing power as that of $100 in July 1950, with a reasonable prospect of continuing to be employed at a return at least that high. That this limitation be not applied if the candidate for marriage be sterilized, or if, on any other ground, a convincing case is made before a designated responsible administrator who certifies his conviction that no social burden will result from the marriage.

6. That no person be given a license to marry except as he or she presents to the licensing officer a physician's certificate evidencing (a) that he or she has had a blood test and such other tests as are necessary to disclose venereal disease; that he or she has no venereal disease, or, if he or she has, it is not in a communicable form or a form that can become communicable; (b) that he or she has no other serious disease.

7. That no woman under the age of 50 years, or man of any age unless he marry a woman over the age of 50 years, be granted a license to marry except as he or she pass an (name of test) I.Q. test with a grade of 90 or more, and except as he or she pass, satisfactorily, examinations demonstrating an education at least equivalent to that which an average student would acquire in six years of schooling, the examinations to be administered by a board set up for that purpose. That this limitation be not applied if the candidate for marriage is sterilized.

8. That no woman under the age of 50 years, or man of any age unless he marry a woman over the age of 50 years, be granted a license to marry, if he or she is an habitual criminal, habitual drunkard, or a drug addict. That this limitation be not applied if the candidate for marriage is sterilized.

9. That no woman under the age of 50 years, or man of any age unless he marry a woman over the age of 50 years, be granted a license to marry if the person be, through heredity, blind, deaf since early infancy, dumb, deformed in serious degree, epileptic, or insane. That every candidate for marriage be examined for these characteristics by an approved examining board, and that the licensing officer be not authorized to issue the license except as a favorable certificate from the said board is in his possession. That these limitations be not applied if the candidate for marriage is sterilized.

10. That any unmarried person who engenders a child, or who becomes pregnant, shall be examined by the licensing officer and the other officials above designated, concerning his or her eligibility for marriage, and if he or she is not eligible, except if sterilized, he or she shall be sterilized through arrangements made by the licensing officer to prevent a repetition of society's misfortune. It shall be the duty of any physician or nurse under whose care the person comes, and of any state, county, or city employee learning of the circumstances, to report such cases to the licensing officer.

11. A person entering this state from another jurisdiction must register within one month with a licensing officer and conform with this law as a citizen would have to, except as he or she can show that residence within the state is temporary and that she will not give birth to a child while in the state. Reports

every two months to the nearest licensing officer are required, with the alternative of being treated as a citizen of this state.

12. That all persons who are given a license to marry must have stipulated on the license, and on the state's record, by the licensing officer, a maximum number of children permitted the couple under the laws of this state. They are required to report each child to the office of the licensing officer six months before its birth and at the time of its birth. After the conception of the final child to which the couple are entitled but before it is born, they may submit to the licensing officer the records of any qualifications which they think may entitle them to a still larger number of children. If they qualify for a larger number, they are to be given, by the licensing officer, a certificate indicating the new maximum. If they submit no evidence, or having submitted evidence, still do not qualify for a larger number, then the mother must be sterilized at the time of the birth, or the father must be sterilized before the child is two weeks old. The physician under whose care the prospective mother has been during pregnancy is to express his opinion as to which is to be sterilized if there is a health factor involved. That opinion is to be controlling. If the physician has no opinion, the agreement of the couple shall be determining as to which shall be sterilized. If they are not in agreement, then the one with the lesser qualifications is to be sterilized. Arrangements for the sterilization are to be made by the licensing officer.

13. That the licensing officer make arrangements for the sterilization without fee of persons for whom it is required under Articles 10, 11, and 12 of this Act, and of such persons as request it for compliance with the provisions of Articles 4, 5, 7, 8, and 9.

14. Couples are to be authorized for reproduction according to the following scale:

Average I.Q. of couple as high as	Average school work completed	Average standing required, in classes having at least 9 students	Children authorized for a couple meeting all three minima
90	6th grade		1
100	6th grade	Top 3/5ths	2
110	High school or College	Top 3/5ths of either	3
120	High school or College	Top 2/5ths of either	4
130	High school or College	Top 1/5th of either	No limit

15. There shall be a State Board of Human Genetics composed of three members appointed by the Governor, one for 1 year, one for two years, and one for three years. Thereafter, each appointment is to be for 3 years. Each appointee must be well trained in genetics, must have a doctor's degree from an institution accredited by the Association of American Universities, and must, as prerequisite to taking office, publicly declare his or her approval of the purposes and method of this law, in the administration of which he or she is to participate. He or she need not previously have been a resident of this state.

16. The Board shall appoint the licensing officers, and shall oversee their work. It shall keep such records and conduct such studies as it thinks appropriate. Funds shall be allocated to their use for the purposes herein set forth.

17. Persons with socially beneficial qualifications which are not regularly allowed for in the foregoing provisions may apply to the Genetics Board for a higher

quota of children than that dependent on their IQ and educational attainment. Musical ability, special achievement in the sciences or the liberal arts, in mechanical invention or in organization, are illustrative. The Board shall consider each case in view of the employment conditions, and the number of special allocations already made, as well as of the likelihood of social contribution by the prospective children. Always the burden of proof is on the applicant, to justify a deviation from the standard quota. Not more than a tenth as many children are to be authorized in any one year by special action of the Board as the number that is authorized under the IQ and education provisions.

However, with the rule of law as an objective, it is provided that the Genetics Board shall not have power to *reduce* the number of children which a person may have under the law. The Board shall have power only to *enlarge* a person's quota.

But the Board is invited to recommend to the Legislature, when it sees fit, any changes in the classifications and quotas which its members believe would be of benefit to the state, setting forth in writing the recommendations and the reasons for them.

18. This state recognizes that the partnership family is less effective than in previous decades as a social agency for reproduction; that the partnership family may not be sufficiently adapted to the urban phases of a civilization to justify its exclusive sanction as the only social agency for reproduction; that the census statistics show that 40 percent of college graduate women in the larger cities are not married. It is possible that re-emphasis on offspring, as an objective worth while for leaders, will revive family life and change the present bases on which men choose their wives. This state recognizes that until such

time, or until the development of a new organization for reproduction, something must be done to
prevent the loss of high quality heredity of women
who remain unmarried. It is therefore enacted that
single women may apply for licenses to reproduce by
artificial insemination, and be authorized for children on the same basis that they may be authorized
when applying for a marriage license, except that
(a) only men with a rating for an unlimited number
of children, or men approved by the Genetics
Board as of world-renowned merit, are to be sires for
their children; and except that (b) the number of
children for whom they are authorized shall be the
same as if the sire's IQ and education is the same as
their own.

19. The Board shall maintain a list of sires who will have
agreed to serve; and at request of a single woman, or
of a couple, authorized for a child, shall act as inter-
mediary. Charge to applicant shall be postage, and
expense of venereal tests and of tests of blood types
for the woman and for the prospective sire. There
is to be no payment for sires. Their opportunity for
participation in the world's improvement is reward
enough. The choice available to the authorized
woman or couple is not to be limited to the Board's
list.

The suggested changes are sweeping; they have to be!
The sluggish, half-dream consciousness that something is
wrong, which characterizes the attitude of most civic-
minded people, is an inadequate response to the overwhelming disaster of the differential birth rate. Revival

of the family institution is appropriately to be desired, but whether or not the family is revived, we must face the fact that it never has been geared to the quantity or quality requirements of a population. Its insufficiency for that objective—its reproduction in reverse correlation with social requirement—twists us anew with every successive presentation of birth statistics. And in the same statistical figures one must see also the futility of the plaintive exhortations of those noble men who limit their aim to leading us back to earlier times when disintegration was slower. Civilization's standardized controls have no leverage; they slap and vibrate without meaning; they fail to take hold. The tail spin to the crash whips faster. We must act. But we must not face the prospects with the illusion that there is no other way to happiness than the way which used to be. In this fast-moving age our social change must be by reasoned adaptation. The lack of suitable measures to overcome the differences of birth rates was an element in the downfall of the earlier civilizations. It is an element in our own civilization and could lead to our own collapse.

This Marriage Law formulation may require some modification to fit some states, or may require auxiliary measures. For example, in the South the educational opportunities for rural people and for Negroes seem to have been less than for urban whites. I doubt if any lower educational qualifications for reproduction should be made for *any* groups—since such a maneuver might damage the incentive structure for the persons who are highly qualified. But measures to equalize educational opportunities should be prompt and thorough. The Marriage Law itself would furnish a great incentive for a person to make the most of his educational opportunities.

Articles 18 and 19 deserve a little more discussion. Those are the provisions for authorized reproduction of high quality single women by artificial insemination from top-flight sires.

Assuming that some one state—your state—adopts the suggested law including Articles 18 and 19, I think it might be helpful if a few ministers, priests, and rabbis in that state should be prepared to officiate at optionally supplementary ceremonials for sanctioning, on request, the suggested procedure. Many of the single women who are currently excluded from reproduction would feel a psychological necessity for religious approval for having children under the plan herein described.

This whole idea of artificial insemination may be new to many of you. It has been going on for about twenty years.

Dr. H. J. Muller, a biologist at Indiana University, a recent Nobel Prize winner for work on mutations, and first President of the American Society of Human Genetics, in a 1935 publication reported having read a paper before a small student organization at Columbia University in 1910 in which he suggested artificial insemination as a means of transmitting the heredity of transcendently estimable men.

The first *published* proposal on artificial insemination was from the pen of an Australian social worker, Mrs. Marion Piddington. It was published in 1916, under the title "Scientific Motherhood." That was followed in 1918 by a booklet, also from Australia, called *Facultative Motherhood,* which presents the same idea, It bears the name of Dr. Henry Waterman Swan as author.

Mrs. Piddington advocated motherhood for high quality unmarried women by the artificial insemination method. She thought of having the state support the unmarried mothers and their scions of geniuses, but my contrasted view is that governments should not get into this phase of living any more than necessary. A single woman who can pass the rest of the tests in the prescribed law can probably support herself and her progeny; and if she can't, let her dad help out, or a discriminating philanthropist here and there. If the state begins supporting children, it will soon be choosing their sires; that will come to be centralized judging of what is worth while in heredity—an extreme as dangerous as the present extreme of laissez faire. Let a woman choose the sire for her child—within such limits as the proposed law sets forth. After all, she is the one who will have to live with the youngster. And since worth-whileness is largely a matter of ethics, she is as good a judge of the positive qualities of a man as any biological bureaucrat could be. Since thousands or millions will be doing the choosing, the future geniuses will be appropriately diversified as to types. Besides, there seems to be no good reason to put a financial premium on single blessedness by making payments to single women bearing children, or to put an additional burden on taxpayers for that purpose. But except for the money angle, Articles 18 and 19 of the law I have proposed are close to the plan which Mrs. Piddington offered to the Australians more than 30 years ago.

It appears that Mrs. Piddington was not only the first person to *distribute* the idea of artificial insemination, but the first to propose the application of the plan to high quality single women. Men, as a rule, marry women of less education than they have themselves. That leaves many of the best educated women unmarried, and in part accounts for the differential birth rate. The world loses in the fact that these women have no children. Mrs. Piddington suggested that their heredity might be saved for the future through artificial insemination.

In America the first publication suggesting artificial insemination was a mimeographed paper by a sociology instructor at the University of Nevada, distributed in the fall of 1925. That was followed in 1934 by a 27-page printed pamphlet by the same author, entitled *Heredity Corporations,* distributed through the aid of Ellsworth Huntington to the members of the American Eugenics Society.

Dr. Muller reports that he lectured on artificial insemination at the University of Chicago in the summer of 1925. It is possible that the Nevada instructor received the basic idea, by way of grapevined student phrases, from Dr. Muller, since he too spent a few days at the University of Chicago in the summer of 1925, although from 1925 to the time of his contact with Muller's 1935 book he believed his own plan was completely original. At any rate, his 1934 brochure, according to my present knowledge, is the first discussion in print in America setting forth possibilities of social benefit from artificial insemination of women.

In England, the *Eugenics Review* published an article in its July 1935 issue entitled "Eutelegenesis." That article, by Mr. Herbert Brewer, appears to have been England's first.

There has been actual practice of the physical methods that those scholars and philosophers were preaching. Sterility or seeming sterility of a husband furnished most of the occasions, but not all. In those cases of seeming sterility, sometimes the artificial method was successful with the husband as sire. He wasn't sterile after all. But often an outside sire was selected.

In the *American Mercury* for April 1948, Clintie Winfrey Kenney told that a British surgeon named John Hunter artificially impregnated a woman in 1790. In the U. S. the first known use of the method was reported by Dr. J. Marian Sims in 1866. Kenney said that in 1927 a French physician, A. A. Schorohowa, reported success in 22 cases, and in 1940 he announced 15 more pregnancies by artificial insemination. By the latter year the practice had become rather widespread in the United States.

It is probable that most artificial inseminations have been by M.D.'s. If a woman is normal, there is no physiological reason why she couldn't apply the method herself, but where a selected sire is used a professional third party is a precaution against jealousies. The third party could as readily be a nurse or a biology laboratory technician as an overworked M.D. As a rule the woman never sees the sire whose heredity has been transmitted to her child, and the sire never sees her. The doctors in many cases were confronted with a problem, and met it, working out the social arrangements that seemed to them appropriate. Secrecy was thorough.

There has been some discussion about possible embarrassment "if the facts were known." Embarrassment there might have been in the pioneer years of the practice. Now that artificial insemination has become established, the need for secrecy is less, if present at all. The situation is much like that in cases of adoption. Few parents keep the facts from the child, or from the public. As one adopted boy boasted: "My parents chose me from a hundred babies; your parents had to take what they got." There is reason for a proper pride in the heredity of a selected sire in the very fact that he has accomplished much, and that he represents heredity which is outstanding.

In 1940 a survey was conducted by the National Research Foundation for Eugenic Alleviation of Sterility, Inc., to determine the extent of artificial insemination in the United States by the medical profession. Dr. F. I. Seymour was Medical Director of that organization, and Dr. A. Koerner was Executive Secretary. The *Journal of the American Medical Association* for June 21, 1941, contains a report of that survey, beginning on page 2747. Aspects of the study were related in *Science Digest,* September 1941, page 52; also by Gretta Palmer in *Coronet* for October 1941, and by J. S. Schock in the *Dickinson Law Review* for May 1942, published by the Dickinson School of Law in Carlisle, Pennsylvania. Some of the details are reported here.

Questionnaires were sent to 30,000 M.D.'s. Replies were received from 7,642 of them, of whom 4,049 reported successful results with artificial insemination. Here are the results:

Pregnancies from artificial insemination	9,489
Children born from those pregnancies	9,238
Children born from artificial insemination with husband as sire	5,728
Children born from artificial insemination with sire other than husband	3,510
Mothers having more than one pregnancy by artificial insemination	1,357

For 85% of the pregnancies, twelve or more inseminations per pregnancy were required, as the following table shows:

Number of pregnancies resulting after the number of inseminations shown opposite	Number of inseminations required to bring about pregnancy
3	1
17	2
409	3
61	8
897	9
4,312	12
1,916	14
1,003	15
367	18
139	20
241	21
124	More than 21 (including 1 after the 72nd)

Where there were twelve inseminations, they usually were three for four months, four for three months, or two for six months.

The number of pregnancies that terminated in births of living normal babies was a higher percentage than among pregnancies in general: 97%. Miscarriages were only about a fifth as many as for pregnancies in the general population.

The proportion of boys among the 9,489 pregnancies was curiously high: at a rate of 148.8 boys to 100 girls, whereas for usual births the ratio is about 105.5 boys to 100 girls.

Those figures resulted from questionnaires sent to about a fifth of the physicians of the country. If returns could have been had from the whole 150,000 or more physicians, the totals would surely have been much higher, though not five times as high. It seems that the questionnaires were sent not in a usual sampling, but were sent to doctors most likely to have engaged in artificial insemination. But a 1940 survey is rather old now, and the practice appears to have been expanding rapidly since then.

A paper by Marie Pichel Warner, M.D., read before the Society of Medical Jurisprudence on February 9, 1948, and published in the June 1948 number of *Human Fertility*, reported an analysis of a hundred cases of artificial insemination.

By the time of the report there had been 59 pregnancies; 19 women had discontinued the artificial inseminations; 22 were proceeding with the method.

Inseminations ranged from one to nine per month, between the 5th and the 23rd days of the menstrual cycle, the days from the 8th to the 16th being most fruitful. Temperature charts appear to have been used to indicate the time of a woman's greatest fertility. Eighteen women conceived in the first month, 17 in the second month. Others took longer.

Thirty-two of the women had previously received artificial insemination unsuccessfully. With different sires, 13 of them were among the 59 who had become pregnant.

From the 59 pregnancies there had been 42 full-term deliveries and 7 miscarriages; ten women of the 59 were awaiting delivery at the time of the report.

The women's ages ranged between 19 and 42 years. The method was 100% successful for women of ages 19 and 20; 61% successful for those of ages 21 to 29; 51% successful for women 30 to 39; and 33% successful for women 40 to 42. Presumably the percentages for success would be increased as the 22 other women continued the inseminations, but it appears that in some way age has a sterilizing effect on many women long before the menopause.

•

Notice the provision in Article 19 of the proposed law, that "There is to be no payment for sires. Their opportunity for participation in the world's improvement is reward enough."

That inclusion is a result of careful consideration of a practice of the Catholic artificial insemination clinic at Georgetown University School of Medicine, as reported in *Time* for September 26, 1938. Hospital interns furnished the sperm cells, according to *Time,* and were paid $25 for each occasion.

As I see the issue, the honor of being selected as a sire —of being called on after serious study and comparison to supply heredity for the generation to come—is as high an honor as can be bestowed. It must not be put on a commercial basis. I grant that an intern has passed a series of severe tests and has demonstrated abilities probably well above the average for the human species, yet compared with other possibilities his merits are a gamble. If his service is commercialized at $25, presumably that of a great inventor with distinguished ancestry is worth well in the thousands. But surely any such charges would stand as a barrier to the prospective advantages to humanity from selected sires. Any man with brains enough to be worth the trust will, I believe, if he will serve at all, serve without charge—for the cause of improving humanity. Interviews I have had on the question with a few men of renown support that belief.

•

Some of "these moderns" with whom I have talked have raised this question: If we are to approve unmarried parenthood for high quality women by present-day Aristotles and Leonardo da Vincis and Ben Franklins, why bother about the artificial method?

It will be readily seen, however, that many of the most distinguished sires are married, and would be unavailable except by the indirect procedure. Also, artificial insemination makes other social barriers unimportant. Thus, age, which would in many cases make a man unattractive as a mate, would make him more desired as a sire. Age would have afforded an opportunity for accumulation of his own accomplishments and for the time testing of the quality of his earlier offspring. Reason, rather than emotion, can be the major basis of a woman's choice when the choice is for paternity rather than companionship.

Differences in folkways between a woman and a prospective sire for her child are of little importance, though they might be very important in other social relationships. One other point: artificial insemination decreases the handicap of distance. That enlarges the choice of sires, and so makes higher quality possible.

Does artificial insemination present an opportunity for control of the sex of offspring? Can a woman somehow arrange that her child shall be a son or a daughter according to her choice? The question has arisen in connection with the rebalancing of the sexes in areas where one sex or the other is outnumbered. In Alaska, for example, there are relatively few women; whereas in most U.S. cities of over 100,000 population the women outnumber the men.

The key to the sex of a prospective child is in the chromosomes of the reproduction cells. "Chromo" refers to color. Chromosomes are called that because they take a dye more readily than the other substance in a cell, and in order to see them under a microscope, geneticists dye them.

All the reproduction cells of all women are just alike in this: that they have no influence on the sex of offspring. All their chromosomes are X chromosomes.

A man's reproduction cells, the sperm cells, are of two sorts. Each of half of them includes a Y chromosome, and when that pairs up with an X chromosome of an ovum, the result is a boy. Half of the sperm cells have only X chromosomes, and when one of those sperm cells fertilizes an ovum, the result is a girl.

The Y chromosomes—the boy-producers—are smaller than the X ones, so some geneticists think they may be able to separate out the sperm cells which contain them. Scientist Marianne E. Bernstein, in *Science Digest* for June 1949, said that biologists at the University of Pennsylvania are trying to do that by centrifugal force.

There are possible methods of sex control other than the actual separation of sperm cells containing Y chromosomes from the sperm cells containing only X chromosomes. Carl Warren had a book published in 1940 by the Orange Judd Publishing Co., Inc., entitled *Animal Sex Control*. He reported that douching female rabbits and mice with a 2 percent alkaline solution before insemination resulted in litters predominantly male. A 2 percent lactic acid solution resulted in litters predominantly female. Also, in *Science News Letter* for October 22,1949, I learned that Dr. Alfred Taylor and Dr. Nell Carmichael of the University of Texas and the Clayton Foundation, of Austin, Texas, have discovered facts that may have an application. They injected large doses of folic acid into mice. Male mice can easily stand doses of the stuff that result in sure death to the females. It will be worth while to try folic acid on the X and Y sperm cells.

But up to the time of this writing the control of sex of human beings had not yet been attained. We can say, however, that if and when sex control becomes possible, artificial insemination is likely to be part of the process.

•

In the same area of population study is a question of the prospects for proxy *mothers*. In *Look* Magazine for January 31, 1950, and in *Science News Letter* for April 1, 1950, are accounts of the transfer of cattle ova from some cows to others. Scientist Raymond E. Umbaugh of the Foundation of Applied Research is conducting the experiments on the Essar Ranch, near San Antonio. Success has already been attained for the method in rabbits, by Dr. Gregory Pincus of the Worcester Foundation for Experimental Biology at Shrewsbury, Massachusetts.

Pincus has found that for rabbits a properly timed injection of pituitary hormone has increased the number of eggs, and Umbaugh has similarly increased the number of eggs in a single ovulation of a cow to as many as 140.

The expected benefit in cattle breeding is in using scrub cattle as incubators in the development of offspring having the heredity of prize-winning stock.

There are similar possibilities for human beings.

Perhaps the possibilities are even greater for the transfer of the ovaries themselves. Dr. Leon F. Whitney is reported in *Science News Letter* for December 31, 1949, to have been successful in transplanting the ovaries of dogs. Dr. Harry S. N. Greene, of the Yale School of Medicine, who worked with Dr. Whitney, believes the method can be used with human beings. Dr. Whitney's experiments have shown that old ovaries, when transferred to a young dog, are rejuvenated. In one such case the ovaries of an 18-year-old cocker were transplanted in a young Dalmatian, which was then successfully bred.

If such transfers can be made in human beings, a woman of exceptionally capable heritage who has demonstrated her own abilities, may, when she grows too old to have babies herself, contribute her ovaries, or one of them, to a young woman. It is not unreasonable to imagine a philanthropic foundation organized to encourage breeding of young women having genius-bearing ovaries. Presumably they would be artificially inseminated with the sperm cells of great sires.

But we must not permit our contemplation of the experimental frontier to becloud our immediate responsibilities. Let's get back to the suggested legislation.

The voters of a state may adopt the proposed legislation in the form presented in the foregoing pages; then as its benefits are demonstrated, another state may adopt

them, and gradually many states. But one state may balk
at the artificial insemination clauses, Articles 18 and 19.
All right; that is not serious. Probably the artificial insemination could as well be implemented by a private
society organized by the prospective mothers themselves.
But with or without the state facilitation of artificial
insemination, there must be sterilization.

An important sponsor for a sterilization law is the
Right Reverend Ernest William Barnes, Bishop of Birmingham, of the Church of England. On November 28,
1949, he told the Rotary Club of his home town, and told
the world, that Englishmen are too numerous, are likely
to be the paupers of the English-speaking world. "We
must preserve the better stocks in the population," he
said, "and hinder the increase of the worse."

What, specifically, did those terms mean?

For one thing, "sterilization of the unfit" is essential,
he said.

To advocate sterilization as a remedy *for overpopulation* may imply a wide application of the method. I think
it does—because if sterilization is only narrowly applied,
the results will not be noticeable in lessening the pressure of population.

And if we use sterilization as a counterbalance for the
differential birth rate, as I think we must, we must use it
in a wide application too. We've got to *reverse* that differential; we got to bring about a larger birth rate among
accomplished people than among society's burdens, and
we've got to reduce the birth rate of society's burdens.

Maybe a little more evidence on that challenge is in
order.

There is more to show that birth-rate differences were
the key cause of the earlier declines than was presented
in the chapter "Prospects for Posterity." To comprehend
the imperativeness of the need for complete and immedi-

ate reversal of policies we should do well to survey other evidence relating to the declines of ancient Greece and Rome.

There are startling parallels with the present time brought out by G. M. McCleary, M.D., in *The Hibbert Journal* for April 1947. McCleary, drawing on Mommsen's *History of Rome,* quotes an ancient Roman:

"Citizens," said Metellus, "if it were possible to go entirely without wives, we would deliver ourselves at once from this evil: but as the law of nature has so ordered it that we can neither live happy with them nor continue the species without them, we ought to have more regard for our lasting security than for our transient pleasures."

I am not supporting the assumption of Metellus as to the reason for nonmarriage; and history has amply demonstrated that neither his exhortation nor anybody's exhortation, by itself, could stem the trend toward bachelorhood. Some of the reasons that I have reported for childlessness, are also reasons for nonmarriage—especially other interests. What I do want you to see is that childlessness, of the accomplished people of the time, augmented by the nonmarriage of a large proportion of them, was conspicuously frequent when Metellus Macedonicus berated the Roman citizens in 131 B.C. Childlessness of the accomplished people was even more frequent and disturbing when Augustus Caesar read Metellus' speech to the Roman Senate over a hundred years later. There is every reason to believe that the decline and fall of Rome was, centrally, the result of the reverse evolution involved in its birth rates. Says McCleary:

"Childlessness was common, and among the upper classes families of more than one or two children were rarely found."

Just as important as the lessons of Rome's birth rates are the lessons of her attempts to stop the drift. Those attempts were essentially like the efforts of various governments now—and equally futile. They lacked wisdom in the use of incentives. The similar measures of our own time are more stupid than those of the ancients in that they misread more experience, and persist in ignoring the psychology of emulation.

Said McCleary:

"many of those who professed eagerness to restore the traditional respect for marriage set no example to the public. Maecenas and Balbus had no children, and Horace, who had urged Augustus to legislate against luxury, immorality and celibacy, was, like most distinguished writers of the time, an unmarried man."

But why be surprised that those men, who in their ripened years had comprehended the meaning of the torrent, were nevertheless unable to escape it?

Exhortation to reproduce failed—because exhortation failed to change sufficiently the incentives *not* to reproduce. According to Augustus, as Brooks Adams reports, the Romans were conscious that sterility must finally deliver their city into the hands of the barbarians. Legislation was passed in 4 A.D. to encourage marriage. Since that legislation was not effective, it was supplemented in the year 9. Some of the nobility protested and asked for the repeal of the laws. Augustus called them to the Forum and gave them a lecture which was passionate, even violent, in its earnestness. Those who were single were the worst of criminals—destroyers of the race. Did they expect men to start from the ground to replace them?

"While the government liberated slaves for the sole purpose of keeping up the number of citizens, the children of the Marcii, of the Fabii, of the Valerii, and the Julii, let their names perish from the earth."

But Augustus might as well have spared his intensity and left his bitter plea unspoken, for "in the reign of Augustus all but fifty of the patrician houses had become extinct."

A subsidy for reproduction was futile too. McCleary reports that that expedient was tried later in the first century A.D.:

"There is ample evidence . . . that the main purpose of the alimenta was to encourage population. The grants were first introduced on a voluntary basis by public spirited citizens in the principate of Claudius, and in A.D. 97 Nerva introduced a state scheme for Italy the details of which have been lost. We have, however, definite evidence of the working of the alimenta under Trajan. Funds were provided from the Imperial Treasury in the form of loans on mortgages to local landowners, at an interest of 5 percent, less than half the usual rate of interest at that time. The funds received in interest were distributed by the local authorities in maintenance grants for needy children. Boys received 16 sesterces monthly up to the age of eighteen, and girls 16 sesterces up to the age of fourteen. In Rome many children were enrolled among the recipients of free corn. . . ."

"There is no evidence," says McCleary, "that the alimenta of Nerva and Trajan or the social legislation of Augustus did anything to check the depopulation of Italy."

I wonder what strange quirk in Nerva's brain could have led him to expect that men of distinction would willingly put themselves in the beggar class! Or that men of less than top rank would fail to follow the envied ones.

"The bearing of children was unfashionable . . . ," says McCleary. "The local bourgeoisie and *nouveaux riches* strove to emulate their betters in Rome. Their families died out."

"In spite of attempts to check the decline of the population of Italy, including extensive settlements of barbarian-born soldiers, depopulation spread, and attacked in succession the provinces of Sicily, Spain, Africa, and Gaul."

Even the Romans should have known their remedies were wrong. After all, they did have before them the experience of Greece.

"In Greece the population began to decline in the fourth century B.C.," reports McCleary, "and the movement spread from Sparta and Athens to other Greek states, though many had laws encouraging the production of large families."

The father of four sons was exempted from all taxation and other burdens of the state, continues McCleary, "Yet the people of Sparta dwindled."

You have done a good job, Dr. McCleary, but I'll have to stop you on that one. The expression should not have been "YET the people of Sparta dwindled"; it should read, "THEREFORE the people of Sparta dwindled." Exemption from taxation is like other baby bonuses in its effects; the only people it stimulates to reproduction, if any, are the people far down in the social pyramid. Its area of greatest failure is among the very people whose heredity is most necessary to the survival of the civilization. Gradually, as the fashion of childlessness takes greater hold, in some countries the practice reaches farther down, till eventually, even the population *totals* decline.

"According to Aristotle," continues McCleary, "the number of fighting men, which, it was said, had once been 10,000, had at the time of the Theban invasion fallen below 1,000. 'The city sank under a single defeat; the want of men was their ruin.'"

McCleary quotes Polybius, out of Thirlwall's *History of Greece,* via Cardinal Angelo Mai, referring to about 140 B.C. Said Polybius:

"All Greece has been afflicted with a failure of offspring, in a word, with a scarcity of men, so that the cities have been left desolate and the land waste; though we have not been visited either with a series of wars, or with epidemic disease.... when men gave themselves up to ease and comfort and indolence, and would neither marry nor rear children born out of marriage, or at most only one or two, in order to leave these rich, and to bring them up in luxury, the evil soon spread. . . ."

That ambition to bring children up in luxury was the inaccurate guess of Polybius as to the reason for the differences of birth rates, and their decline. Polybius got close to the target but never hit the bull's eye. With the help of Thorstein Veblen and his *Theory of the Leisure Class* we know now that people, in their gregariousness, strive to do those things by which they can show that they are as worthy as their neighbor, and if possible a little more so. The people who are capable enough, or fortunate enough, to have a choice of achievements, try for that achievement which will most set them up as leaders. Others try to keep up. Under our present social arrangements there is no glory in having a baby—any bum can have a dozen of them. And babies get in the way of recognized achievement. The only way to make babies sufficiently desired so that the desire for them will more than offset their bother is to set up high standards for parenthood; in other words to make the babies hard to get. Then getting them will be evidence of their parents' having arrived. On that basis people will tend to have as many as they are entitled to.

Better look over again that Marriage Law at the beginning of this chapter. I didn't expect you to like it the first time.

Chapter 15

World Aid to End the Need for Aid

The evidence is overwhelming that for the world as a whole there is not "enough food for everyone"; there is, in fact, such a stringent scarcity that at least 1,500,000,000 people are receiving less than enough for health. Yet even to feed the present population of the world in the present partial measure of its need, the soil is being mined. If and as the population expands, the soil destruction is likely to be more rapid, the proportion of people in want will be a larger proportion, and the deaths from malnutrition will be more numerous. These conditions and prospects threaten the whole structure of our civilization.

And an even more insidious and basic menace is the differential birth rate, which saps our brain power, our problem-solving ability.

One of the objectives of conscientious parents has been to teach their children "to leave the world a better place than they find it," and yet, generation after generation have left the world a worse place—because they have misinterpreted the essentials: care of the land, fitting the numbers to the land, and safeguarding the quality of the people.

"Looks hopeless, doesn't it?" said a friend.

"Not at all," I answered. "One thing that is necessary is that human beings apply to *re*production the same degree of intelligence they have applied to production." Thus far they have been governed in reproduction mostly by emotion unrestrained—as other animals are. And the blind have led the blind—as when politicians have complimented the parents of large families irrespective of the qualifications of those parents.

The results of reckless reproduction are too serious to permit us to file the subject away and do nothing about it. If we forfeit the civilization we have, there will be dark ages of ignorance and tyranny and pain and suffering before another civilization can evolve; better correct those ways that lead us to the downfall.

The direction for our correctives is clear. It points unmistakably to the field of preventive checks to population. I have already made definite suggestions for action for the United States and for its tiny satellite, Puerto Rico. Now let us look at the world as a whole.

First, however, we must examine a few concepts which, by keeping the possessors of those concepts in comfortable error, have tended to keep the world's sufferers in torment.

Probably most pernicious of such concepts is that of a Federal World Government with universal suffrage, in which each adult would have as much political power as any other adult.

There are three times as many people in China as in the U.S., so the people of China would have three times as much vote power in the World Federation as the people of the U.S. would have, and 40 times as much influ-

ence as the people of Canada. The population of the
Orient is more than half the population of the world.
The United States has only 6 percent of the world's people. It is inescapable, then, that the poverty-stricken
Orient, in complete control of the proposed World Federation, would arrange for dividing up the wealth of the
U.S. The TVA's that would blossom in every Chinese
valley might increase China's productivity somewhat, but
one of the tragedies of the situation would be that it
could only minutely and temporarily improve the Chinese level of living because the Chinese birth rate would
absorb the increased productivity as soon as it became
available.

In the U.S., which would be bearing most of the cost,
the level of living would rapidly decline. We should soon
be in the position of Ireland after the year 1800. In that
year the Irish parliament in Dublin adopted the Act of
Union, providing for Irish representation in the British
Parliament. There the Irish constituted a small minority.
They were helpless to prevent whatever the English
wanted to put over. That Federation brought only frus-
tration to the outnumbered Irish. Home rule—getting
out of the Federation—became their chief ambition;
achieved in 1921. And the U.S., voted to impotence in a
World Federation with suffrage for all, would have no relief from exploitation except by getting out.

Sometimes the structure of the U.S. is assumed for the
World Federation: a house of representatives with its
membership based on comparative populations, and another legislating body, comparable with our Senate, representing countries as such, in an equality with other
countries. In that second legislating body the U.S. would
have one vote in perhaps 57. In such a body the U.S.
would be almost as vulnerable as with a one-house parliament with representation in proportion to populations.

Our protest against tax measures would be as ineffective as the protest of our Southern states has been against tariff duties of Northern design.

One organization proselyting for a global government, the United World Federalists, trusts blindly in a world *constitution* as a protector of the people of the U.S.

A study of the inability of any state of the United States to resist the pressure of the national Government shows how risky is that dependence on a constitution. Even under the most carefully worked-out constitution that ever existed, the supposedly sovereign states have been unable to stand against the will of the Federal legislators. By the 10th Amendment to the U.S. Constitution our early citizens thought they had secured to the states all those sovereign powers not delegated to the central government. But the taxing power which they gave to the Federal Government is a tool for usurping all other powers. Florida provided against a state inheritance tax. The Federal Government cut the ground from under it by legislating a national inheritance tax which credits inheritance tax payments made to states under state laws. In that arrangement the Federal Government discriminated against Florida by keeping the money of its dead men, while crediting to the other jurisdictions the payments made from the estates of their deceased. Thus taxing, and then remitting the tax to states that line up in the pattern set by the Federal Government, avoids the Constitution in bringing about conformity.

Another instance of it is in the Social Security Act of 1935. In its unemployment insurance clauses that Act levied a Federal tax on payrolls. The legislature of a state could reclaim some of the purchasing power thus taxed away only by passing a state unemployment insurance law.

Another means of by-passing the Constitution is used in that Social Security Act. The Federal Government ar-

ranged grants to a state from money raised by taxes, on
condition that the state use some of its own funds in specified ways.

Please understand that I am not discussing the desirability or undesirability of the measures that have been
instituted through circumvention of the U.S. Constitution. The point is merely that the taxing power of a central government can and does take away the independence of other governments that may be intended to have
some retained sovereignty.

A constitution leans strongly in the direction of the
philosophy of the court that applies it. There is no reason to expect a world court to defend the interpretations
that our 6% of the world's population would put on a
world constitution. So U.S. citizens in a world government would pay the taxes that would increase the numbers of people in the lands of reckless reproduction.

In a world in which population breeds with thoughtless abandon, government itself is a population phenome-
non, in part. Government by the people of all the world
in equal representation would lead rapidly to equality of
incomes *at a subsistence level.*

And in recent plans that have received wide notice,
participation in world government has not been conditioned upon restraint in reproduction. Fundamentally
our troubles are mostly derived from unwise relationships of men with the supporting soil. No government,
whether a world government or a national one or a state
organization, can improve the prospects for the future of
its citizens unless it unequivocally faces the population
problems.

Warren R. Austin in *Harper's Magazine* for May 1949
analyzes additional dangers from the world government
delusion.

Though the position of the United World Federalists
is thoroughly untenable it is exercising wide influence,

many of its members making large financial contributions in its support. The 1949 expenditures of the organization for Congressional lobbying alone amounted to $291,672.

•

Another dangerous development is the recent campaign for increasing our immigration.

To open the migration gates of the United States would be a speedy way to local and global disaster. The U.S. birth rates would fall. I explained that in *Human Breeding and Survival*. Yet the country's population total would increase—as California's total has increased with the trek of people from other states. Guy Irving Burch showed, in the *Population Bulletin* for September 1948, that

"the only thing that prevents our level of living from sinking rapidly to that of the most destitute country of the Old World is our immigration restriction legislation and the power to enforce it."

And from the standpoint of the world's welfare, *as this country filled up, the greatest area of agricultural surpluses would cease to have agricultural surpluses.* Grain exports would decline as beef exports declined many years ago. The level of living of all those parts of the world which depend on our abundance of food would sink.

Any prospective benefits, then, which large-scale immigration might yield to the immigrants themselves would be accompanied by harms not only to people already here, but to the people remaining in foreign lands.

•

A third misconception that leads to harmful action is that *giving* will benefit the world—giving with no strings attached. The theory has been that if the level of living of a people is raised by regularly supplementing their earnings, the tendency to reproduce will be reduced. The inapplicability of that reasoning has been discussed in previous chapters. Just as in colonial America and the early U.S. the tremendous surpluses of goods had to hold the level of living high *for several generations* before the birth rates fell, similarly any other means of holding up the level would have to operate *for several generations* before the resulting change of interests would register in substantially lower birth rates. As I have pointed out, the first effect of the doles would be not a lower birth rate but a lower death rate, and so a higher survival rate. The rapid increase of population that would come about from that high survival rate makes it impossible to carry through a program of giving. The goose that would be trying to lay the golden eggs would be worn out long before the golden eggs could hatch. And when the giving terminated, as eventually it would have to, more people than before would be left stranded on meager resources.

Even the Marshall Plan, though possibly justifiable in delaying Russia's accumulation of power, is almost sure to fail in most of the supposed beneficiary countries as a means of stabilizing their economies, because of their birth rates. The Marshall Plan funds are intended to stimulate productivity in those countries, and presumably they will do that. But there is little chance that the increase in productivity will exceed the increase in people; little chance, then, that the *average* per person productivity will be increased, and particularly, little chance that the per capita average productivity of *food* will be increased.

Aid is wasted if not conditioned on a program of population restriction.

The people who are responsible for the Marshall Plan
are at last catching faint glimmerings of the unpromising
outlook. They are still befuddled as to the population
causes, however, so their further planning is just as be-
nighted. The *Wall Street Journal* under the headline
"After ECA, What?" summarized an unpublished report
from the Economic Cooperation Office in Paris. That
report attempted to show that the billions of dollars
going into the Marshall Plan may be wasted if there isn't
a follow-up aid program. The point to be realized is
that the follow-up aid money will be wasted too if the aid
is not conditioned on a program of population restriction.

•

Clearly, many of the world's problems call for a population approach. The long delay in recognizing that fact
is partly due to the supersentimentality that makes people welcome illusion when the truth hurts. In America,
too many soft hearts are accompanied by soft heads. The
Russians are not bothered by either; and there is some
reason to believe that they are—for China—actually
thinking in population terms.

We learned in Chapter 2 that industrialization in
China cannot be a cure for the misery there—a misery
that stems from the fact that there are too many people
for the amount of good land available.

Now what about the direction of *Russian* action? Even
yet we can be only speculative as to the details. The
New York Times for January 29, 1950, plus a United
Press news item of February 1, 1950, and *Time* Magazine
for February 6, 1950, and the Russo-Chinese Treaty as released February 15, 1950, give us basis for the specula-
tion.

A million Chinese are to be sent to Siberia. Presumably most of them will be illiterate, so they cannot report their hardships back to their home areas. A few of them will be pampered, and those will be used for propaganda purposes later. Probably most of the million will die within a few months—as most prisoners from Eastern Russia die in Siberia. That will not prevent the Russian leaders and the Chinese Communist leaders from issuing glowing accounts of the success of the experiment and will not prevent their alleging that the migrants are happy.

Within three or four years the movement to Siberia of a hundred million Chinese will be under way. Of course it will have to be rapid so that its prosperity effect in China will not be concurrently neutralized by new births. Who will be selected to go? Again, persons who cannot write their actual experiences to the people back home. Areas will be organized in China for collective farming. The success of the collective farms will be made more likely by removing half of the inhabitants. And how will the selected victims be induced to volunteer to leave? By directed hunger in China, and a promise of plenty in Siberia. That the promise is empty will be of no concern to those who make it.

The subsequent stream of humanity to Siberia will be made up of Chinese who do not fully co-operate with the collectivization program in China. In a few generations the greater prosperity in China which will come about as a consequence of a better balance of people with land will lead to a lowering birth rate, and a relaxation of population pressure comparable to that in the U.S.

I have been asked if I thought the Russians have a better understanding of the dynamics of population than Americans have. I do not think so. Almost every American knows that the main cause of China's suffering is overpopulation—knows it when he is not struggling to conceal the truth with some soothing deception. The simple fact of overpopulation is probably all that the Russians know about it too. But the Americans are more sentimental. Instead of facing the truth, they cringe, and paste a false label on the problem. The Russians, in contrast, say, "Too many people? Get rid of some of them!"

Summarizing:

The American State Department plan for crowded lands is industrialization—Truman's Point Four. As we saw in Chapter 2, it will not work. The Russian plan, if I have pieced it together correctly, will work—just as the Black Death, in the 15th century, worked to the benefit of remaining Englishmen.

But the Russians' prospective action is horribly harsh on those hundreds of millions who are to go to their deaths in Siberia—and that harshness is unnecessary. If sterilization were used instead, with a plan after the pattern of that which I have described for Puerto Rico—the prosperity would be assured without the suffering.

•

America has adopted the policy of bailing out countries that get themselves in a jam. Consequently America must give attention to the constant invitation to further trouble which is present in the reproduction chaos in those countries.

There is a penetrating 1949 book bearing on the subject, published by the Macmillan Company. It is a symposium entitled *New Compass of the World,* edited by Hans W. Weigert, Vilhjalmur Stefansson, and Richard Edes Harrison. I must mention particularly its last four articles—by G. C. L. Bertram, Warren S. Thompson, Irene B. Taeuber, and J. Russell Smith. They interpret the amassing populations as a threat of aggression.

Dr. Thompson is the same Warren S. Thompson whose textbook on population problems I panned in Chapter 9. In matters of heredity I think he is in the Dark Ages, and his shortcoming in that field throws off his recommendations; but in projecting population numbers and consequences of numbers the man has had some big moments. He had a considerable part in working up data for that Pitkin book to which I referred in Chapter 1, the book entitled *Must We Fight Japan?*, and Pitkin gave special credit to him in the foreword. That book, way back in 1921, accurately reported Japanese population prospects for the decades to come. Its writers foresaw the part of Japan in World War II twenty years before the war started. And in contributing to that book Thompson was one of the men who led me to center my life interest in POPULATION. The man was so right, when most of the U.S. was so wrong, so uncomprehending, so disgustingly stolid!—war-bound but too sentimentally superficial to believe it even when the facts were laid out logically before them.

Well, we had the war that Thompson foresaw. And now, since he has written about closely similar facts again, I think you will want to see what he has to say.

He examines population trends in South and East Asia. Java's population, under the orderly government of the Dutch, grew from a probable figure of 4.5 millions in 1816 to 40.7 millions in 1930 and an estimated 49 to 50 millions in 1940. The Philippines have had a comparable though lesser increase, and, says Thompson, "except for a small class in Manila there is no evidence of a decline in the birth rate and every improvement in health leads to a larger natural increase."

French Indo-China, Burma, Siam, and Malaya are experiencing the same trends. As production has increased, population has increased; and now, possible improvement cannot come fast enough to sustain an increase of people such as occurred in the last four or five decades. The native people "will more and more feel the need for larger resources" and "we may expect violent efforts to gain access to these resources as soon as they feel strong enough." They will feel that "war must be resorted to for the determination of the right to settle on and use" the unexploited lands.

Says Thompson: "We can ignore the population problems of South and East Asia only at great peril to our children and our children's children."

Then Irene Taeuber presents the population predicament of Japan, Formosa, Korea, and Manchukuo, with a prospect for Japan proper of 88 to 95 millions by 1960—if that many can exist.

J. Russell Smith takes the theme and shows that death control without birth control leads to disaster. He shows that our modern inventions are not likely to help matters. People live on tiny acreages; of what use would American tractors or power discs or grain drills or combines be to them? And how would they pay for the fuel to run them? The people "have no surplus." Mechanization would reduce the harvest, and starvation would result. The people are so crowded that malnutrition is normal, and crop failure is deadly because the people "have no margin, no surplus."

"If there ever was a need for a crusade for self preservation," concludes Geographer J. Russell Smith, "that need has presented itself. That need is for a campaign of birth control among the peoples of Asia and other countries also."

G. C. L. Bertram says: "If education and demonstration are insufficient, it may, however regrettably, be necessary for a time to resort to coercion. An unpleasant doctrine indeed; yet what is the alternative?"

•

The basic position of those writers is the same as mine; namely, that preventive checks to population are essential.

However, when Mr. Bertram writes of *coercion,* one wonders what he has in mind—just as one wonders what the writer of the article in Tokyo's newspaper *Yomiuri* had in mind when, as I mentioned in Chapter 1, he called on the Japanese government to outlaw births above a designated limit for each family. Coercion seems hardly possible in birth control in its usual meaning of rubber and chemical contraception.

At any rate I believe that there need be no more coercion on governments than that which occurs in the U.S. when the Federal Congress induces a state to adopt a law by Federal appropriation of money to match money provided by the state for a specified purpose. Earlier in this chapter I referred to the Social Security laws. In 1946 the Federal Government agreed to stand two-thirds of the burden of care of the aged and the blind. U.S. Congressional Acts of that contingent type, I am convinced, would lead to the adoption of effective co-operating laws for population control by Oriental countries.

And as to individuals, they would be in much the same position as the Oriental governments. They would need to conform to the provisions of the plan only as a prerequisite to getting free rice. There would be no coercion applied. The provision would not be, for example, like our vaccination laws, except in its purpose of serving the general well-being. In contrast with our vaccination laws, and our school attendance laws, and our Army registration laws, the population law would not be compulsory.

To be effective, however, our preventive check must usually be sterilization. Birth control in the more usual meaning seems to me dangerously inadequate. The JAPAN BIRTHCONTROL INSTITUTE is making remarkable strides, I understand, in establishing a following. Its program includes a mothers' clinic, publications, and lectures—all intended to popularize rubber and chemical contraception. It issued the first number of a *Japan Planned Parenthood Quarterly* in March 1950, well edited by Doctors K. W. Amano and F. Y. Amano, and printed partly in English, partly in Japanese. The quarterly is published at 12 Shinryudocho, Azabu, Minatoku, Tokyo, Japan.

Give the noble Doctors Amano an A for effort—and for accomplishment too, for that matter; but don't expect miracles.

C. Langdon White, geography professor in Stanford University, suggested to the Stanford alumni at their 1947 meeting that American aid to the countries of the Far East might well be made contingent on their popularization of birth control.

That seems to suggest government initiative in spreading the good word.

To require steps which will avoid chronic crises is surely a reasonable condition to our relieving a present need—and the principle applies to European aid as definitely as to aid in the Orient. And is there any question now that in all parts of the world contraception information should be available?

But, again, the population problems of the world cannot be solved by rubber and chemical contraception alone.

The spread of birth-control information has been slow, even in countries of widespread education. In countries with a large amount of illiteracy, contraception has been known and used almost solely by the literate. Its nonuse among the illiterate has been due partly to distorted ideas among educated people as to the role of birth control. I remember that even in our own country, not very many years ago, the city council of a large city in New York state had antisocial ideas of the exclusive right of the educated class to contraceptive knowledge. An educator of considerable ability and prominence was scheduled to give a lecture on the need for birth control. The council refused a permit for the lecture. Birth-control advocates listed the council members, tabulated the number of years each council member had been married, and the number of his children. The tabulation, considered with the statistical fact that when married people "let nature take its course" they will have a child about every two years, on an average, led to the conclusion that the council members were somehow avoiding the natural consequences of marital relationship. Their attempt to confine contraceptive knowledge, like a trade secret, to their own class seemed out of keeping with democratic government. In the face of the council's opposition to birth control education the newspapers saw headline material in the council members' moderate paternity. In view of the prospects for publicity about their antisocial discrimination, the council members hastened to get in touch with the sponsors of the lecture to reverse their earlier action on the permit.

Yet the occasional effort to monopolize contraceptive knowledge is not the only reason for the slowness of its spread, either here or in other parts of the world. And the attempt of the Catholic clergy to put a religious label on biological facts is only part of the story. Significantly, the narrow scope of the mental processes of uneducated people makes them relatively unready to grasp opportunities of any sort—including opportunities for birth-control knowledge.

An experiment reported by Christopher Tietze, M.D., and Clarence J. Gamble, M.D., in *Human Fertility* for June 1948, supports the conclusion that ignorant people are slow to grasp their opportunities. Doctors Tietze and Gamble wanted to test the effectiveness of a type of contraceptive suppositories, but doctors who otherwise would have been glad to help felt that, to persons who came to them for birth-control information, they must advise techniques which had a degree of effectiveness already known. With the aid of the Alabama State Board of Health and the Alabama League for Planned Parenthood the test was arranged in the venereal disease clinics of two counties. The suppositories were offered without charge to women being treated for syphilis. The offer was accepted by 709 patients. These women already had an average of 4½ pregnancies, and 3.7 live-born children. However, 142 cases were closed in less than a month; a fifth of the women failed to return. Per hundred women in the test in one of the counties, only 52 were known to be using the method after six months; 36 after one year; 27 after two years. In the other county 64 percent were using the method after six months; 45 percent after a year; 18 percent after two years.

The method under test seems to have been moderately successful among those who actually used it.

"Most of the shortcomings of the Alabama investigation appear to be connected with the population that had to be used for the test," say the investigators. "Although there must have been numerous exceptions from this generalization, as a group the patients drawn from the venereal disease clinics were backward, poorly educated, shiftless, and irresponsible." That's what I mean! Ordinary contraceptive practices will not work among the people whose reproduction must most surely be prevented!

The people who, for the well-being of society and of themselves, should have fewest children are usually the ones who are least likely to have, and use, a knowledge of contraception. *Sterilization* can helpfully be made available to them as a means of birth control.

And how can they be convinced that they should be sterilized?

By tying our world gifts to sterilization of the individuals who receive them.

The principle is important that those individuals who are burdens should not increase the burdens by reproduction. As John Stuart Mill worded it (Ashley edition, page 364) :

"If a man cannot support even himself unless others help him, those others are entitled to say that they do not also undertake the support of any offspring which it is physically possible for him to summon into the world."

Professor White's idea of giving aid only if the recipients follow a program which will remove the need for aid is sound, but birth control in the usual meaning of chemical and rubber contraception, as a means of removing the need for financial aid, is not everywhere workable. If White's specific suggestion were followed literally and only that were done, the population problems would still be with us a century from now, as bad as ever in their quantity aspects, worse as to quality. Ordinary birth control must be supplemented by sterilization programs.

•

A final roundup of principles will point the way to a program:

1.   There is a tendency for people to increase.

2.   When the tendency of people to increase has not been restrained by birth control it has led to hunger, malnutrition, and disease. Those involuntary checks cause direct suffering for individuals.

3.   When the tendency of people to increase has been restrained by birth control, a difference of birth rates has developed, the practice being more widespread among alert, capable, accomplished people. In other words, when the need for restriction of population *quantity* is met solely on an individual initiative basis, the *quality* of a people declines, and, in time, because of consequent bad judgments, suffering results.

4.   Thus, either the involuntary checks to population growth (hunger, malnutrition, and disease), or the usual voluntary checks (contraception, late marriages, etc.), eventually, if not promptly, lead to misery. There is a better check, voluntary for the group, often involuntary for the individual: namely, sterilization.

•

We must recognize our limitations in our *direct* influence in salvaging a damaged world. Better not spread our substance too thin. A thorough demonstration in one or a few countries would probably be followed by comparable home-grown programs in other lands which are now shackled to starvation.

The basic principle is that we help carry a burden only on condition that the burden be decreased with reasonable rapidity. Since the burdens are primarily the result of too many fathers and too much fatherhood, specific measures for reducing total reproduction and for shifting reproduction to persons best qualified must be agreed upon.

Details of a sterilization program could appropriately vary to fit the circumstances of the country in which the program is applied. And if the inhabitants of an area prove not co-operative in sufficient numbers to make the area's early self-support likely, the program can be transferred to a more promising nation.

Relief may be direct or indirect. If directly by an agency of the U.S. government to *individuals*, then individuals are to qualify for a dole, or for employment at a minimum wage guaranteed by our agency, only if there is agreement to sterilization when offspring reach a designated number. The number is to depend on the I.Q. of the dole receiver, or his other objective accomplishment. The indirect type of relief would involve grants to *a government,* or to separate enterprises, industrial or agricultural, for developmental purposes, on condition that some general law be adopted and enforced which will reduce the quantity and improve the quality of the population. The formulations herein for Puerto Rico and for the U.S. are illustrative. Definitely the provisions must attach to individual persons; no vague generalizations to the effect that a government will "encourage sterilization" can be sufficiently effective.

For a country so absurdly overcrowded as India, direct doles would seem to be appropriate, sterilization to be applied to a husband as prerequisite to a dole when his first child is born. For a family already large, the sons as well as the husband should be sterilized, except the son who tests highest, and those who rank among the nation's highest testing 20 percent. The higher the dole is made, the more people will be attracted by it, and the more rapidly will the country's level of living be improved.

In the Introduction to *Population on the Loose* I expressed confidence that we can shape the long future, but obviously we cannot do that if we cling blindly to traditional ways. Tradition is good as a direction stabilizer, but where facts and reason show that our civilization is headed for disaster, the traditions must yield, so that the direction can be changed. It is traditional for society to exercise its control over reproduction only to the marriage threshold. Since the results of that tradition have come to be horrible for everybody, the conditions of the right to paternity must be redefined.

The limitation of the right of reproduction even of married people would be a balancing action for our previous interference with biological laws. Human beings establish co-operation, preserving the weak more surely than the strong. That action leads to too many people and to a decline in heredity. If, promptly, we offset the bad effects, we need not relinquish the benefits of co-operative ways, but right now we are speeding back toward the jungle, where the devil takes the hindermost.

People are waking up! It seems probable that in the last five years more copies have been published of discussions relating to population than in all the previous centuries of history. And great segments of the public, realizing that all other approaches to large problems have failed, at last are questioning the misleading rationalizations that have ignored basic causes, and are examining the population analyses with open minds. You, the reader, must be one of those with a strong interest in population as it affects the world's well-being. Now is the time for you to throw in the clutch—to gear that interest to action!

THE END

Index of Names

A

Acheson, Dean, 61
Adams, Brooks, 193-195, 200, 209, 216, 353
Adams, Clifford R., 165
Alexander, Robert J., 83
Alvarado, Mrs. Carmen de, 314
Amano, Fumiko Y., 20, 371
Amano, K. W., 371
Anderson, Clinton P., 133, 312
Armes, Irene H., 272
Aristotle, 295, 355
Arsena, Salvatore, 112
Ashida, Hotashi, 15, 16, 20
Austin, Warren R., 361

B

Bach, 207
Balbus, 353
Bailey, Harry, 113
Ballinger, Willis J., 194
Barnes, Ernest William, 148, 351
Beach, Frank A., 186
Beard, Charles A., 193
Beard, Mary R., 166
Beethoven, 207
Belaval, Jose S., 315
Bengtson, Nels A., 252
Bennett, H. H., 200, 267
Bernstein, Marianne E., 348
Bertram, G. C. L., 368
Besant, Annie, 159, 308
Blake, Carl Harvey, Jr., 330
Blodgett, Ralph H., 23, 171
Bradlaugh, Charles, 159, 308
Brewer, Herbert, 342

Brink, Mrs. Jesse, 145, 228
Brahms, 207
Bray, Joseph, 145
Breidenthal, Oren W., 116
Buck, John Lossing, 57, 108
Bunsen, 207
Burch, Guy Irving, 42, 200, 285, 362
Burt, Cyril, 189
Butler, Fred O., 272, 274

C

Caesar, Augustus, 212, 352
Calitsounakis, Demetrious, 295
Calwell, Arthur A., 80
Carlson, A. J., 142
Carmichael, Leonard, 186
Carmichael, Nell, 349
Carney, Francis W., 292
Cattell, R. B., 189
Chandrasekhar, S., 1-3, 120
Clark, Colin, 31
Claudius, 354
Coe, George A., 162
Coogan, Thomas Francis, 152, 172
Cook, Robert C., 285
Cooper, Robert A., 316
Confucius, 9
Connolly, Vera, 308
Corner, George W., 290
Costello, Bill, 18
Cotterman, C. W., 271
Crespi, Leo P., 177, 189
Crookes, William, 49

D

Davis, Kingsley, 88
Darwin, 279

379

Dawson, Pat, 260
DeJong, Pieter, 43
Denny, Ludwell, 26
DeVoto, Bernard, 42
Dibelius, Otto F. K., 28-30
Dice, Lee R., 277
Dickinson, Robert L., 272, 274
Dight, Charles Fremont, 276
Dillard, Harrison, 181
Dorn, Harold F., 180
DosPassos, John, 136
Drysdales, 308
Dunn, Halbert L., 11, 12
Dupre, Anthony, 112
Durand, Loyal, Jr., 261

E

Eastman, Max, 88
Ebon, Martin, 301
Enzler, C. J., 311
Evans, J. W., 69, 139

F

Farnham, Marynia, 172
Fawcett, C. B., 119
Ferrero, Guglielmo, 211
Finnigan, Edward L., 181
Flugel, J. C., 154
Flux, A. W., 46
Forsyth, William Douglass, 79
Frank, Tenny, 211
Franklin, Benjamin, 92
Fryer, Douglas, 162
Funk, John, Jr., 113

G

Galileo, 122
Gamble, Clarence J., 272, 373
Gaylord, Gladys, 315
Genghis Khan, 208
George, Henry, 88
GilFillan, S. Colum, 196, 200
Gilgallen, George and Edna, 115

Godwin, William, 17
Goethe, 207
Geothe, C. M., 271
Goldberg, Rube, 12
Gordon, Eve B., 176
Gowder, J. Mack, 268
Grajdanzev, Andrew J., 13, 67
Greene, Harry S. N., 350
Greene, Marc T., 80
Griser, Arthur and Irma, 112
Gutermuth, C. R., 262
Guttmacher, Alan F., 282

H

Hailey, Foster, 10, 12
Haldane, J. B. S., 186
Hall, Calvin S., 186
Hammurabi; Hammurapi, 208
Handman, Lillian, 176
Hankins, Frank H., 285
Hansen, Alvin, 38
Harper, Floyd, 35, 69-72, 200
Harper, Roland M., 118
Harvey, William W., 114
Harrison, Carter H., 288
Harrison, Richard Edes, 367
Herndon, Nash, 278
Hertzler, J. O., 4, 212, 214
Hofsten, Nils von
Hooton, Earnest A., 224
Horace, 353
Humboldt, 207
Humphreys, Edward J., 270
Hunter, John, 342
Huntington, Ellsworth, 45, 65, 66, 70, 205, 209, 252, 342
Hutchison, Claude B., 9, 10
Huxley, Aldous, 53, 69, 211

I

Ipuwer, 212
Ise, John, 169
Ives, David O., 85

J

Janer, Jose L., 93
Jevons, W. Stanley, 45, 55, 62, 63
Jewkes, John, 73
Joshi, Hriabai, 8

K

Kato, Mrs., 20
Kenney, Clintie Winfrey, 342
King, Marguerite N., 320, 322
King, Willford I., 285
Kinsey, A. C., 164
Kiser, Clyde V., 164, 167, 168
Kiser, Louise K., 284
Kleberg, Robert Justus, Jr., 179
Knowlton, Charles, 159
Koerner, A., 343
Kornhauser, Arthur, 188

L

Lamb, Harold, 208
Landis, Paul H., 236-245
Landsteiner, Karl, 176
Lashley, Karl S., 186
Leacacos, John P., 25
Lentz, T. F., 189
Leonard, John D., 29
Lerch, Walter, 292
Lester, Richard A., 31, 32, 33
Light, Richard U., 15
Little, Clarence C., 275, 285
Long, L. D., 99
Lord, Daniel A., 292-311
Lord, Russell, 261
Lorimer, Frank, 170, 189
Lowdermilk, W. C., 200, 201, 267
Lucretius, 193
Lundberg, Ferdinand, 172

M

Maecenas, 353
MacArthur, Douglas, 17, 19, 20
Macleod, John, 182
Madigan, Albert E., 329

Malthus, Thomas Robert, 17, 21, 40, 51, 53, 237, 279, 300
Marin, Luis Munoz, 94
Martin, C. E., 164
Martin, Joe, 144, 145
McCleary, G. M., 352-355
McDaniels, James and Doris, 115
McDonough, James, 292
Mencken, H. L., 286
Mendel, 207
Metellus, 352
Michanovich, Clement S., 292
Mill, John Stuart, 38, 41, 308, 329, 374
Moffatt, Robert Scott, 52
Moore, Wilbert E., 5, 86
Morgan, Clifford T., 186
Morley, Felix, 194
Mozart, 207
Muller, J. H., 270, 340
Munn, Norman L., 187
Murphy, Gardner, 178, 187
Mussolini, 23

N

Nehru, 62
Nerva, 354
Nicholas, William H., 55
Notestein, Frank, 228, 284

O

Oden, Melita H., 147
Olden, Mrs. Marian S., 166, 272
Oliver, Clarence P., 277
Orr, John Boyd, 142
Osborn, Fairfield, 2, 35, 200
Osborn, Frederick, 189

P

Palmer, Gretta, 343
Patton, F. Lester, 40
Pearson, Frank A., 35, 69-72, 200
Peattie, James and Pearl, 113
Pendell, Elmer, 200, 285, 362
Piddington. Mrs. Marion, 340

Pincus, Gregory, 349
Pinero, Jesus T., 94
Pitkin, Walter B., 14
Plato, 295
Pollock, Channing, 211
Polybius, 356
Pomeroy, W. B., 164
Ponder, Eric, 182
Poole, Sidman P., 6
Pope, Maude Ethel, and Bill, 113
Prentice, E. Parmalee, 49, 138, 200

R

Ramos, Menendez, 97, 98
Reed, Margaret S., 256
Reed, Sheldon C., 277
Renne, Roland R., 51, 65
Renner, George T., 253
Rhoad, A. O., 179
Ricardo, David, 41
Rich, Charles C., 119
Riddle, Sam, 175
Roosevelt, Franklin D., 95, 98-100
Roosevelt, Theodore, 194
Rife, D. C., 278
Roberts, Fraser, 189
Robinson, Mrs. James, 111
Rolon, Jose A. Lanauze, 314
Ross, Edward A., 285
Ryel, Lavern J., and Alice, 114

S

Salter, Robert M., 140
Sanger, Margaret, 30, 279, 281, 308
Sargon, 207
Sawyer, Charles, 61
Sax, Karl, 285
Schacter, Nathalie L., 167
Scheibel, Kenneth, 128
Scheinfeld, Amram, 289
Schiller, 207
Schock, J. S., 344
Schorohowa, A. A., 342

Sears, Paul B., 84
Senior, Clarence, 93
Seymour, F. I., 343
Shryock, Henry S., 284
Sidoti, Vincenzo and Mary, 116
Sims, J. Marian, 342
Sismondi, 153
Smee, Gordon, 154, 327, 330, 331
Smith, Adam, 33
Smith, J. Russell, 84, 368
Smith, T. Lynn, 247
Smith, Wallace P., 162
Snodgrass, Mary Elizabeth, 87
Snyder, Lawrence, 278
Somervell, D. C., 202
Sorokin, Pitirim, 196, 215
Spengler, Joseph J., 285
Spengler, Oswald, 195, 200, 209
Stecher, Herbert M., 279
Stefansson, Vilhjalmur, 196, 200, 236, 367
Stern, Edith M., 323
Stevens, Fayette B., 278
Stone, Abraham, 279
Stone, Calvin P., 186
Strandskov, Herluf H., 176, 271
Svec, M. Melvina, 261
Swan, Henry Waterman, 340

T

Taeuber, Conrad, 5
Taeuber, Irene Barnes, 284, 368, 369
Taylor, Alfred, 349
Terman, Lewis M., 146
Tompkins, Edward W., 329
Thompson, Godfrey, 148
Thompson, Warren S., 227-235, 259, 368
Thorndike, Edward L., 163
Tietze, Christopher, 307, 314-321, 373

Torrens, Robert, 41
Torres, Mrs., 316
Toynbee, Arnold J., 193, 202, 216-218
Trajan, 354
Tugwell, Rexford Guy, 94-107
Turgot, 40
Truman, Harry, 140, 367
Tryon, R. D., 187

U

Umbaugh, Raymond E., 349

V

Vance, Rupert B., 52
Van Royen, William, 252
Veblen, Thorstein, 234, 356
Velie, Lester, 120, 132
Visher, Stephen Sargent, 206, 285
Vogt, William, 41, 83, 84, 86, 200, 285

W

Wagasky, William, 146
Walker, Francis A., 41
Ware, Hudnall, Jr., 288
Warnecke, Frederick J., 288
Warner, Dennis, 19
Warner, Marie Pichel, 345

Warren, Carl, 349
Warren, Earl, 131
Watson, John B., 185
Weigert, Hans W., 367
Welles, Sam, 42
West, Edward, 40
Whelpton, P. K., 167
White, C. Langdon, 253, 371
Whitney, C. V., 182
Whitney, Leon F., 350
Weiner, Alexander S., 176
Weintraub, Philipp, 274
Willison, George F., 203
Wintrobe, M. M., 278
Wise, T. A., 107
Wisehart, M. K., 48, 124
Wiskemann, Elizabeth, 26
Wolfe, A. B., 285
Wood, H. Curtis, 149, 272
Wood, Leland Foster, 288
Woodside, Moya, 272
Wright, Warren, 182

Z

Zapata, Candido, 88
Zoroaster, 214
Zimmerman, Carle C., 196-200

Index of Subjects

A

Achievement
  evidences capacity, 183, 215
  and IQ of children, 146-148
  and number of children, 144-174,
    155
Aggression of 1960's, 16
Agriculture (see also Farming)
  is basic, 34-72
  in China, 2, 57-63
  in civilization, 201
  diminishing returns in, 36-72
  in Korea, 13, 67-68
  mission, 9
Aid, World, 357-377
Alabama, 281, 373
American Association on Mental
    Deficiency, 270
American Eugenics Society, 270,
    283
American Forestry Association, 260
American Geographical Society,
    260
American Genetics Association, 270
American occupation, 17
American Society of Human Genet-
    ics, 270
American Statistical Association,
    258
Appeasement, 228
Area
  of Australia, 79
  in China, 9
  in England, Germany, Italy, 27
  world, 70

Artificial insemination, 338-351
  extent of, 344-346
  society for, 351
Asia, 11, 35, 57-60, 368
  manufacturing in, 45
Australia, 79-82

B

Baby (see also Children)
  bonus, 169, 170, 234, 241, 242,
    243, 354
  and birth rates, 170
  failed in Sparta, 355
  in Italy, 23
  in Japan, 15, 16
Bachelors penalized, 22
Backward individuals overlook op-
    portunities, 373
Behaviorism, 185, 186
Biological evolution
  and civilization, 203-209, 219-222,
    331
  makes individuals different, 222
  misinterpreted, 230
  must be paralleled, 225
  of the Pilgrims, 203-206
  reversed, 166, 224, 241
Birth control (see also Steriliza-
    tion), 7, 85
  alternatives to, 18, 102, 294, 297,
    298, 307, 308
  approved, 160
  attitudes, 121, 282, 291, 292, 304,
    311, 338

385

Birth control (*contd.*)
"automatic" population check, 11, 101, 143, 243
background facts, 288-291
to balance men and land, 95
benefits U.S., 125
by the alert, 102, 373
Catholic clergy on (see Catholic clergy)
Catholic practice of, 152, 172, 281, 305, 318
church sponsorship, 282
Clinical Research Bureau, 279
clinics in Japan, 20
clinics in Puerto Rico, 314-321
compulsory, 20, 370
depended on, 102, 312
determines numbers, 312
and differential birth rate, 102, 167, 309
in England, 159, 302
Fortune poll on, 311
for India, 7, 8
for or in Japan, 15, 371
knowledge required, 333
knowledge withheld, 118, 372
law
against, in Italy, 22
in Puerto Rico, 105, 315
MacArthur on, 17
and marriage, 330
is moral, 311
needed, 369
neurosis as, 17, 18
objections to, 12
organizations, 280, 287
permits wholesome living, 290
procedure, 290
and prosperity, 110, 125
for or in Puerto Rico, 94, 96, 102, 314-321, 326
requires brains, 374

Birth control (*contd.*)
is slow, 319, 372
sterilization as, 321-326, 371
success varies, 168
tied to doles, 371
too much, 126
training in, 279
worry as, 17, 18
Birth rate
"automatic" decline of, 11, 101, 143, 243
and baby bonus, 170
balanced by death rate, 9, 306
cancels emigration, 9
cancels improved yields, 137
decline (discussed mainly with "differences"), 159
differences, 144-174, 211, 240
affect civilization, 199, 210, 220, 222
affect heredity, 189, 210
in ancient civilizations, 211-214, 352-356
the big problem, 320, 352, 357
and birth control, 310
in California, 244
and education, 150-153
and IQ, 246
can reverse, 351
among Catholics, 152, 172
causes of, 103, 153-174, 210, 239, 240
in France, 244
in Ireland, 302
and late marriages, 302
and levels of living, 11
among Negroes, 151
in Puerto Rico, 320
in Russia, 171
a social blunder, 183
and social security, 242
and survival, 230

Birth rate (contd.)
of distinguished women, 166, 167, 214
of French Canadians, 119
and immigration, 173
in India, 3
of Kentucky mountaineers, 121
lag in decline, 11
lowered by prudence, 154
must be controlled, 47, 143, 225
and old people, 306
and prosperity, 102, 110
in Puerto Rico, 93
reflects degree of sex restraint, 144
and relief, 145
and success, 166
of syphilis patients, 373
in U.S., 123, 144, 305
Black Death, 367
Blood types, 176
Breeding from numbtops, 220
Bureau of the Census, 259

C

California, 146, 244, 276
Canada, 49-53, 69, 170, 295
Canadian French, 119
Capacity, mental, 175-179
Caterpillar Tractor Co., 134
Catholic
artificial insemination, 346
birth rate differences, 152
clergy (see below)
laymen passed birth control law, 317-318
practice of birth control, 172, 281, 305, 318
revenues, 122
vote is 18%, 318
women approve birth control, 311

Catholic clergy
breeding program, 122, 152
dictatorship, 172
distorts government, 19, 20, 97
dogmatism, 122
invites poverty, 126
misguidance, 2, 292-312, 314, 320
perversion, 19, 172, 292-312
in politics, 19, 281, 315, 317, 318
power, 19, 20, 82
prefers war to birth control, 304
worsens birth rate difference, 310
Catholic Physicians' Guild, 292
Celebacy of tadpoles, 291
Census of U.S.; 1940, 149, 210
Central America (see Latin America)
Central Valley, 130
Centralization
destroys civilization, 193, 194, 225
destroys democracy, 194
leads to crash, 225
Check to population increase, 17, 370
Chile, 83, 170
Children
as badges of honor, 232, 326
as evidence of quality, 331
gifted, 147
have to be supported, 240
IQ of, 148
qualifications for bearing, 332-339
sold in Japan, 16
starved in Shanghai, 9
suffer in Europe, 139
and tax exemption, 22
too too many, 111-121, 123, 139, 145, 155
two too many, 115
unfashionable in Nerva's Rome, 354

China, 9-10, 298, 358
  agriculture in, 2
  can manufacture little, 59
  civilizations in, 190
  diminishing returns in, 57-60
  erosion in, 201
  farm production, 58
  of Genghis Khan, 208
  under Russia, 366
CIO faces immigration, 91
Cities
  depend on food, 51
  rule of growth, 51
Civilization, 190-226
  an accumulation, 220
  Babylonian, 207
  collapse, 220
  as a cycle, 193, 195
  definition of, 72, 190, 191, 219,
    220, 224, 358
  depends on
    agriculture, 201
    biological evolution, 203-209,
      218
    brains, 175-179, 207, 220-222
    creative individuals, 202, 217
    culling, 203-209
    heredity, 199, 203-209, 215, 354
    selection, 203-209, 331
  family in, 196, 197, 225
  is farther north, 196
  follows laws, 194, 224
  has no permanence, 190, 192
  lags, 220-222
  may be salvaged, 222-224
  Mayan, 217
  related to interests, 200
  reverses biological evolution, 209-
    215, 219, 220
  Sumerian, 207, 217

Civilization (contd.)
  unbalances incentives, 220, 223,
    353
  undermines heredity, 209-215,
    219, 223, 377
  threatened, 72, 357
  weakened
    by birth rate differences, 209-
      215, 219, 220, 224, 352
    by centralization, 194
    by erosion, 200, 201
    by government, 226
    by overpopulation, 199, 200
    by security, 224
    by specialization, 198
Concentration of power (see also
    Centralization)
  and birth rates, 157
Conservation (see also Resources,
    Soil conservation), 131
  cost, 128
  service, in Mexico, 86
  of water, 130
Constitution, 360
Contraception (see Birth control,
    and Sterilization)
Cotton pickers, 120
Creative individuals, 202, 215, 216,
  217
Crime can be reduced, 330
Croatans, 118
Cycle
  of civilization, 193
  man-sperm-man, 289
  weather, 69, 133

D

Death rate, 9, 11
Decline of the West, 195
Delaware, 276
Demand for laborers, 32

Democracy
  a phase of civilization, 194
  endangered, 194, 211
Density of population (see Population density)
Dependance on America for food, 69
Depopulation, 355
Dight Institute for the Promotion of Human Genetics, 276
Diminishing returns, 31-72, 74, 76, 80, 81, 238, 255, 296, 298
  basis for, 39
  in China, 57-60
  corollary of law of, 63-64
  definition, 36
  different from
    decreasing fertility, 36
    depletion of resources, 48
    diminishing productivity, 36
  in education, 178
  forced extensive cultivation, 48
  fundamental, 36
  importance of, 40, 42
  in Japan, 42
  leads to manufacturing, 54
  from mental effort, 183
  prevents manufacturing, 59-61
  and per acre production, 57
  a resistance of earth, 40
  table showing, 37, 58
  a tie between economics and geography, 31-72
  and total production, 57
  transfer of, 48, 51, 81
Dutch, 12, 43, 65, 368

E

ECA (see also Marshall Plan), 26, 365
Education
  and baby bonuses, 170

Education (contd.)
  in birth control, 94, 167
  and birth rate differences, 150-153, 167
  lost to the family, 197
  of married women, 341
  as pre-requisite, 336
  a problem in, 249
  scanty, a population problem, 4, 112
  of various groups, 248
Egypt, 212
Emigration (see also Migration), 6, 29, 90, 109
Engel's law, 56
England, 44-51, 63, 73, 74, 170, 300, 342, 351
English, 46-53
Environment, 175-189
Erosion, 134
  control plants, 266
  districts, 263
  endangers civilization, 201
  in Latin America, 82, 83, 87
  in Puerto Rico, 98, 100
European Recovery Program (see Marshall Plan)
Evolution (see Biological evolution)
Exports of U.S. food, 139
Expanding economy, 44

F

Family (see also Marriage), 196-199
  allowances (see Baby bonus)
  limitation (see also Birth control, Sterilization) necessary, 233
  wage (see Baby bonus)
Famine, 81
  cause of, 111
  in India, 1, 8
  is lack of reserves, 78
  and population, 81

Farm machinery, 108

Farming, large scale, 120

Farms in conservation districts, 263

Fascists on birth control, 22

Fathers, too many, 175-189

Fertility services, 281

Florida, 360

Food
from afar, 27, 63
area producing, 71
and civilization, 201
in crowded countries, 65, 79
distribution, 34
for England, 46
enough tomorrow, 140
exports, 35, 69, 139
in India, 1
and machinery, 108
main objective, 35
necessary for cities, 51, 65
needs, 107
not enough, 140, 142, 357
one source only, 69
is prime necessity, 57, 59
priority in producers, 35, 44, 59
and prosperity, 34
scarcity, 1, 124
surpluses, 69, 79, 89, 298

Food and Agriculture Organization, 268

Foreign trade (see Trade, Exports, Food exports)

Forest
fires, 84, 128, 129
reserves shrinking, 78, 84
as water tanks, 130

Forest Service, 129, 135

France, baby bonus, 234

French Canadians, 119

Friends of the Land, 261

G

Genetics
Board, 336
laboratory, 278
in a Population Department, 250-255

Geography
has relation to population courses, 236
importance for food, 69-72
in a Population Department, 250-255
tied to economics by the concept of diminishing returns, 31-72

Germany, 27-30, 206

Gifted children, 147

Girl Scouts, 256

Giving
with no strings, 243, 363
and sterilization, 376

Government
destroys civilization, 226
pattern on population, 80

H

Haiti, 83, 88, 105

Hammurabi, code of, 213, 214

Heredity, 175
affects blood, 176, 182
affects civilization, 195, 199, 209, 215
affects IQ, 177, 246
affected by birth control, 96
affected by birth rates, 189
affected by late marriage, 302
basis for achievement, 215, 232
belief in, and birth rates, 158
beyond price, 346
of brain and brawn, 176
brushed aside, 229-230
changes, 96, 148-153, 177, 182,

Heredity (*contd.*)
changes (*contd.*)
188, 189, 204, 206, 216, 302, 324, 377
clinic, 277
deteriorating, 144-174, 166, 177, 178, 189, 246, 302
improved by hardships, 204, 206
of learning capacity, 187, 246
of musical talent, 189
must be built up, 232, 324, 341
neglected, 186, 229
organizations, 257, 270-287
of Pilgrims, 203-206
plays leading role, 188
in a Population Department, 250-255
studied, 255
vs. environment, 175, 185
weakened by civilization, 377
of women, lost, 338, 341
History
in cycles, 193
Housing
in Chile, 83
in India, 1, 3, 4
in Italy, 23
in Puerto Rico, 99
a population problem, 115, 116
Human Betterment Association of America, 271-274
Human Betterment Federation, 275
Human Betterment League of North Carolina, 275
Hunger (see also Famine), 21
in Catholic countries, 82
in England, 63
for land in Italy, 26

I

Immigration (see also Migration)
and birth rates, 109, 173

Immigration (*contd.*)
danger, 362
potential, 28
Importers
depend on surpluses, 52
Incentives
affected by specialization, 199
corrected, 326, 327-356
socially made, 231
unbalanced by civilization, 220
up-side-down, 123, 233, 235, 242, 244, 246, 353
Income
high, and diet, 72
low in Italy, 23, 26
India, 1-8, 74, 81, 376
Indiana, 276, 328
Indonesia (see also Java), 10
Industrial Revolution, 35, 295
Industrialization (see also Manufacturing), 67
in Puerto Rico, 100, 106
futile, 107
Industry
as birth control, 17
in crowded countries, 61-68
no cure for hunger, 35, 52, 59, 106
Interests and birth rates, 103, 162-166, 200
Institutionalism, 186, 194, 228-249
Intelligence (see IQ)
IQ
and achievement, 147
in avoiding pain, 194
and birth rates, 149, 246
basis in heredity, 148, 177, 180, 246
declining, 148, 178, 189, 246
and employment, 148
high, desirable, 179, 185
low among criminals, 273

IQ (*contd.*)
    of parents and children, 148
    for reproduction, 333, 336, 376
    and salaries, 147
Iraq, 214
Ireland, 102, 302, 303, 359
Italy, 22-26, 31, 302, 303

J

Japan, 13-20, 42, 43, 304, 368-371
Java, 10-13, 65, 66, 368
Juvenile delinquency, 273

K

Kansas, 134
Kentucky mountaineers, 121
Korea, 13-14, 67

L

Laboratory of Human Genetics, 278
Laboratory of Vertebrate Biology, 277
Laborers
    demand for, 32
    shortage of
        defined, 74
        how measured, 74
        rare, 74
Lag
    in birth rate, 11
    in civilization, 220-222
Land (see also Area, Resources, Soil)
    conservation, 130-136
    constant, 36
    high price of, 66
    in food production, 71
    -man ratio (see Man-Land ratio)
Latin America, 82
Level of living, 27, 61, 101, 134, 138, 143, 248, 362
    affected by birth rates, 303, 306, 359

Level of living (*contd.*)
    affected by population, 22, 43, 71, 81, 248, 303
    affected by reserves, 75, 81, 127, 135
    at expense of others, 51, 105
    at expense of the future, 130
Life span, 291
    affected by population, 306
Lobbying, 362

M

Machinery on farms, 67
    no cure for overpopulation, 107, 108, 369
Maine, 328
Malthusian League, 279
Man-land ratio, 23, 27, 31, 34, 36, 42, 56, 71, 74, 88, 97, 99, 109, 111, 127, 142, 248, 255, 259, 312, 326
    in Asia, 11
    in China, 10
    in England, 301
    in Greece, 295
    in Ireland, 302
    in Italy, 22, 24, 25
    in Java, 10
    in Korea, 13
    in Puerto Rico, 97, 313
Man-o'-War, 175
Manu, Code of, 4
Manufacturing (see also Industry)
    centralized, 68
    depends on markets, 27
    depends on raw materials, 27
    in India, 61, 62
    in overpopulated countries, 61-68
    retarded by diminishing returns, 56
Margaret Sanger Research Bureau, 279

Market, foreign (see also Food exports, Trade), 27, 43, 44, 45, 59, 62
Marriage
  after sterilization, 330
  age of, 330
  and prosperity, 46
  avoidance of, 352
  bonus in Japan, 14, 16
  denied to some, 330
  laws, 327-356
    can reduce poverty, 329
    can stimulate education, 339
    sample, 332-338
  license
    importance of, 327-332
    officer duties, 327-335
  qualifications, 327-340
  regulated reproduction, 329
  relation misused, 111-121
  a time for testing, 331
Marshall Plan, 6, 24, 139, 363, 365
Massachusetts, 203-206
Metropolitan Life Insurance Co., 259
Mexico, 84, 86, 87, 132
Michigan, 277
Migration (see also Immigration)
  doesn't help, 6, 228
  helped Ireland, 302
  of 1960's, 15
  unwelcome, 25, 28, 362
  within Puerto Rico, 98
Milbank Memorial Fund, 280
Mississippi, 244, 281
Myth of open spaces, 79, 89

N

National Council of Geography Teachers, 261

Natural resources (see Land, Resources and Soil)
Natural Resources Council of America, 262
Navajo Indians, 117
Netherlands (see also Dutch), 43
New Hampshire, 276
New Zealand, 170
North Carolina, 281, 291, 327, 328
  Engenics Board, 275
North Dakota, 276
Norway, 329

O

Old people, 245
Opportunities, economic, 32
Optimum population (see under Population)
Organizations in population work, 256-287
Orient (see also separate countries, and Asia), 2, 9, 359
Ova, transplanting of, 349
Ovaries, transplanting of, 350
Overgrazing, 135
Overpopulation (see also Population)
  basis of problems, 8
  in China, 2, 10, 366, 369
  complicates problems, 226
  defined, 297
  deliberate, 15
  an enemy, 2
  in England, 301
  Fascists and, 22
  in Greece, 295
  and hunger, 21
  in India, 2, 21, 376
  in Italy, 23
  in Japan, 14, 368
  in Java, 368
  in Korea, 13, 369

Overpopulation (contd.)
　　and lack of reserves, 78
　　and manufacturing, 61-68
　　and migration, 18
　　in the Philippines, 368
　　preventable, 279, 325, 351
　　results of, 18
　　in Salvador, 85
　　in South America, 82
　　under false labels, 367
　　and war, 18
　　weakens civilizations, 199
　　world's, 21
　　worried Aristotle, 295

P

Pakistan, 1
Palestine, 208
Papal infallibility, 223
Parenthood should be planned, 288
Pennsylvania, 328, 329
Persia, 214
Pilgrims, 203
Planned Parenthood (see also Birth
　　control, Sterilization)
　　clinics, 284
　　Federation, 9, 16, 20, 114, 148,
　　　280-284
　　organizations, 280-287
Point Four, 61, 367
Pope, 19
Population (see also Birth rates,
　　Overpopulation, Reproduc-
　　tion)
　　affects level of living, 138
　　in America, 2
　　of Asia, 44
　　Association, 284
　　a broad subject, 236, 237
　　and buying power, 45

Population (contd.)
　　of California, 131
　　checks, 18, 297
　　control (see also Birth control,
　　　Sterilization)
　　　required, 10, 12, 19, 85, 86
　　　or starvation, 102
　　courses, 250-255
　　density, 27, 71
　　　and interests, 172
　　　in Korea, 13
　　department recommended, 250
　　and housing, 62
　　increase, 12, 26, 27, 39
　　　brings suffering, 69, 142, 357
　　　in Britain, 159
　　　in Canada, 50
　　　cancels improvements, 137,
　　　　140, 142
　　　in China, 9
　　　decreases food exports, 54
　　　in Germany, 27, 28
　　　in Italy, 26
　　　invites disaster, 7, 140
　　　in Japan, 14, 16, 18, 19
　　　in Latin America, 82-86
　　　and level of living, 125, 138,
　　　　248
　　　and poverty, 88, 314
　　　threatens civilization, 72
　　　in U.S., 111-144, 124
　　　in various areas, 93, 94
　　　was frightening, 95
　　　in world, 21, 39
　　　in India, 3, 4
　　infinitely expansible, 85
　　knowledge spreading, 377
　　optimum size, 39, 81
　　of Orient, 359
　　and poverty, 88, 231, 314
　　pressure, 5, 9, 10, 12, 228

Population (*contd.*)
  principles (A principle is a general truth—a truth of wide application though not necessarily a universal. There must be about 200 population principles in this book; too many to list here. The italicized sentence on page 189 is illustrative. And here is a simple but very important population principle: "Reproduction is something that can easily be overdone."
  problems, 8, 10, 18, 111-118
    slums as, 100
    start from couples, 111-118
  quality, 144-226
  reduction necessary, 70
  Reference Bureau, 286
  regulation required, 19
  -resources ratio (see also Man-land ratio), 31, 71
  rule of growth of cities', 51
  "under", 31
    advantages of, 31, 33
    of U.S., 359
    world, 21, 39
Population Association of America, 284
Population Reference Bureau, 285
Posterity, prospects for, 121, 190-226
Poverty
  avoidable, 323, 329
  caused by ignorance, 77
  a cause of ignorance, 77
  in Italy, 24
  in Java, 10
  in Korea, 13
  and population, 88, 231, 314

Poverty (*contd.*)
  in Puerto Rico, 92-110, 313
  and resources, 77
  transition to, 78
Priestly perversion, 19, 172, 292-312
Production, 14, 136, 137
Productivity
  average, 74
  elements in combination, 70
  of laborers, 74
  low in crowded lands, 299
  low in Korea, 67
  low in some years, 69
Progress, 193
Prosperity
  affected by birth control, 110, 125
  affected by reserves, 77
  and low birth rates, 102
Puerto Rico, 90-110, 173, 273, 298, 313-326

Q

Quality of population, 144-226
Qualifications for marriage, 327-340
Quantity of population (see other topics under Population)

R

Rainfall, 133
Ratio
  of farmers to population, 53
  man-land (see Man-land ratio)
  of men to beef animals, 48
  population-resources (see under Population)
  sex, 345, 348
Reciprocal trade agreements, 29
Relief (see also Aid, Giving), 114, 118, 376

Relief (*contd.*)
  a bar to marriage, 329
  via birth control, 315
  and birth rates, 145
Reproduction (see also birth rates)
  by artificial insemination, 337-349
  correctives necessary, 72, 225, 232, 358
  easily overdone, 9, 111
  encouraged, 22, 23, 174, 331
  in England, 300
  of feebleminded, 273
  incentives (see also Incentives), 185, 231-233, 331, 353
  in India, 3
  in Italy, 26
  moratorium on, 30
  now lacks honor, 231, 232, 235, 356
  for pay, 171
  policy for Japan, 16
  prevented, 331
  recklessness, 19, 42, 95, 111-121, 123, 130, 358
  regulated by marriage, 329
  should have pre-requisites, 358
  standards appropriate, 232, 327-356
  subsidy for (see Baby bonus)
  vs. reserves, 78
  without intelligence, 2
Reserves (see also Resources), 22
  of brainpower is small, 223
  in Britain, 73
  durability as, 76
  economy of, 127
  education as, 77
  in engineering policy, 75
  excess capacity, as, 73
  as insurance, 73-77, 81

Reserves (*contd.*)
  lack of, brings famine, 78
  in land, 15, 35, 73
  and levels of living, 75, 127-138
  need for, 84, 137
  not waste, 73, 74
  water, 132
Resources
  definition, 5
  depletion, 35, 129
  destruction of, 42, 128
  "human", 5
  as insurance, 73, 81
  limit numbers, 131
  overworked, 255
  in ratio with people (see also Man-land ratio, Population resources ratio, Ratio), 10, 127
  as reserves, 73
  struggle for, 27, 52
  and wages, 34
Rice (see Food)
Rome, Ancient, 193, 211, 235, 352
  affected by erosion, 201
Roscoe B. Jackson Memorial Laboratory, 275
Royal Commission on Population, 158, 167, 245-247
  is inconsistent, 246
Russia, 170
  in China, 365

S

Salvador, 83-86
San Joaquin Valley, 120
Scripps Foundation, 259
Security (see also Social Security), 230
  kills itself, 219, 224
  made safe, 225

Semites of Akkad, 207
Sex
  determination, 348
  ratio, 345, 348
Siam, 66
Slums
  in Italy, 24
  in Puerto Rico, 98-100
Social Security Laws, 242, 360, 370
Soil
  can be improved, 38
  conservation, 130-136
    districts, 263
    practices, 264
    service, 201
  destruction in U.S., 133
  resistance, 24
  vital, 34
Soil Conservation Service, 263-268
South Africa, 295
South America (see also Latin America), 82, 295
  food exports, 69
South Carolina, 281
Specialization
  affects incentives, 199
  increases centralization, 225
  necessary to a civilization, 191
  weakens a civilization, 198-200
  weakens the family, 198
Standard of living (see also Level of living), 169
Standards for parenthood, 327-356
Statistics in a Population Department, 253
Sterilization, 103
  as birth control, 168, 321, 371, 374
  does not unsex, 273
  effects of, 322
  essential, 351

Sterilization (contd.)
  without fee, 335
  for inadequate persons, 274, 330
  and marriage, 330
  organization for, 271-276
  program, 324
  in Puerto Rico, 105, 316, 321
  saves taxes, 274
  in various states, 275, 276
  by worry, 17
Subsistence level, 85
Success
  and birth rate, 166
  evidences ability, 231
Surpluses (see also Reserves, Resources), 69, 89, 138, 228, 298
  basis for cities, 51, 59, 65, 68
  basis for civilizations, 138, 191
  basis of prosperity, 52, 73-82, 127, 137-139
  basis of sales, 34
  depend on population control, 86
  essential
    to Catholic church, 122
    to civilization, 191
  are insurance, 4, 73, 82, 120
  necessary to efficiency, 74, 369
  preclude appeasement, 228
  are small, 176-178, 243
  vs. increase of people, 34, 138, 362
  win wars, 80
Survival rate, 11, 59, 72, 230
Syria, 201

T

Tax power can destroy, 360
Texas, 132, 134, 281, 295
Trade, foreign
  an unsafe reliance, 27, 29, 39, 43, 51, 52, 62

Trade (contd.)
  may decline with population increase, 54
Trusteeship, earth in, 127

U

Underpopulation, wholesome, 31, 33
Unemployment
  and birth rate, 157
  in Italy, 26
  transferred to U.S., 107
United Nations
  UNESCO, 269
  Food and Agriculture Organization, 268
  Population Commission, 269
  Statistical Commission, 259
  Statistical Office, 259
United States, 13
  doles for Italy, 26
  doles for Japan, 16
  failed in Puerto Rico, 99, 104, 314
  food exports, 69
  Forest Service, 269
  population, 124
  as Santa Claus, 16, 18, 367
  South, 54
United World Federalists, 360
Utah, 276, 278

V

Virginia, 206, 281, 288
Voluntary Parenthood League, 287

W

Wages
  in America, 31, 32

Wages (contd.)
  in colonies, 31
  differences, 31
  and diminishing returns, 54
  in England, 31, 32
  fund doctrine, 41
  maximum, 32
  in Puerto Rico, 106, 107
  and resources, 34
War
  deaths and population, 28
  effectiveness, 80
  not avoided by appeasement, 228
  Thirty Years, 206
Water, 130-132
Who's Who, 205
Women
  of achievement, 166, 167, 206
  approve birth control, 311
  of the Caesars, 211
  differ
    in birth rates, 150-153, 167
    in fertility, 346
  education of, 248
  get sterilized, 322
  heredity lost, 338
  independent in Babylonia, 214
  status in India, 4
  their choice, 347
World
  acreage, 70
  aid, 357-377
  food, 69
  government, 358-362
  population, 21, 39

Y

Yield per acre, 136